Ralph Waldo Emerson

American Intellectual Culture

Series Editors: Jean Bethke Elshtain, University of Chicago, Ted V. McAllister, Pepperdine University, Wilfred M. McClay, University of Tennessee at Chattanooga

The books in the American Intellectual Culture series examine the place, identity, and public role of intellectuals and cultural elites in the United States, past, present, and future. Written by prominent historians, philosophers, and political theorists, these books will examine the influence of intellectuals on American political, social, and cultural life, paying particular attention to the characteristic forms—and evolving possibilities—of democratic intellect. The books will place special, but not exclusive, emphasis on the relationship between intellectuals and American public life. Because the books are intended to shape and contribute to scholarly and public debates about their respective topics, they will be concise, accessible, and provocative.

When All the Gods Trembled: Darwinism, Scopes, and American Intellectuals
    by Paul K. Conkin
Heterophobia: Sexual Harassment and the Future of Feminism
    by Daphne Patai
Postmodernism Rightly Understood: The Return to Realism in American Thought
    by Peter Augustine Lawler
A Requiem for the American Village
    by Paul K. Conkin
A Pragmatist's Progress? Richard Rorty and American Intellectual History
    by John Pettegrew
The Next Religious Establishment
    by Eldon J. Eisenach
A World Made Safe for Differences: Cold War Intellectuals and the Politics of Identity
    by Christopher Shannon
Ralph Waldo Emerson: The Making of a Democratic Intellectual
    by Peter S. Field
Intellectuals and the American Presidency: Philosophers, Jesters, or Technicians?
    by Tevi Troy

Ralph Waldo Emerson

The Making of a
Democratic Intellectual

PETER S. FIELD

ROWMAN & LITTLEFIELD PUBLISHERS, INC.
Lanham • Boulder • New York • Oxford

ROWMAN & LITTLEFIELD PUBLISHERS, INC.

Published in the United States of America
by Rowman & Littlefield Publishers, Inc.
4720 Boston Way, Lanham, Maryland 20706
www.rowmanlittlefield.com

12 Hid's Copse Road
Cumnor Hill, Oxford OX2 9JJ, England

British Library Cataloguing in Publication Information Available

Library of Congress Cataloging-in-Publication Data

Field, Peter S., 1962–
      Ralph Waldo Emerson : the making of a democratic intellectual / Peter S. Field.
            p.   cm.
      Includes bibliographical references and index.
      ISBN 0-8476-8842-9 (alk. paper)
      1. Emerson, Ralph Waldo, 1803–1882—Political and social views.   2.
Democracy—United States—History—19th century.   3. United
States—Intellectual life—19th century.   4. Democracy in literature.   I. Title.
PS1642.P64 F54   2002
814'3—dc21   2001041698

Printed in the United States of America

∞ ™ The paper used in this publication meets the minimum requirements of
American National Standard for Information Sciences—Permanence of Paper
for Printed Library Materials, ANSI/NISO Z39.48-1992.

For my mother and father

CONTENTS

ACKNOWLEDGMENTS

E merson's great essay notwithstanding, self-reliance is overrated when it comes to writing books. This book would not have been written but for the assistance of many individuals whom I am pleased to acknowledge. In addition, two universities provided crucial resources for the completion of this project. A year at Princeton University as a fellow at the Center for the Study of Religion enabled me to complete an entire first draft in the most congenial surroundings. Similarly, my tenure in the history department at Tennessee Tech, where I went fresh from graduate school, proved highly conducive to furthering my research. Besides being situated in the idyllic Upper Cumberland region, Tennessee Tech is home to a coterie of generous and sympathetic scholars, including Leo McGee, Jack Armistead, and William Brinker, who relentlessly stripped me of each and every excuse, other than personal lassitude, for not completing the project.

The first fumblings out of which this book eventually took shape were presented in 1997 at the Center for the Humanities and Department of American Studies at Princeton University under the title of "Ralph Waldo Emerson and the Problem of Democracy." Similarly, the Shelby Cullom Davis Center for Historical Studies afforded me the opportunity to return to Princeton in 1999 to share the results of my research. It is a pleasure to acknowledge the Davis Center participants for their trenchant and good-natured criticism, as well as the hospitality of William Chester Jordan, Anthony Grafton, Kenneth Mills, and Eduardo Cadava.

An early version of chapter 6, under the title "Emerson and Political Antislavery," benefited from a first hearing at Yale University, where participants of the seminar at the Gilder-Lehrmann Center for the Study of Slavery, Resistance, and Abolition offered a number of incisive suggestions. My thanks go to Robert Forbes for being a gracious host and to David Brion Davis for his generous and lucid commentary.

The manuscript itself was completed during a fruitful year of uninterrupted writing at Princeton's Center for the Study of Religion, where I accumulated a number of large debts. Thanks to Anita Kline and Lorraine Fuhrmann for steering me in the right direction, to the faculty of the Department of Religion for their hospitality and encouragement, and especially to the CSR's directors: Marie Griffith, Al Raboteau, Leigh Schmidt, John F. Wilson, and Robert Wuthnow. Several preliminary versions of early chapters benefited immeasurably from the suggestive criticism of the brilliant fellows at the CSR, Melani McAlister and Patrick Rael, and from Princeton graduate students Tom Bremer and Tisa Wenger. To John Wilson, William Hart, and Michael Sugrue, each of whom read every word of the manuscript and whose generosity made them virtually co-conspirators during my year in 1879 Hall, I am particularly grateful.

I have borrowed, pilfered, or otherwise appropriated ideas from conversations and correspondence over the past several years with an excellent group of interlocutors. Foremost among them are Jim Shenton, whose biting belief that Emerson belonged more in the boardroom than the classroom I have relentlessly tried to overcome, and Eric Foner, who not only read several chapters of this project but who has continued to offer me sage advice over many years. Thanks as well to those friends and colleagues who critiqued various portions of the manuscript: Michael Birdwell, Charles Capper, Mary Cayton, Helen Deese, George Kateb, Mark Larrimore, Lou Masur, John Recchiuti, Jeff Roberts, and Jeffrey Stout. Other forms of encouragement came from Lesley Baier, Jamie Bronstein, Richard Bushman, Phyllis Cole, Nancy Field, John Gager, Len Gougeon, Dean Grodzins, Susan MacKenzie, Shaun Marmon, Robert Richardson, Louis Ruprecht, and Matthew Shipman. Finally, I am grateful for the inimitable assistance provided by Paul Conkin, Andrew Field, and Darren Staloff who offered detailed and searching critiques of the entire manuscript.

Wilfred McClay and Ted McAllister, along with Jean Bethke Elshtain, the editors of the American Intellectual Culture series at Rowman & Littlefield, have been of great assistance both in terms of their critical readings of several drafts of the manuscript and their unstinting enthusiasm for the project. Their excitement greatly contributed to making this book a collaborative endeavor. The same may be said of R&L editors Steve Wrinn and Mary Carpenter, for whom the author feels a special affection. Together with Lynn Gemmell, Ginger Strader, and Tanya Tremewan, they did a masterful job of turning words on a page into a handsome volume.

A version of chapter 6 appeared as "The Strange Career of Emerson and Race" in *American Nineteenth Century History,* and portions of chapters 4 and 5 were published in the *Journal of the Early Republic* as "The Transformation of Genius into Practical Power." I am obliged to Martin Crawford,

John Lauritz Larson, and Michael Morrison for permission to reprint some of this material.

Thanks of a different magnitude go to Helen, Abigail, and the members of our extended family. My debt to my mother and father, to whom this book is dedicated, is of another order entirely.

ABBREVIATIONS AND SHORT TITLES USED IN NOTES

CEC
The Correspondence of Emerson and Carlyle. Ed. Joseph Slater. New York: Columbia University Press, 1964.

Collected Works
The Collected Works of Ralph Waldo Emerson. Vols. 1–5. Ed. Alfred E. Ferguson et al. Cambridge: Harvard University Press, 1971– .

Early Lectures
The Early Lectures of Ralph Waldo Emerson. 3 vols. Ed. Stephen E. Whicher et al. Cambridge: Harvard University Press, 1961–72.

Emerson's Antislavery Writings
Emerson's Antislavery Writings. Ed. Len Gougeon and Joel Myerson. New Haven: Yale University Press, 1995.

JMN
The Journals and Miscellaneous Notebooks of Ralph Waldo Emerson. 16 vols. Ed. William H. Gilman et al. Cambridge: Harvard University Press, 1960–82.

Journal
Journals of Ralph Waldo Emerson. 10 vols. Ed. Edward Waldo Emerson. Cambridge: Riverside Press, 1909–14.

Letters
The Letters of Ralph Waldo Emerson. Vols. 1–6. Ed. Ralph L. Rusk. Vols. 7–10. Ed. Eleanor M. Tilton. New York: Columbia University Press, 1939 and 1990–95.

Sermons
The Complete Sermons of Ralph Waldo Emerson. Ed. Albert J. von Frank et
al. Columbia: University of Missouri Press, 1989–92.

Works
The Complete Works of Ralph Waldo Emerson. 12 vols. Riverside Edition. Ed.
Edward Waldo Emerson. London: Routledge, 1898–1900.

Young Emerson Speaks
Young Emerson Speaks: Unpublished Discourses on Many Subjects. Ed.
Arthur Cushman McGiffert Jr. Boston: Houghton Mifflin, 1938.

Equidem beatos puto, quibus deorum munere datum est aut facere scribenda aut scribere legenda, beatissimos vero, quibus utrumque—

—Pliny the Younger

[To my mind, I think happy those whom the gods have endowed either to do what must be written or to write what must be read; but happiest are those endowed to do both.]

INTRODUCTION

A s the United States enters the twenty-first century Ralph Waldo Emerson remains one of the shining luminaries in the American intellectual firmament. Anyone intent on coming to terms with American society and culture must engage with Emerson in some fashion. Arguably no American intellectual has contributed more to the culture than he has. As a poet, preacher, lecturer, Transcendentalist, abolitionist, and author, Emerson made his mark in such a way that more than a century after his death scholars and thinkers continue to find him worthy of detailed examination. The Concord sage draws attention from beyond the academy as well. Naturalists, novelists, philosophers, poets, and even the occasional politician find that Emerson repays reading.[1]

What is more, Emerson is wonderful to read. So much so that it is tempting to direct would-be readers of this book to put it aside in favor of the original. As the consummate preacher of self-reliance, Emerson would seem to command us to forsake biography and such secondary ephemera in favor of direct experience. Instead of reading "biographies, histories, and criticism," as he wrote in *Nature*, one should consult the man himself to obtain "an original relation to the [Emersonian] universe." On the other hand, Emerson was himself a prodigious consumer of biographies and history, whose voracious intellectual appetite made him one of the most widely read Americans of the nineteenth century; from his youth he read the life histories and autobiographies of many of the great figures of religion, philosophy, politics, literature, and art. He also delivered many extremely popular biographical lectures on such personages as Shakespeare, Plato, Goethe, Montaigne, Napoleon, and George Fox, as well as a few Americans. He converted a highly successful series of biographical public lectures into *Representative Men*, a selection of concise vignettes that became one of his best-selling publications. Following Emerson's own method, I have strived in the ensuing pages not so much to be comprehensive as to distill the essence of his character and expose his singular impact upon nineteenth-century American culture. Within a biographical structure, I have included only those facts and events that most effectively elucidate his search to become what I call a democratic intellectual.

Emerson surely would balk at the amount of study devoted to him and his writings since his death in 1882. A veritable cottage industry exists devoted to the scrutiny of his life and the Transcendentalist circle of which he was the key figure. Library shelves groan under the weight of hundreds of specialized studies of every size and dimension, with his writings alone filling some forty volumes. There is precious little we do not know about Emerson's essays, poetry, lectures, correspondence, personal reading, family, travels, illnesses, politics, and reform activities. One scholar has even assembled *An Emerson Chronology* that reconstructs as nearly as possible every day of his life. On the basis of this ever-growing list of scholarship, Emerson's would seem to constitute one of the most transparent lives in American history. Despite this cornucopia of scholarship, or perhaps in response to it, the last decade has witnessed the publication of many fine new works on Emerson and his New England cohorts. Highlighted by the new Harvard University Press *Collected Works of Ralph Waldo Emerson* (five volumes of which have appeared by 2001), scholars can now consult virtually complete collections of everything Emerson wrote. As for biographies, readers can feast upon many worthy biographies including three works from the past decade alone, each more than 600 pages in length.

For the most part, scholars and biographers in the six score years since his death have been highly laudatory of Emerson, finding in him far more to praise than to disparage. Readers of "Self-Reliance," "Experience," "Fate," or any other of his famous essays will not find it hard to see why. Here is a gifted essayist and wordsmith, who seems at once to be a poet, preacher, and thinker of the first order. Romantic and ecumenical, intellectual and accessible, American and yet not insular, Emerson emerges from his essays as a strangely compelling national prophet. Nineth in a line of Congregationalist ministers, Emerson eschewed the Puritan "fire and brimstone" Jeremiad so effectively and famously deployed by revivalists from George Whitefield and Charles Grandison Finney to Billy Sunday and Billy Graham. Instead he resigned his pastorate and left the church in order to be the nation's irenic pastor of the Deutero-Isaiah type. Simultaneously Emerson was avuncular, stern, passionate, patriotic, and protreptic—all without pandering to a people intent on being alternately praised and entertained. Like so many of the scholars of the twentieth century, I too have found far more heroic than craven in Emerson.

Those conversant with Emerson's life may perhaps find few facts in this book with which they are unfamiliar, for admittedly there is scarcely anything that we do not already know about the man. What they will discover, I hope, is a novel study of a familiar figure that offers several new insights into Emerson's aspirations, vocational struggles, and public career. As my title suggests, in contrast to many biographers, especially those of a literary bent, I argue that Emerson's public life and career represent the very marrow of his biography.[2] Not the inner life, the spiritual search, the religious struggle, or the isolated, individualist odyssey but the vocational search for a public role commensurate with Emerson's awesome ambition constitutes the heart of this project. Searching for what even in his teens he called that "*aliquid immensum infinitumque*" (something awesome and infinite), Emerson disdained the academy, renounced his ministry, and quit the church in order to create a new, broader public role for American intellectuals like himself.[3] Utterly disaffected with the self-satisfied Boston Brahmin establishment into which he had been born, he set forth first to Concord and thence through the nation to assume the role of conscience, critic, and gentle exhorter to the people. Hardly an apologist for Americans as they were, Emerson sought to elicit in his compatriots moral and intellectual aspirations as strong as their headlong pursuit of material gain. Throughout his life, he expressed confidence in the promise of a uniquely able and democratic American nation.

Like so many intellectuals, Emerson more than once professed a preference for the privacy of his study to venturing out among an amorphous and often indifferent audience. For many decades scholars took Emerson at his word, citing for example an 1844 letter to Thomas Carlyle in which he labeled his recent participation in the fight to abolish chattel slavery as "an intrusion . . . into another sphere, and so much loss of virtue in my own."[4] From Arthur Schlesinger's apolitical outsider and Stanley Elkins's "intellectual without responsibilities" to Carlos Baker's Concord "eccentric" and Taylor Stoehr's "nay-sayer," students of Emerson have drawn a compelling portrait of an isolated individual whose philosophical idealism ensured at best a tangential relationship to Jacksonian politics and society.[5] More recently, critics of contemporary American society have seen in Emerson an early apologist for the self-centered, individualistic, alienated culture in which we live today. His rejection of many antebellum institutions, particularly the Unitarian church, in favor of "going alone," as he exhorted his audience at the Harvard Divinity School Address, provides them with ample evidence for portraying Emerson as the champion of a woefully misguided, self-reliant individualism that trumps such collective values as those of community, family, and institutional religion. For some deeply thoughtful intellectuals of both the right and the left, Emerson extols precisely those bourgeois, Lockean liberal, and ultimately hollow nostrums that conspire in the United States to reduce ideas into ideology and turn human communities into islands of isolated individuals.[6]

On the whole the last years of the twentieth century witnessed a revision of the earlier critical assessments and their more recent expressions. A growing number of scholars have sought to diminish the rhetorical distance between an idealist Emerson culled from selective readings of his essays and the real-life figure devoted to his family, friends, and beliefs. They have sympathetically explored Emerson's political philosophy, turned his famous lack of systematization and technical rigor into a precursor to pragmatism, and even made his common-language philosophical investigations into a proto-Wittgensteinian gambit. By doing so, such eminent scholars as political scientists George Kateb and Judith Shklar and philosophers Cornel West and Stanley Cavell have cast doubt on the old shibboleths, instead underscoring Emerson's intimate connection to the political culture of his day. Kateb has brilliantly contextualized Emerson's vaunted individualism and, along a similar line, Richard Poirier has written that Emersonian self-reliance "gives way recurrently to its opposite, to self-dissolution."[7] In more historically based works, Len Gougeon and Albert von Frank have stressed Emerson's participation in reform activities, especially abolitionism, and Richard Teichgraeber, utilizing Michael Walzer's term *connected critic*, has situated Emerson and Thoreau squarely in the emerging market culture of their times.[8]

My work extends this recent trend insofar as, significantly more than earlier scholars, I portray Emerson as engaged with the people, events, and politics of his day. Like Teichgraeber I see Emerson as far more conscious of and connected to the burgeoning market economy and turbulent social movements of the Jacksonian period. And with Gougeon and von Frank I understand Emerson's antislavery activities, despite his profound and grave reservations about African Americans' intellectual abilities, to be more central, more powerful, and more effectual to the movement to abolish chattel slavery in the United States than has been perceived by previous generations. For me, the old formulaic Emerson as the avatar of the isolated, irresponsible intellectual will no longer wash. As the following pages demonstrate, he became perhaps the critical intellectual figure of his time whose significance extends far beyond his Concord study and Transcendentalist Romanticism.

As a social history of intellectuals, this work stresses social, personal, and political preoccupations over the more traditional Hegelian history-of-ideas constellation of religious, philosophical, and literary concerns. I have situated Emerson more squarely in the political and social environment that impinged on a Harvard-educated, Unitarian-trained New England minister in the early American republic, with the central concerns of his life stemming from his unique attempt to right himself with his times and with a growing nation beyond the parochial confines of Boston and Cambridge. Emerson pursued national relevance and recognition in an expanding, opportunity-filled, adolescent America that in his estimation represented the democratic promise of the Western world. Not Transcendentalism, socialism, idealism, or Romanticism but living Americans and their potential served as the focus of Emerson's aspirations, vocational pursuits, and greatest public efforts.[9] Examining Emerson's youthful tribulations, his Harvard education, and his turbulent career as preacher, lecturer, abolitionist, and author reveals a young man with an exalted faith in his own abilities, as well as the public intellectual who could remind his fellow citizens of their higher duties. His greatest challenge, by which so much of his life can be understood, proved to be his struggle to overcome the nagging insularity that stalked his Unitarian brethren and his Transcendentalist cohorts and that still lurks in American intellectual circles today. Craving relevance, Ralph Waldo Emerson fashioned himself into what I call the first democratic intellectual in American history.

As part of Rowman & Littlefield's American Intellectual Culture series, this book is meant to be more than a biographical study of an American icon. Rather than minutely examining the mundane details of Emerson's biography, I have instead explicated his crucial, often excruciating search for a suitable vocation, one in which he could simultaneously put to effective use his high cultural training and reach as broad an audience as possible. It is precisely in the throes of this search that Emerson emerges as the principal intellectual of the nineteenth-century United States. Perhaps more than any other intellectual career, Emerson's life serves as a counterpoise to the ubiquitous figure of the American thinker isolated in academia or ignored by the public and all but irrelevant to the nation at large. In contrast to Henry Adams and George Santayana and their notion of intellectual duty characterized by a "sacred rage" against American philistinism, Emerson holds out the possibility, however minute, that an intellectual of great ability and democratic sympathies might well obtain and occupy a position of moment in American society. Without being overly sanguine, it is possible to discern in Emerson a public intellectual admirably struggling against the ferocious tendency in democracy toward the dulling conformity of what Tocqueville aptly described as the tyranny of majority opinion. Emerson was virtually alone in blaming intellectuals' alienation from the crowd not on democratic leveling but on the infirmities and effeminacy of the thinking class. He deemed it the responsibility of intellectuals like himself to harness the attention of the American people. For the democratic intellectual the great task was to procure an audience without pandering

to philistine tastes, to teach and exhort instead of merely entertaining. This
was the goal Emerson set for himself.

Formidable problems inhere in writing on Emerson. Accordingly, a few
disclaimers are in order. From Santayana, William and Henry James, and Oliver Wendell Holmes Sr. over a century ago to Vernon Parrington, F. O. Mattheissen, and Perry Miller in the middle of the twentieth century to Cavell,
Kateb, Harold Bloom, and Sacvan Bercovitch in our own time, some of the
nation's foremost intellectuals have offered powerful assessments of the Concord sage. Indeed, so many others have written about him that it is easy to
write more about the critics than about the subject himself. I have assiduously
avoided citing other scholarly works in the body of the text for fear of relegating the narrative thread to the background. Readers are directed to the notes
at the conclusion of each chapter for reference and commentary on the institution that is Emerson's legacy.

A second and no less daunting hazard for the biographer inheres in the
subject himself. Emerson is famously elusive, often exasperatingly so. Not
surprisingly, the person who declared "mad contradictions flavor all our
dishes" never fetishized consistency. Fully aware of his own limitations when
it came to "systematic philosophy" (he was hopelessly inept at mathematics),
Emerson turned vice into virtue by celebrating his freedom from philosophical
rigor. Insofar as he comprehended that he was not up to systematic logical
analysis on any sophisticated level, he readily granted to others the tasks of
refuting, for example, the radical empiricism of David Hume and resolving
the great technical puzzles of academic philosophy. Because of this, I find
curious the arguments of such eminent thinkers as Cavell, B. L. Packer, and
Eduardo Cadava who read Emerson with what I consider a misplaced analytical precision. Equally strange are comments by biographers who write, for
example, that Emerson "had studied the British epistemologists, rejected
Locke in college, worked himself free of Hume's skepticism, and settled confidently on Berkeley's idealism" without suggesting just how much of a gloss
his rejection, freedom, and settlement actually were.[10] Some college papers
excepted, Emerson did not write philosophical discourses or analyses; and
though the aphoristic style of his essays and lectures have a certain similarity
to those of Friedrich Nietzsche, and his prose, like that of Ludwig Wittgenstein's *Philosophical Investigations*, can baffle us with the contents of his
broom closet, we ask too much to read Emerson as philosophically precise.
Without publications remotely equivalent to either Nietzsche's systematic refutation of Schopenhauer or Wittgenstein's austere and exact *Tractatus Logico-
Philosophicus*, it seems to strain credulity to embrace Emerson as a rigorous
or precise philosophical thinker. Even as a precursor to pragmatism, as West

and Poirier eloquently lay out, Emerson barely gets passing marks. Like John Dewey he sought to broaden the appeal and provenance of the "public philosopher," but unlike Dewey, he produced nothing comparable to *Experience and Nature* or *Reconstruction in Philosophy*. He simply was not up to it.

Emerson might well be considered a vital and original contributor to the Western intellectual tradition but for reasons other than the rigor of his analysis. His awesome breadth of reading, lifelong dedication to intellectual inquiry, preoccupation with ethics, and his very Wittgenstein-like devotion to an unimpeachable intellectual honesty make Emerson a philosopher in the broad sense of the term. In fact his lack of analytical ability proved to be a blessing, as a great deal of his popularity in his day and his continued relevance in our own stems from his monumental imprecision as well as his affection for the plain language study of everyday life that nature's necessity determined would be his lot. His greatness arose from his lyrical sympathy for the beautiful, comprehensible, useful, and pedestrian.

Emerson's disdain for systems presents another problem for any would-be biographer. When it comes to explaining a great many of his ideas one must come to terms with the multitude of vagaries and inconsistencies in his prose. From the most profound issues, such as his explication of human nature, the conduct of life, or the origins and legitimacy of private property, to more trivial matters, such as Andrew Jackson or the contemporary press, Emerson's writings, both public and private, can be maddeningly ambiguous. Even when he is not contradictory, the Concord sage almost never defines his terms, preferring instead to gesture at them with general descriptions, fanciful allusions, and the generous employ of metonym and metaphor. Even such vitally Emersonian terms as *individualism, idealism,* and *the oversoul* fail to elicit "each and only" definitions; in undertaking an examination of Emerson's ideas, it is virtually impossible to pin down precise meanings. The only solution, and the one I have put to use, is to read each line of Emerson in context of the sum of his writings in an effort to tease out his message. The overall tenor and concerns of his voluminous writings prove far more consistent than the individual parts. Bearing this in mind, one must approach Emerson with profound respect, constantly resisting the temptation to allow his lack of analytical rigor to lure one into condescension. Emerson is a deep thinker, whose masterful use of irony demands the reader's careful and undivided attention. The even vaguely sympathetic biographer must not be bamboozled by his unsystematic and open-ended style, just as one should not expect the author of "a foolish consistency is the hobgoblin of little minds" to approach his subjects as a professional philosopher would. More poet than philosopher, he needs to be read as the unique poet-preacher-prophet that he was. In sum,

Emerson demands to be understood as he attempted to create himself—as a unique, irenic prophet to the American people.

NOTES

1. Most literate Americans have read an Emerson essay or chanced across some Emersonian aphorism.

2. The most compelling and persuasive case for the "inner life" as well as for its distinction from public life is Stephen Whicher, *Freedom and Fate: An Inner Life of Ralph Waldo Emerson* (Philadelphia, 1953).

3. *JMN* 2:239.

4. Emerson to Thomas Carlyle, 12/31/44, *CEC* 373.

5. Arthur Schlesinger Jr., *The Age of Jackson* (Boston, 1945); Stanley Elkins, *Slavery: A Problem in American Institutional and Intellectual Life* (Chicago, 1959); Taylor Stoehr, *Nay-Saying in Concord: Emerson, Alcott, and Thoreau* (Hamden, Conn., 1979); and Carlos Baker, *Emerson among the Eccentrics: A Group Portrait* (New York, 1996).

6. See for example Wilfred M. McClay, "Mr. Emerson's Tombstone," in *Community and Tradition: Conservative Perspectives on the American Experience*, ed. George W. Carey and Bruce Frohnen (Lanham, Md., 1998); Christopher Newfield, *The Emerson Effect: Individualism and Submission in America* (Chicago, 1996); and Sacvan Bercovitch, *The Puritan Origins of the American Self* (New Haven, 1975) and *The Rites of Assent: Transformations in the Symbolic Construction of America* (New York, 1993).

7. George Kateb, *The Inner Ocean: Individualism and Democratic Culture* (Ithaca, 1992); George Kateb, *Emerson and Self-Reliance* (Thousand Oaks, Calif., 1995); Judith Shklar, "Emerson and the Inhibitions of Democracy," *Political Theory* 18 (4) (1990), 601–14; Stanley Cavell, *Conditions Handsome and Unhandsome: The Constitution of Emersonian Perfectionism* (Chicago, 1990); and Cornel West, *The American Evasion of Philosophy: A Genealogy of Pragmatism* (Madison, Wis., 1989). Writes Shklar: "Emerson may not have been what is conventionally called a political philosopher, but political considerations played a more subtle part in his thinking than mere expressions of opinion on public affairs suggest" (601). A good review of some of this literature is Cyrus Patell, "Emersonian Strategies: Negative Liberty, Self-Reliance, and Democratic Individuality," *Nineteenth Century Literature* (March 1994), 440–79. See also Richard Poirier, *Poetry & Pragmatism* (Cambridge, 1992), 20; with Kateb, he argues that "Emerson is actually opposed to individualism in the customary or social sense in which the term is most often used" (29).

8. Len Gougeon, *Virtue's Hero: Emerson, Antislavery, and Reform* (Athens, Ga., 1990); Albert von Frank, *The Trials of Anthony Burns: Freedom and Slavery in Emerson's Boston* (Cambridge, 1998); and Richard F. Teichgraeber III, *Sublime Thoughts/Penny Wisdom: Situating Emerson and Thoreau in the American Market* (Baltimore,

1995). On Emerson and the emerging market economy, see Michael Gilmore, *American Romanticism and the Marketplace* (Chicago, 1989), ch. 1.

9. George Santayana had it right when he claimed that "at bottom" Emerson "had no doctrine at all." George Santayana, *Interpretations of Poetry and Religion* (1900; rep. Gloucester, Mass., 1969), 218.

10. Gay Wilson Allen, *Waldo Emerson: A Biography* (New York, 1981), 259.

1

FROM EMERSON TO EMERSON

O n the evening of July 15, 1838, Ralph Waldo Emerson delivered his famous tour de force, the Harvard Divinity School Address, to an intimate gathering of graduating divinity students, elite professors, Boston ministers, and invited guests. The address on the "evil of the church now manifest" represented the great turning point in Emerson's professional life, thrusting the aspiring intellectual into the role of chief critic of the Unitarian elite of eastern Massachusetts. In the preceding months he had published *Nature* and delivered his Harvard Phi Beta Kappa oration, "The American Scholar," but neither had really attracted the attention or sparked the kind of vitriolic reaction of this summer discourse before the Unitarians. The address in Divinity Hall proved to be nothing less than an American intellectual parricide in which Emerson accused the Unitarians of engendering the "famine of our churches" that had left "the worshiper defrauded and disconsolate."[1] The ministers of the Unitarian church, Emerson lamented, "accept another man's consciousness for their own, & are in the state of a son who should always suck at his mother's teat."[2] In the address, he openly declared what he had been writing in his private journal for almost a decade, the denomination his father had helped to create "was founded on nothing & led to nothing."[3]

Emerson was a Harvard Divinity graduate himself. A former ordained minister and still an occasional preacher, he had responded warmly to the divinity students' invitation when they had first approached him on a "cold windy clear day" the previous March.[4] These had been fertile, productive months for the blossoming author and lecturer. The invitation to speak to the graduating class promised him an ideal opportunity to elaborate upon his rather awkward relationship with Unitarian Congregationalism, the faith of his father, mother, and virtually all his family and friends. Acutely conscious of his audience, Emerson directed his remarks toward the divinity students—all six of them—who had asked for his counsel. Having already convinced himself that he would say and write only that which was uniquely his own, Emerson realized that these young men deserved nothing less than a candid

11

assessment of the present state of the profession upon which they were about to embark. Perhaps his personal ruminations would help them find fulfillment where he had not, and in doing so they might rescue Unitarianism from what Emerson believed it was lurching toward: oblivion.

Emerson's address was neither offensive nor impolite. It was measured in scope, moderate in tone, and full of Emerson's characteristic optimism. Not here did Emerson accuse the Unitarians of being "corpse-cold."[5] Minister of Boston's prestigious Second Church until his resignation in 1832 and still engaged by Congregational churches throughout eastern Massachusetts, Emerson had in fact been preaching the basic sentiments of the address for the previous several years. Now, in Divinity Hall, the very *axis mundi* of Unitarianism, Emerson urged these novices to follow him by following their own inner path toward enlightenment and spiritual truth. Forsake the past for the present, he declared; "show us that God is, not was; that he speaketh, not spake."[6] Typically Emersonian, his call to look within for meaning, for hope, for God resonated in *Nature* and would in his subsequent works. "Let me admonish you, first of all," he urged, "to go alone."[7]

It seems Emerson was unaware that this brief address without a proper title would rank with Channing's "Unitarian Christianity" sermon as the Ur-text of the Unitarian-Transcendentalist controversy or that it would, as Bronson Alcott aptly asserted, "stagger the slender faith of many."[8] A few months earlier, Emerson had confided in his journal that "I always find that my views chill or shock people at the first opening."[9] With the exception of this aside, his journals and correspondence betray little apprehension that his remarks might produce an adverse reaction from Andrews Norton, Henry Ware Jr., and Divinity School Dean John Gorham Palfrey, the high priests of Unitarianism who were present that July evening in Cambridge.[10] Paying scant attention to the representatives of the establishment and scarcely bothering himself with the likely repercussions from disturbing the equilibrium of the old guard, Emerson concerned himself almost exclusively with the students who had invited him to speak and with aspiring ministers such as Theodore Parker, whom he hoped to inspire.[11] The firestorm that ensued from his call to "dare to love God without mediator or veil" surprised Emerson and left him speechless, literally, as he refused to respond publicly to his critics.[12] As Thomas Carlyle called the controversy nothing more than a "tempest in a washbowl," so Emerson seemed unaware that the Divinity School Address would be his last public act as a member of good standing in that exclusive Unitarian community his father had been instrumental in creating and into which he had been born.[13]

That Emerson's father, William Emerson, who had suddenly died in

1811 just days before his son's eighth birthday, was one of the leading lights of the incipient Unitarian movement at the turn of the nineteenth century lends even greater significance to the Divinity School Address. If William Emerson had lived longer—and there is ample evidence of longevity in the family—he surely would have been in attendance at his son's 1838 commencement address. It is equally certain that the "graceful and gentlemanlike" Emerson Sr. would not have responded warmly to the Divinity School Address, which he would have associated with the New Light party of the previous century.[14] In his posthumously published *Historical Sketch of the First Church in Boston*, he is critical of Jonathan Edwards, whom he associates with James Davenport, and contemptuous of the many New Light ministers whose doctrines he believed threatened the social order.[15] His professional sentiments carried over into his personal life too. Emerson Sr. disparaged Joseph Emerson and Daniel Bliss, two family members who had preceded him in the clergy, who were New Lights and had sided with Edwards; he heaped praise instead upon Charles Chauncy, his predecessor at First Church and staunch defender of rational religion. He even named two of Ralph's brothers after his Old Light heroes, John Clarke and the aforementioned Charles Chauncy. If the elder Emerson's concerns about his sister Mary's beliefs are any indication, there can be no doubt that he would have found his son's advocacy of personal intuition in place of denominational consensus a distinct threat to the social order. Perhaps he, and not Andrews Norton, would have called his son's speech "the latest form of infidelity."[16]

According to his sister, Mary Moody Emerson, William Emerson was a rather typical father whose principal shortcoming was his propensity to spend too much time and effort cultivating his professional and social standing.[17] Looking back many years later, the younger Emerson (he called himself and was called Ralph until his college years when he went by Waldo) thought his father to have been a "social gentleman, but severe to us children." When William Sprague asked Ralph for information on his father for his monumental *Annals of the American Pulpit*, he demurred, writing that his recollections were so vague as to be of little or no meaningful assistance. Sprague would have to consult someone else.[18] The fact that William Emerson died comparatively young and that his son barely knew him should not detract from the profound connection between father and son, both of whom followed their fathers into the Congregational church.

At the time of his death at the age of forty-one, Emerson Sr. was the esteemed pastor of Boston's venerable First Church, the post once held by John Cotton and other Puritan luminaries. Well liked and highly respected by his exclusive parishioners, he was the very embodiment of the Boston elite minister and at the prime of his career. Harvard-educated, refined, status-conscious, and rather cold, William Emerson proved pivotal in maintaining the social status of Boston's Congregational ministers in the first decade of the nineteenth century. With Jeremy Belknap, Joseph Stevens Buckminster, John Thornton Kirkland, Peter Thacher, and several others, he helped to create that uniquely Boston brand of Congregationalism that came to be known as Unitarianism.[19] Emerson never used the term self-referentially, instead alluding to himself and his colleagues as "liberals." Intent on conveying their catholicity, and openness to doctrinal differences, these Congregational ministers self-consciously—and accurately—avoided a specific doctrinal appellation. Today, *liberal* connotes a political stance more closely associated with the Jeffersonian party than that of these ardent New England Federalists. These Boston ministers were liberal, or latitudinarian, on doctrinal issues, but were conservative in virtually all social and political matters. The term *Brahmin* seems preferable to liberal. Unlike liberal, Brahmin does not refer to a political orientation; in the Hindu religion, it denotes simultaneously the highest intellectual and social rank in society. Like Dr. Holmes's postbellum Brahmins, these clerical intellectuals shortly intermarried with the emerging mercantile elite among their parishioners. They formed, as Henry Adams observed, "a social hierarchy in which respectability, education, property and religion united to defeat the unwise and vicious."[20] The term *Brahmin*, then, most accurately conveys their class consciousness, their social connection to the mercantile elite, and their status as one of the first coterie of professional intellectuals in American history.[21] Few individuals did more to foster the Brahmins' literary and social credentials than William Emerson.

The birth of the Brahmins dates to the beginning of the nineteenth century. At the moment when Jefferson's election to the presidency of the United States signaled the denouement of Federalist dominance, Boston's mercantile elite began to encourage the coalescence of a special clique of ambitious Congregational clerics. Affluent Bostonians, flush from a decade of economic expansion, pursued a new type of minister, such as Emerson Sr., Kirkland, and Buckminster, to fill their Boston pulpits. They sought to bring to Boston clerical intellectuals, with whom they had attended Harvard, and of whose hermeneutic and rhetorical skills they were highly impressed, if not envious. They promised fine salaries in exchange for literary Sunday sermons; at least as importantly, they pledged themselves to patronize their ministers' literary and high cultural ambitions. A unique symbiotic relationship developed out of this alliance of clerical intellectuals and a culturally committed bourgeoisie, in which the latter gained a new type of legitimacy and the former accrued an amount of intellectual and financial freedom unmatched in the brief history of the nation.

Patronage of the arts became wealthy Bostonians' civic virtue, as eastern Massachusetts rapidly emerged as the intellectual capital of the country. The Brahmins and their patrons sought to cure New England of being a cultural backwater, in time making it the rightful heir to Athens, Rome, Florence, and London. Cultural institutions, they believed, would command respect from many quarters and confirm American nationhood in a way that political institutions could not. "The time will arrive," wrote William Tudor, one of the brilliantly successful Boston mercantile family,

> when the contention will not be which state has the best soil, which has the largest city, and which city has the best market; but which state had made the most eminent discoveries in science, . . . where have the muses been propitiated to shed inspiration; which cherishes the artists, whose names are to be enrolled with those of Phidias and Apelles, of Michael Angelo and Raphael.[22]

Literary historian William Charvat concludes, "in no other period of American history has the economically dominant class exhibited such an interest in the arts."[23]

At the turn of the nineteenth century, Boston's nine Congregational churches stood out as something of an island in the Massachusetts Standing Order. The Constitution of 1780 had decreed that every incorporated town support "publick Protestant teachers" by public assessment. Article III of the Bill of Rights required citizens to pay a tax for the maintenance of the minister of their town, even if they did not attend church at all, unless they could demonstrate membership in a recognized dissenting sect with its own "publick Protestant teacher." Significantly, the Bay State constitution exempted Boston and Salem citizens from this assessment on behalf of religious instruction. Holding themselves up as more pious but in fact simply wealthier than anyone else in the state, Bostonians had long eschewed the notion that any form of coercion was necessary for the maintenance of their churches. Accordingly, in contrast to the rest of the state, Boston clerical maintenance continued on the same voluntary basis it had enjoyed since the late seventeenth century.[24] For more than one hundred years the wealthy had been accustomed to renting or purchasing pews on the main floor—the middling sorts were relegated to the galleries—and by this voluntary means funding the church society. This uncoerced maintenance system guaranteed that Boston's churches would be distinct from their rural counterparts in several significant respects. A boring, unexceptional minister in a country parish was relatively assured of getting his salary, as paltry as it may have been. His Boston counterpart, if particularly unpopular, risked his salary and the financial viability of the church if he antagonized his congregation. With a variety of choices readily at hand, residents of the capital joined whatever church they desired. In this sense, Boston ministers were more vulnerable under the voluntary system than their rural colleagues, for failure to attract a sizable audience could jeopardize their livelihood and their church's solvency. The case of Joseph Eckley, minister of Old South Church, which for decades was the only orthodox congregation in the city, is instructive. When he insisted on reverting to the seventeenth-century practice of refusing to baptize the children of attendees not in "full communion," he alienated so large a proportion of his church that "from the largest society in Boston," wrote Rev. William Bentley, "the Old South had become the smallest."[25] Edward Dorr Griffin, the ultraorthodox minister of Park Street Church, suffered a worse fate. His harangues and zealous denunciation of the Brahmins proved so caustic and disagreeable, particularly with the well heeled, that he regularly preached to a half-empty church. In no time Park Street found itself hugely in debt. The church deacons felt compelled to demand Griffin's resignation in 1812, barely two years into his tenure, lest the church become insolvent.[26] In Boston, clearly, parishioners voted with their feet.

The voluntary system also had its distinct material benefits. Ministerial salaries depended upon the overall size and, therefore, the satisfaction of the congregation. While it is not precisely the case that the size of the congregation and the minister's salary were directly proportional, the two were related. Federal Street Church, upon calling Jeremy Belknap to its pulpit, effectively offered him a year-end bonus if he augmented the society's membership. "In the case our society shall increase, and the pews be all occupied," the offer stipulated, "the salary shall then be increased to a comfortable support."[27] Ministers had more than just an ideal interest in abandoning sermons of fire and brimstone. Their increasingly well-to-do parishioners believed they were neither sinners nor in the hands of an angry God.

Largely as a result of the voluntary maintenance system, Boston churches differed in another crucial respect from the rest of the commonwealth. In contrast to most congregations where the church communicants—those who had publicly confessed their faith—held the bulk of the power, in Boston the pew proprietors held sway. Power to choose and confirm the minister, to determine his salary, and to decide other matters of church governance largely devolved to the proprietors, particularly those who held the most expensive pews. Since their rents, not state taxes, funded the society, pew proprietors' influence within the church was significantly greater than that of their counterparts outside the capital. This is not to say that there was not a significant overlap of proprietor and communicant; the key point is that the two groups were constituted on entirely different grounds: proprietors by wealth and communicants by professed devotion. And this made all the difference. In Boston religious societies, "the most influential man was also the richest."[28]

In the decades after independence, the Congregational clergy complained endlessly about two issues above all others: meager pay and doctrinal disputes with obstreperous church communicants. Country ministers' diaries and correspondence, including those of William Emerson, are replete with such grievances. As a result of the voluntarist system and the growing wealth of the mercantile bourgeoisie, Boston's churches promised relief from these two sources of unceasing complaints. If a minister could secure a position in Boston, or to a lesser extent one of the other burgeoning seacoast communities, he was assured of significantly greater creature comforts than those of his Congregational colleagues in the hinterlands. A call to a Boston pulpit entailed a dramatically different existence from anywhere else in Massachusetts, or in the nation as a whole. While salaries were not great, when combined with an ample parsonage and other accoutrements, they provided for a decidedly comfortable lifestyle. With the promise of fine salaries and other benefits, Boston's pew proprietors, drawn from the increasingly wealthy mercantile families, fostered the evolution of an exclusive clique of Brahmin ministers. The wealthy parishioners of Boston's Congregational churches—Brattle Street, First Church, Second Church, Federal Street, indeed eight of Boston's nine churches—called to their pulpits a remarkably talented group of ministers, including Peter Thacher, Samuel Cooper Thacher, Kirkland, Belknap, Buckminster, and William Emerson.

Boston's leading proprietors helped to transform the ministry by altering their expectations of the office. More heterodox than their rural counterparts, proprietors and communicants sought in their ministers men of a more literary than doctrinal persuasion, who welcomed the relief from being beholden to the more doctrinally rigid church communicants of the countryside. Boston proprietors encouraged their ministers to pursue more literary and artistic endeavors, often in lieu of performing traditional pastoral chores. They expected enlightened, entertaining, and edifying Sunday sermons to keep the pews full, but as only one aspect of the clerical intellectuals' larger preoccupation with shepherding an indigenous high culture. In addition to paying fine salaries, Bostonians began the first major patronage of the arts in the United States. They opened their purses to support the creation of institutions of high culture, underwriting the publication of the *Monthly Anthology and Boston*

Review, endowing the nation's first great private social library, the Boston Athenaeum, and engineering the takeover and transformation of Harvard College. The combination of merchants' largesse and clerical intellectuals' aspirations resulted in the first steps toward the creation of an indigenous secular high culture in the United States.

The emerging alliance of minister and merchant produced benefits for both parties. In addition to greater personal financial security, Boston's clerical intellectuals gained an outlet for secular interests as well as the patronage vital to their fledgling cultural institutions. For their part, the merchants' growing support of the arts, like their rekindled ardor for the pastoral ideal, served as a bridge between republicanism and liberalism. Patronage of the arts served to assuage the wealthy's uneasiness about their extraordinary acquisition of personal fortunes. Ministers publicly proclaimed that support of cultural institutions was a public good. Philanthropy legitimated the amassing of wealth in the hands of a few.[29]

When Boston's Brattle Street Church called Peter Thacher, pastor of the Congregational church in Malden, Massachusetts, to its pulpit in 1785, it transgressed the long-standing, if unwritten, policy of the Congregational Standing Order that when congregations settled a minister in their pulpit, he would serve for life. This "deep-seated prejudice" against changing pulpits—Congregationalists called it translation—meant above all else that one church should not lure away another's minister, as stealing a sister congregation's settled ministers was looked upon as un-Christian. When Brattle Street broke this covenant by enticing Thacher to depart Malden, other Boston churches quickly followed suit. In short order, Belknap and Emerson fled rural parishes to take positions in the capital. Boston had fractured the covenant "thou shalt not covet thy neighbor's pastor."

It was not by accident that William Emerson fled his obscure pulpit in rural Harvard, Massachusetts, for Boston's First Congregational Church. "Much more than ordinarily attractive" and possessing "a passionate love for the strains of eloquence," Emerson believed himself to be cut from the same cloth as his hero Charles Chauncy.[30] He intimately grasped the difficulty of heeding his ambitious adolescent remonstrance to "Arise to industry! To glory!" as pastor of Harvard's little congregation, even as he stoically wrote in his 1792 acceptance letter that "it is God who assigneth us our station in life."[31] Writing to his family and friends, Emerson frequently complained about his small, miserly, and contentious congregation as well as his cultural isolation. "It may be well for you to come and see how we *up in the country folks* live," he complained to William Farnham. "The taste of our homely fare will give new and pleasing relish to the dainties of *Port*."[32] Desperate for the "life of a scholar" and the other social amenities that went with being a Boston minister, Emerson frequently made the thirty-mile trip from Harvard to the capital. On one such trip in June of 1796 he asked Ruth Haskins, the daughter of a successful distiller, for her hand in marriage. Fourteen weeks later, Ruth Haskins Emerson accompanied her husband on the return trip to their modest home in the country. Into their rural if hardly bucolic life Ruth brought domestic tranquillity and two children, Phebe Ripley and John Clarke, but this domestic prodigality only made William that much more eager to escape his exile. Now, in addition to his social and professional isolation, he felt the pinch of poverty. "We are poor and cold," he lamented, "and have little meal, and little wood, and little meat."[33]

When the Ancient and Honourable Artillery Company of Boston offered him the chance to preach its Election Day sermon in 1799, Emerson readily grasped the significance of the invitation. Important members of Boston society would be in attendance, so there was every likelihood that a first-rate effort would lead to a highly coveted offer of a pastorate in Boston. For weeks Emerson worked feverishly on this sermon, subsequently published under the title *Piety and Arms*, as well as on the one he was to deliver before the First Congregational Church in Boston that same day. To his considerable joy, Emerson's efforts and eloquence produced the desired effect. First Church extended an offer to the ambitious young cleric a few weeks later. On September 22, 1799, while suffering from a severe cold, Emerson preached his first sermon from the pulpit of First Church. He was now the successor of John Cotton as well as his idol Charles Chauncy.

Emerson's old parish in rural Harvard could never have hoped to match his smart new salary of fourteen dollars per week. Even if it could have, it was a foregone conclusion that Emerson would move to Boston, where his "courtly manners and studied pulpit rhetoric," as Phyllis Cole styles it, would find a welcome audience and many kindred spirits.[34] To assuage the bruised feelings of the Harvard congregation, Emerson and First Church sought the intervention of Peter Thacher, himself a defector to Boston from the hinterlands, in negotiating with Emerson's former congregation. Harvard's disgruntled communicants argued that First Church had breached the "almost universal understanding that ministers were ordained for life, and that it was sinful to separate them, except in cases of imperious necessity." Since by general practice and tradition it was especially egregious for "ministers to leave their people for more eligible situations," Harvard argued strenuously that at the least it should not have to absorb the considerable cost of settling a new pastor.[35] In the absence of a Presbyterian system in which to air its grievances, however, Harvard had little recourse but to consent to the settlement its Boston sister society offered. It ultimately accepted a payment of one thousand dollars, "which sum you will consider our ultimate [offer] and will not be exceeded," curtly wrote First Church Treasurer David Tildon.[36] Rural churches like Harvard resigned themselves to the inevitable encroachments of the larger and wealthier Boston congregations.

Underpaid and at odds with their churches, William Emerson, Thacher, and Belknap had leaped at the opportunity to move to Boston. Harvard College graduates, learned, and loquacious, these young ministers fully comprehended that a move to Boston spelled a seismic shift in their professional and social circumstances. In societies where wealthy parishioners dominated, they no longer were obliged to face off against dogmatic church communicants, who resisted innovation. An acquiescent church promised an end to those old theological squabbles that constituted such a bitter nuisance for rural pastors who were often less orthodox than the communicants of their churches. In addition, these same well-to-do pew proprietors who offered their new ministers generous salaries began to patronize their ministers' literary and artistic aspirations. When New South Church extended its pastorate to John Thornton Kirkland, his former mentor, David Tappan, Hollis Professor of Divinity at Harvard, congratulated him on his "chosen lot" of being called to a Boston Church, because it signaled his entrance into that elite circle that Cleveland Amory styled "Proper Bostonians." Finding himself welcome in the best houses in Boston, Kirkland "lived on the most intimate terms with all the leading men of his time in this part of the country."[37] No sooner had Peter Thacher been called to Brattle Street Church than he received social invitations from Boston's most prominent families. Thacher's "society was constantly sought by Bowdoin, [Governor] Hancock, and all the dinner-giving gentry of that day."[38] Longtime Harvard President Josiah Quincy went so far as to claim that "on the top most round [*sic*] of the social ladder stood the clergy."[39]

A decade into the new century, Boston's churches had transformed themselves into elite institutions with brand-new, bigger meetinghouses and young, ambitious ministers who would keep their pews and coffers filled. Benjamin Austin of First Congregational, or Old Brick, Church lampooned in verse these all-too-worldly alterations.

> Farewell Old Brick,
> Old Brick farewell,
> You've bought your minister,
> And sold your bell.[40]

Having been "bought" by First Church, William Emerson quickly became the very embodiment of the new Brahmin minister. Relieved of the more onerous tasks usually associated with the pastorate, Emerson had time to undertake the creation of what was for the United States a number of novel cultural institutions. With his colleagues and connections, the peripatetic minister of First Church spearheaded the establishment of a professional library devoted to theological study, a literary club called the Anthology Society, which published the *Monthly Anthology*, and the Boston Athenaeum, where Boston's intellectual elite mingled with their wealthy patrons amid the nation's greatest private collection of books and periodicals. Emerson most assuredly heeded the advice of his colleague and friend, Joseph Buckminster, when he declared, "Go to the rich and tell them of the substantial glory of literary patronage."[41]

A cursory analysis of one of these endeavors, the "Society of Gentlemen," or Anthology Society, which published the *Monthly Anthology*, reveals the novel ambitions of Emerson and his Brahmin colleagues. Founded in 1803 by Phineas Adams, a Boston schoolteacher, the *Monthly Anthology* would have died in infancy if Emerson had not taken over the cash-strapped journal. Armed with his elite connections as well as the conviction that his wealthy parishioners desired their minister to foster an indigenous high culture outside the traditional bounds of religion, Emerson boasted that he "could give to our charge these expensive advantages."[42] Among the first members of the Anthology Society were six ministers of Boston-area churches. In addition to Emerson, the "clerical band" included Brattle Street's Buckminster, New South's Thacher, Thomas Gray of the Third Church of Roxbury, Chelsea minister Joseph Tuckerman, whom Daniel Walker Howe called "as close as an American could come in his day to being a genuine aristocrat," and John S. J. Gardiner, rector of Trinity Church in Boston.[43] Later members of the clergy to join the Anthology Society included Kirkland, Joseph McKean, John Pierce, and Sidney Willard, each of whom was a Congregational minister as well as professionally affiliated with Harvard College.

That the Congregational clergy proved so prominent in the publication of the *Monthly Anthology* is striking because from the first issue, the anthologists made it clear that they had no intention of focusing on issues of Congregational doctrine or on religious preoccupations generally. Latitudinarians to be sure, the anthologists, William Emerson declared in 1803, the year of Ralph Waldo's birth, "religiously avoided the metaphysical subtleties, with which some adherents of Calvin bewilder themselves and their hearers."[44] As if to prove the point, the Anthology Society tapped John Gardiner, an Episcopalian and rector of King's Chapel, to be its first president. "On the solemn and awful mysteries of some of the subjects of theology," editor-in-chief Emerson declared in the *Monthly Anthology*'s opening remarks, "many of us are unqualified to judge. . . . We feel ourselves therefore pledged to the support of no system, and when any theological work passes under our examination, it will only be in the regular survey of the literature of our country."[45] Buckminster minced no words in explicitly declaring the Brahmins' increasingly secular interests. "Theology," he exclaimed, "is the subject upon which much of our genius and learning has been employed, and not seldom wasted."[46]

It would be anachronistic and misleading to read into the Brahmins' statements and actions the non-Christian theism characteristic of contemporary Unitarianism and Universalism. Deeply spiritual to be sure, Buckminster, Kirkland, Emerson, and their colleagues never wavered in their devotion to Christianity. Yet for them a call to a Boston pulpit and membership in the Anthology Society signaled a welcome release from old theological debates and doctrinal hairsplitting. Freed from having to sermonize on "man as a fallen and apostate creature," the Brahmin ministers looked to this nascent literary high culture as a source of vital intellectual nourishment and an outlet for their artistic ambitions.

Anthology Society members declared in their little periodical their intentions to embrace a novel role, to promote themselves as New England's cultural gatekeepers. Openly espousing the Society's secular interests, Kirkland acknowledged that the anthologists' "design" was to foster "useful knowledge and harmless amusement, sound principles, good morals, and correct taste."[47] Finding diminished intellectual nourishment in rehashing stale theological debates, the ministers who published the *Monthly Anthology* eschewed many of the traditional pastoral activities, replacing them with literary and cultural enterprises. In doing so, the Brahmins hoped to foster an internationally acclaimed high culture. The flowering of literary culture, often called the New England Renaissance, in which William Emerson's son Ralph played a central role, was their offspring.

Not long into the successful run of the *Monthly Anthology*, the membership of the Anthology Society decided to explore the possibility of raising money for the establishment in Boston of an exclusive library society with grand social pretensions. Undaunted by the estimable cost that would be needed to build up a considerable book and periodical collection, the ubiquitous William Emerson doggedly pursued his friends and patrons among what was becoming Boston's grand bourgeoisie for funds to bring the project to fruition. Emerson had already helped to establish Boston's first theological library a few years earlier, but this effort proved an undertaking of an altogether different magnitude. In 1807 his efforts met with a resounding success as the Anthologists and their benefactors founded the Boston Athenaeum. From the first subscription, it was clear that it would become much more than the convenient meeting place of the wealthy and the learned in the heart of the capital, in short order becoming the very embodiment of the emerging Brahmin union of aspiring intellectuals and a thriving mercantile bourgeoisie.

In contrast to the *Monthly Anthology*, which could be read by any literate American, the Boston Athenaeum was an elitist institution from start to finish. Membership was exclusive, restricted to those who bought shares. Initially priced at three hundred dollars, later subscriptions went for over ten times that figure. In addition to the minister-founders who enjoyed special dispensation, only Boston's wealthy could afford to purchase shares. Owning a share in the Athenaeum soon became a distinct badge of honor belonging to only the most exclusive elite of Boston. Shares in the Athenaeum became so coveted—and scarce—that the first families rarely relinquished them, usually bequeathing them to their heirs.[48]

The only nonsubscribers welcome in the Athenaeum's drawing rooms and encouraged to use the library's considerable holdings were members of the intellectual elite. The founders ensured that the charter guaranteed Boston's Brahmin ministers and Harvard professors access to the collections. Similarly, the Athenaeum charter left it up to the discretion of the members whom to exclude. The members studiously banned from the premises orthodox Congregational ministers such as Jedidiah Morse and the other editors of the strident *Panoplist* magazine that, like the *Monthly Anthology*, was also published in Boston in the first decades of the nineteenth century. Similarly, the conservative membership withdrew the privilege of using the Athenaeum's ample collections from Lydia Maria Child after the publication of her first abolitionist tract.[49] The Athenaeum embraced only those intellectuals who toed the party line.

By 1820 the Athenaeum's custodians, Treasurer William Shaw in particular, had assembled the largest private collection in the nation. The Athenaeum boasted holdings of over twenty thousand volumes. The collection proved so large that one generous family, the Perkins clan, donated its Pearl Street mansion to be the Athenaeum's new home. Others contributed significant sums to the institution, with several bequests in excess of ten thousand dollars. Within two decades, the vision of a few Anthology Society members had become one of Boston's most conspicuously endowed cultural institutions.

The publication of a relatively modest journal and the more ambitious project of creating the Boston Athenaeum paled in comparison to the Brahmins' efforts to take over Harvard College. Not only was it New England's most venerable cultural institution, Harvard was a quasi-public university, responsible for almost two centuries for the training of ministers of the Standing Order. The Brahmins and their State Street allies faced powerful opponents both in the state government and the Congregational church. Their ultimately successful struggle to assume control of Harvard created bitter opposition among the orthodox clergy and precipitated a bifurcation in the Standing Order that eventually led to the disestablishment of the Congregational church in 1833.

The fight for Harvard began with the deaths within a year of one another of David Tappan, the Hollis Professor of Divinity, and the university's president, Rev. Joseph Willard. When Acting President Eliphalet Pearson assembled the Harvard Corporation members in the fall of 1805 to fill the Hollis vacancy, he was "shocked and greatly disturbed" to discover that the leading candidate was Henry Ware, the venerable minister of Hingham, Massachusetts.[50] Trusted colleague of William Emerson and one of the leading Brahmin ministers in the Bay State, Ware contributed to the *Monthly Anthology* and enjoyed membership in the Athenaeum. Accordingly, Pearson and his orthodox ally, Jedidiah Morse, who as Charlestown's minister held a seat on the Harvard Board of Overseers, believed that appointing Ware to this most prestigious chair of divinity in the nation "would threaten a revolution in our university."[51] Working feverishly during the winter of 1805–6 to find some means of denying Ware the Hollis appointment, Pearson and Morse ultimately claimed that Ware's warm rejection of doctrinal rigidity disqualified him because of the explicit call for an "orthodox" candidate in the original bequest of Thomas Hollis to Harvard, dating from the 1730s. Since Ware acknowledged himself to be a liberal—that is, a latitudinarian who like Emerson and his Brahmin brethren eschewed doctrinal debate and hairsplitting—he could not possibly be "of sound and orthodox principles," as the contract stipulated. Pearson and Morse were virtually alone in this judgment. Most of the Harvard community agreed with Corporation member and Anthologist John Pierce that theirs was a specious argument utterly without merit.[52] In the winter of 1805–6 the Board of Overseers confirmed Henry Ware as the Hollis Professor of Divinity.[53]

Desperate to stave off this "revolution," the ever-fractious Jedidiah Morse leapt into print, publishing a scathing pamphlet about the controversy in which he skewered the Brahmins. *The True Reasons on which the Election of a Hollis Professor of Divinity in Harvard College was Opposed at the Board of Overseers* proved to be the opening salvo in a protracted fight between the orthodox and Brahmin camps. Significantly, while Morse had erroneously contended that the Hollis Professor must be one of his own orthodox party, he accurately prognosticated that the Ware appointment signaled the beginning of the Brahmin transformation of Harvard. With Ware's installation as Hollis Professor, Harvard, like Boston's Congregational churches, came to embrace a religious latitudinarianism that was characterized less by a rejection of Calvinism or Trinitarianism than by an air of catholicity. Together with the Corporation, the Harvard faculty—still ministers for the most part—acknowledged that an upright character, personal comportment, and intellectual depth were the qualities they sought in their colleagues and attempted to inculcate in their charges. When Jedidiah Morse warned of a revolution in the religious sentiment at Cambridge, he was only half right. Ware and his Brahmin supporters did reject orthodoxy, but not in favor of a competing set of doctrines. The real revolution rested in the Brahmin movement away from doctrinal debate of any kind. The traditional theological preoccupations no longer interested them. Therein lay the revolution.

At least as important to the transformation of Harvard as the Hollis fight was the completion of the West Boston Bridge in 1803. By cementing the connection of Harvard and the mercantile elite of Boston, the West Boston Bridge facilitated the movement of Boston money in one direction and Harvard graduates—"the scholar and gentleman united"—in the other.[54] In contrast to the admonitions of Timothy Dwight, the orthodox president of Yale, who feared that the proximity of Boston to Harvard was a paramount danger, the members of the Harvard Corporation were immeasurably relieved at the prospect of renewed Boston patronage, which arrived not a moment too soon. By the beginning of the nineteenth century, Harvard was in dire financial straits. The buildings had been badly damaged while serving as headquarters for the Continental army; the endowment, invested in Continental currency, had been devastated by inflation; and the commonwealth was in no mood to grant the school additional funds. Virtually bankrupt, the college needed far more than occasional gifts from its faithful supporters. Harvard had to find an alternative and regular source of income.[55]

The transformation of Harvard's financial regime and educational mission commenced in earnest with the installation of John Thornton Kirkland to the presidency of Harvard in 1810. A Harvard graduate—all the Brahmins were—and until his appointment minister of the New South Church, Kirkland was a member of the Anthology Society as well as one of the founders of the Boston Athenaeum. He no less than William Emerson was the very model of the new Brahmin minister. Under his benign reign, Harvard's Corporation and Trustees transformed the institution from a religious seminary into a formidable institution of higher education. Harvard's leadership secularized many features of the institution, moving rapidly to establish professional schools in medicine and law, while simultaneously relegating the training of ministers to a separate school of divinity. Ralph Waldo Emerson would be one of the first students to live in Divinity Hall in Cambridge. During his seventeen-year tenure, Kirkland forcefully leaned on the mercantile elite of Boston to give generously to their Cambridge neighbor. And did they ever. What had been for the previous two hundred years essentially a publicly funded seminary became by the 1830s a privately funded institution that depended upon the generous annual contributions and bequests of the Brahmins' patrons. One contemporary quipped that with Kirkland, "there is scarcely a limit to his influence with the rich men of Boston."

The Brahmin takeover and transformation of Harvard, a far more public act than the founding of the Athenaeum, precipitated a schism in the Congregational ranks that would ultimately bring about the disestablishment of the Standing Order in 1833. Coalescing around their defense of Harvard, Trinitarians, Moderate Calvinists, Consistent Calvinists, and other Brahmin opponents formed an orthodox party. Led by the vitriolic and contentious Jedidiah Morse, the orthodox sought to expose the dangerous heterodoxy of their erstwhile Congregational brethren. Morse, Leonard Woods, Joshua Huntington, Jeremiah Evarts—all Yale graduates—and others created the institutional means to defeat the Brahmins and drive them out of the church. When William Emerson and the Brahmins began publishing the *Monthly Anthology*, Morse and the orthodox countered with their own publication, the *Panoplist*. The takeover of Harvard necessitated the creation of a seminary for the training of a devout clergy, so the orthodox established the Andover Theological Seminary. Finally, in an attempt to establish a more forceful presence in the capital, the orthodox party formed the Park Street Church, appropriately named Brimstone Corner, in the heart of Brahmin Boston.[56]

The members of the orthodox party, particularly those on the editorial board of the *Panoplist*, known as the Friends to Evangelical Truth, were convinced that true religion was in desperate straits in New England and in the nation at large. Threatened on all sides, orthodox ministers deplored the deism and demagoguery of Thomas Jefferson, which they associated with Brahmin heterodoxy, and simultaneously fretted over the rising tide of Baptism and Methodism. Perhaps suffering from what another generation of scholars called "status anxiety," these devout and doctrinaire ministers warned of a grave declension in the religious fervor of the region. Echoing the lamentation of the prophet, *Panoplist* writers called for a renewal of national piety through revivals and regeneration. They saved their most scathing attacks for their Brahmin opponents, convinced that the declension they witnessed all around them was directly attributable to the heterodox and latitudinarian sentiments of the Brahmins. "Should it please the exalted Redeemer to address the churches in New England, especially in the Commonwealth," stated a *Panoplist* contributor, we have reason to conclude that his language would not be unlike that, which he used to address the Asiatic churches. He would certainly find as little to approve, and as much to condemn, as he found there. Not a single erroneous opinion or practice existed among them, which does not, in substance, exist among us.[57]

Something had to be done to squelch the heterodoxy within the Congregational church.

The orthodox party betrayed its disgust with Brahmin latitudinarianism by refusing to engage in ministerial fellowship with its ideological opponents and by seeking to adopt creeds and examinations to ensure orthodoxy. Edward Griffin, the ill-fated first minister at Park Street, so vociferously condemned his Boston colleagues that he shortly wore out his welcome with even his orthodox parishioners. In a similar vein, the refusal of Dorchester's minister, John Codman, to exchange pulpits with virtually anyone in the Boston Association of Ministers precipitated a crisis in that church. Desirous of hearing the preaching of Boston's well-known latitudinarian ministers, members of Codman's parish threatened to remove him if he continued to refuse his pulpit to any but other orthodox pastors. Successive ecclesiastical councils failed to convince or compel Codman to "be more generous in his exchanges." As a result, in 1810 Dorchester's church split in two, with the largely latitudinarian parish dissolving its bonds with Codman and his orthodox supporters.[58]

The Dorchester controversy was a harbinger of things to come. For the next two decades the Congregational churches of eastern Massachusetts fractured along Brahmin-orthodox lines. Whatever the immediate cause, whether an orthodox pastor refused to exchange pulpits—a critical safety valve for diverse congregations—or a latitudinarian minister offending the orthodox in his congregation, the result was usually separation. The class nature of the Brahmin appeal is unmistakable in these controversies. In Dorchester, Princeton, Taunton, Sandwich, Dedham, and other towns, the wealthier parishioners proved more latitudinarian than the church communicants. As in Boston, where the voluntary maintenance system prevailed, well-to-do parishioners sought Brahmin ministers who, as Joseph Stevens Buckminster noted, "do not require men . . . to throw their wealth into the sea or to inflict upon themselves unnatural austerities."[59] In contrast, church communicants, who constituted themselves on the basis of religious conviction and public testimony, felt their traditional status within the church and in the community to be under siege. Together with orthodox ministers, they sought to extirpate the latitudinarian elements within the congregation and thus revitalize Christian piety. This is not to suggest that parishioners and communicants did not overlap; rather, as fewer wealthy parishioners confessed their faith yet continued to attend church, they were not going to have their choice of minister or other issues of church policy dictated to them by church communicants. In this sense, the Congregational societies surrounding Boston merely caught up to those in the capital where parishioners' pew rents already determined that they would control their church societies.[60]

In 1814 Jedidiah Morse thought he had uncovered irrefutable evidence of the Brahmins' "open infidelity" that he had long suspected. The proof came in the form of a copy of Thomas Belsham's pamphlet on Unitarianism in America. Morse published a review of the work in the *Panoplist*, convinced that he had finally exposed the rank apostasy of his enemies. While few Brahmins agreed with James Freeman whom Belsham quoted as asserting the Unitarian faith was making "fast and irresistible progress," they did not rush into print defending themselves.[61] Virtually all the Brahmin ministers had disavowed Calvinism and considered Jesus to be the Son of God only in an attenuated and metaphorical sense. On this point, Morse was right. Yet, the Brahmin ministers shared neither a creed nor a strict set of doctrines. Some were Socinians, others Arians and Arminians. When William Ellery Channing openly adopted the name Unitarian in his "Unitarian Christianity" sermon, delivered in Baltimore in 1819, which did at least reflect the Brahmin disbelief in the triune nature of the deity, he did so as an attempt to suggest what beliefs the Brahmins minimally held in common. It proved no easy task, and a deeper, more penetrating theologian likely would have despaired of achieving even partial success. Still, for better or worse, the party of Emerson, Buckminister, Kirkland, and Channing became known as the Unitarians.

When William Emerson died in 1811, neither he nor Channing called themselves Unitarians. To them, their specific doctrinal convictions, such as they were, proved of little import, which is why their Boston Association of Ministers had ceased to examine candidates about their specific beliefs. What Emerson and his latitudinarian colleagues constituted was a coterie of clerical intellectuals who were no longer preoccupied with "metaphysical subtleties of theology." In the pages of the *Monthly Anthology*, at the genteel sitting rooms of the Boston Athenaeum, and in the classrooms of Harvard University, they demonstrated their social sensibilities and high cultural tastes. In forging an alliance with the mercantile elite of Boston, who patronized their literary interests, and with whom they intermarried, these thinkers fashioned themselves into an intellectual upper crust.

Ralph Waldo Emerson delivered his Divinity School Address a score of years after Channing's Baltimore sermon. For the speaker this homily was intended as an insider's attempt to warn his colleagues, both present and future, that their elitism had gone too far, that they were in grave danger from a self-inflicted wound. Not only had "coldness & continually increasing superficialness" resulted in the "continually thinning of our ranks," as he wrote in his journal subsequently, but the Brahmin ministers had utterly lost influence in society at large.[62] The radicalism of Emerson's words that July evening in 1838 stemmed from his assertion that in becoming Brahmins, William Emerson and his colleagues had sacrificed the Puritan notion of a covenant with the community as a whole for a class compact with the rich. Accordingly, when Andrews Norton attacked the address as "the latest form of infidelity" and other Unitarians worried over the dangerous ideas it contained, its author was sorely tempted to offer some sort of public rejoinder, convinced that the Unitarian elite had misunderstood his remarks. The ninth in a line of Congregational ministers and son of one of the leading Brahmins, Emerson believed that his tapping into the deep vein of antinomianism that dated back at least to Anne Hutchinson and could be found in the writings of virtually all the Puritan greats since the first decades of the settlement of Massachusetts Bay proved hardly radical, much less a form of infidelity. Playing Luther to Norton's Leo X, Emerson understood himself to be stating the obvious in an attempt to rescue the Unitarian faith from itself. In matters of faith Emerson and the Transcendentalists, who were deeply religious Christians for the most part, differed only marginally from their Unitarian parents and teachers.[63] Like the author of the Divinity School Address, James Freeman Clarke, Theodore Parker, Frederic Hedge, and other Transcendentalists remained at least nominally Unitarian ministers of the Gospel.[64] Similarly, Unitarians like Norton and his Harvard colleagues espoused such rationalistic, essentially Arian doctrines that the Transcendentalists simply took the next logical step along the path laid out for them by the previous generation. As Jedidiah Morse, Lyman Beecher, and other orthodox stalwarts had been arguing since the turn of the century, the Unitarians had long ago let the Trojan horse of science into the citadel of religion. More recently, James Turner has written that the intellectual bloodlines of "unbelief in America" run through the first Unitarian pulpits of New England.

Emerson's address was less about dogma or doctrinal issues than it was a denunciation of intellectual and social elitism. As society had become less deferential, as politics had turned democratic, and as Boston and the nation as a whole had become more open, his own professors and his father's ministerial associates had by 1838 chosen a smug exile. The Unitarians of Boston and Harvard and the *North American Review* had developed a distasteful snobbery. Whether they knew it or not, they had become irrelevant. "Merely spectral," Emerson had called them.[65] The very success of his father's cultural projects, such as the Boston Athenaeum and the Brahmin takeover of Harvard, had led to a dreadful class stratification, out of which the Unitarians had lost touch with those who most needed converting. The Divinity School Address, much like his 1836 *Nature*, was Emerson's pointed intellectual admonition.[66] When he urged the divinity students to "go alone," he was telling them to be honest with themselves, to acknowledge that their Unitarian mentors were members of an effete, elitist community that had lost touch with the vitality of the nation. Disdainful and fearful of democracy, they had barricaded themselves in their elite Cambridge and Boston institutions. Anyone who trusted their own sensibilities could see that Unitarianism had already reached its apogee and would never extend beyond the parochial confines of eastern Massachusetts. It was time to "abandon the church of our fathers" in order to do God's work in the world.

In the Divinity School Address, Ralph Waldo Emerson explained why he could no longer be a Brahmin. Ambitious, peripatetic, brilliant, and optimistic, Emerson sought, as he put it, "a new theatre, a new art," in which he could come into communication with a real audience that was not so smug as to think it was not in need of conversion.[67] At Divinity Hall on Harvard's campus Emerson made public his personal and political rationale for rejecting so much of New England's intellectual inheritance. Everyone could divine that the old institutions had become irrelevant. In the same journal entry where he despaired of a faith "founded on nothing & [which] led to nothing," Emerson noted that for almost a decade he had "wondered at the patience of people" who sustained the shell of the Unitarian belief.[68] Just as his own patience had run out, so he held that but for a few Boston Brahmins the patience of all the people had largely evaporated. Craving relevance beyond the borders of Boston and Cambridge, Emerson clamored for his colleagues to undertake a sort of democratic conversion. To save themselves and the faith, they had to look beyond Boston.

From William Emerson to Ralph Waldo Emerson, then, the intellectual culture of one section of the United States took a most intriguing course: from Brahmin rejection of a popular calling in the name of high culture to a protreptic embrace of culture in the name of the American people. Child of one of the principal founders of the Boston Brahmins, Emerson resolved to show his fellow New England intellectuals the way.

NOTES

1. "The Divinity School Address," *Collected Works* 1:85.
2. *JMN* 5:465.

3. *JMN* 5:58.

4. *JMN* 5:471.

5. *JMN* 9:381.

6. "Divinity School Address," *Collected Works* 1:89.

7. "Divinity School Address," *Collected Works* 1:90.

8. Odell Shepard, ed., *The Journals of Bronson Alcott* (Boston, 1938), 103.

9. *JMN* 5:471.

10. For differing interpretations of Andrews Norton's reaction to Emerson's address, see Robert D. Habich, "Emerson's Reluctant Foe: Andrews Norton and the Transcendental Controversy," *New England Quarterly* 65 (1992), 208–37; and Perry Miller, *The Transcendentalists: An Anthology* (Cambridge, 1950), 210–13.

11. Perhaps Norton and the others recoiled so violently from the address precisely because it had come from one of their own. Emerson was virtually a family member. In their eyes his message proved so dangerous because its exponent was more than an enemy; he was an apostate, a traitor. Or perhaps, as Perry Miller observed, the Unitarians, already reeling from the Abner Kneeland trial and the growing threat of Universalism (despite their ultimate merger in 1961), sensed that they would shortly suffer assaults from Theodore Parker and Orestes Brownson. As Mary Cayton notes, "perhaps the Unitarian clergy would have allowed Emerson his say with less uproar had they not already been under siege." See Mary Kupiec Cayton, *Emerson's Emergence: Self and Society in the Transformation of New England, 1800–1840* (Chapel Hill, N.C., 1989), 173.

12. *JMN* 1:90; Lidian, Emerson's wife, pressured her husband not to respond to his critics, declaring that, as Emerson transcribed into his journal, "this whole practice of self justification & recrimination betwixt literary men seemed every whit as low as the quarrels of the Paddies." Emerson replied, "But what will you say, excellent Asia, when my smart article comes out in the paper, in reply to Mr A & Dr B? 'Why, then,' answered she, 'I shall feel the first emotion of fear & of sorrow on your account.' But do you know, I asked, how many fine things I have thought of to say to these fighters? They are too good to be lost.— 'Then' rejoined the queen, 'there is some merit in being silent.' " *JMN* 7:112.

13. Emerson to Carlyle, 11/7/38, *CEC* 200.

14. See Lowell's letter in William B. Sprague, *Annals of the American Pulpit,* 9 vols. (New York, 1865), 8:244. Perry Miller makes exactly this case in "Jonathan Edwards to Emerson," first published in the *New England Quarterly* 13 (1940), 589–617.

15. William Emerson, *Historical Sketch of the First Church in Boston* (Boston, 1812). Note that the use of Sr. in the text is to distinguish father and son only.

16. It is also possible that Emerson might have had his father in mind instead of Barzallai Frost, his Concord pastor, when composing the address. For the relevance of Frost, see Conrad Wright, "Emerson, Barzallai Frost, and the Divinity School Address," in *American Unitarianism, 1805–1865,* ed. Conrad Edick Wright (Boston, 1989).

17. Phyllis Cole, *Mary Moody Emerson and the Origins of Transcendentalism: A Family History* (New York, 1998), 121–22, 130.

18. Emerson to William Emerson, 2/10/50, *Letters* 4:179; see also Sprague, *Annals*, 8:244–45.

19. In 1803, the year of Emerson's birth, Unitarianism was on the outer fringe of American Christianity. The Boston ministers, who, following Channing's lead, assumed the name Unitarians in the 1820s, held as anathema the materialist teachings of Joseph Priestly and his European followers. Calling themselves liberals, clerics such as Ralph Waldo Emerson's father, William, subscribed to a set of beliefs that John Adams and others called Arminianism, but more resembled Arianism than the teaching of Jacobus Arminius. The liberals, or Brahmins, as I prefer to call them, adopted a rationalistic posture toward the Bible and historical Christianity that originated in New England in the writings of Jonathan Mayhew, Ebenezer Gay, and Charles Chauncy. They self-consciously eschewed dogmatism, often criticizing the Puritan Congregationalists for surreptitiously adopting creeds and confessions into what was an avowedly free church tradition. Like their old light predecessors, these Boston ministers defined themselves in opposition to those denominations that warmed to revivals, religious enthusiasm, and an overtly emotionally charged oratorical style. When pressed, the Brahmins rejected the notion of a triune deity, claiming that Jesus was the Son of God in only a metaphorical, attenuated sense.

20. Henry Adams, *History of the United States during the Administration of Jefferson and Madison*, ed. and abridg. Ernest Samuels (1921; rep., Chicago, 1967), 56.

21. For a fuller discussion of the applicability of the term *Brahmin*, see Peter S. Field, "The Birth of Secular High Culture in America: The *Monthly Anthology and Boston Review* and Its Critics," *Journal of the Early Republic* 17 (winter 1997), 575–609.

22. William Tudor, *Monthly Anthology and Boston Review* 9 (1810), 160.

23. William Charvat, *The Origins of American Critical Thought: 1810–1835* (Philadelphia, 1936), 173.

24. See Charles H. Lippy, "The 1780 Massachusetts Constitution: Religious Establishment or Civil Religion?" *Journal of Church and State* 20 (1987), 533–49; see also John D. Cushing, "Notes on Disestablishment in Massachusetts," *William And Mary Quarterly*, 3rd ser., 26 (1969), 169–90.

25. William Bentley, *Diary of William Bentley*, 4 vols. (Salem, Mass., 1905–14), 4:18.

26. H. Crosby Englizian, *Brimstone Corner: Park Street Church, Boston* (Chicago, 1968).

27. *Church Records of Federal Street*, cited in Sprague, *Annals*, 8:77.

28. Anne Rose, "Social Sources of Denominationalism Reconsidered," *American Quarterly* 38 (1986), 251.

29. Scholars continue to portray the mercantile elite's patronage of the arts as a self-conscious push toward cultural hegemony. For what I consider to be the overly reductive Marxian view of intellectuals as servants of the "constituent classes" of society, see Antonio Gramsci, "The Formation of Intellectuals," in *The Modern Prince and Other Writings* (New York, 1957). Tamara Plakins Thornton in *Cultivating Gentlemen:*

The Meaning of Country Life among the Boston Elite, 1785–1860 (New Haven, 1989) and Ronald Story in *Harvard and the Boston Upper Class: The Forging of an Aristocracy, 1800–1870* (Middletown, Conn., 1980)—following Gramsci and Georg Lukacs—fail to give intellectuals as a constituent class of society their due.

30. See Ralph L. Rusk, *The Life of Ralph Waldo Emerson* (New York, 1949), 12.

31. *William Emerson Journal* (1), October 13, 1795, Houghton Library, Harvard University Archives.

32. Emerson to William Farnham, 4/24/92, Emerson Collection, Massachusetts Historical Society.

33. Rusk, *Life*, 6.

34. Cole, *Mary Moody Emerson*, 103.

35. *Records of the First Church*, September 20, 1799; reprinted in the Colonial Society of Massachusetts *Collections* 40 (Boston, 1961), 585–603.

36. *Records of the First Church*, September 20, 1799, 601–2.

37. Alexander Young, "Memoir of John Thornton Kirkland," in *American Unitarian Biography*, ed. William Ware (Boston, 1850), 292.

38. Sprague, *Annals* 1:721.

39. Josiah Quincy IV, *Figures of the Past, from the Leaves of Old Journals* (1883; rep., Boston, 1926), 303.

40. Austin also wrote alternatively: "Alas, Old Brick,/you're left in the lurch,/You bought your minister,/and sold the church." See the (Boston) *Independent Chronicle*, July 5, 1808.

41. Joseph Stevens Buckminster, *Works,* 2 vols. (Boston, 1854), 2:428–42.

42. William Emerson, "Preface," *Monthly Anthology* 1 (1804), ii.

43. Daniel Walker Howe, *The Unitarian Conscience: Harvard Moral Philosophy, 1805–1861* (Cambridge, 1970), 313.

44. William Emerson, *A Sermon on the Decease of the Rev. Peter Thacher, D.D.* (Boston, 1803), 20.

45. *Monthly Anthology* 5 (1808), 586.

46. *Monthly Anthology* 5 (1808), 586.

47. *Monthly Anthology* 5 (1808), 586.

48. Ronald Story, "Class and Culture in Boston: The Athenaeum, 1807–1860," *American Quarterly* 27 (1975), 178–99; see also Peter S. Field, *The Crisis of the Standing Order: Clerical Intellectuals and Cultural Authority in Massachusetts, 1780–1833* (Amherst, Mass., 1998), 103–10.

49. See Deborah Pickman Clifford, *Crusader for Freedom: A Life of Lydia Maria Child* (Boston, 1992), 47–51.

50. For a fuller discussion of the "fight for Harvard," see Field, *Crisis*, ch. 4; and Conrad Wright, "The Election of Henry Ware: Two Contemporary Accounts," *Harvard Library Bulletin* 17 (1969), 245–78.

51. Jedidiah Morse, *The True Reasons on which the Election of a Hollis Professor of Divinity in Harvard College was Opposed at the Board of Overseers, Feb. 14, 1805* (Charlestown, Mass., 1805), 19.

52. Pierce believed that Pearson was intent on securing the Hollis Chair for Morse, while Morse, as Hollis Professor, would then cast the deciding vote for Pearson to be made university president outright. See John Pierce, "Memoirs and Memorabilia," *Proceedings of the Massachusetts Historical Society* 7 (1891), 305–18.

53. Eliphalet Pearson promptly resigned not only from his position as Harvard's acting president but as Hancock Professor of Religion as well. His bitter letter of resignation, never published, remains in the Pusey archives of Harvard University to this day.

54. *Monthly Anthology* (1806), 3:18.

55. Samuel Eliot Morison, *Three Centuries of Harvard* (Cambridge, 1936), 180–88.

56. Field, "High Culture," 577–81.

57. *Panoplist* 1 (1806), 541–42.

58. Conrad Wright, "Institutional Reconstruction in the Unitarian Controversy," in Wright, *American Unitarianism,* 3–29.

59. Buckminster, *Works*, 2:228.

60. It is no irony that the status of full communion declined simultaneously with the remarkable influx of women into the ranks of church communicant. For an analysis on the meaning of this transformation, see Ann Douglas, *The Feminization of American Culture* (New York, 1977).

61. Jedidiah Morse, *Thomas Belsham's "American Unitarianism: Or a Brief History of the Progress and Present State of the Unitarian Churches in America"* (Boston, 1814).

62. *JMN* 8:355.

63. See David Robinson, *Apostle of Culture: Emerson as Preacher and Lecturer* (Philadelphia, 1982).

64. The German idealism transplanted to America as Transcendentalism surely went beyond anything in Unitarianism. Yet Unitarians such as Joseph Stevens Buckminster had for a generation championed the higher biblical criticism prominent in German universities. As early as 1810 the Unitarians had founded the Dexter Lectureship at Harvard, and as a result had embraced a critical stance toward the New Testament and the divinity of Jesus. Doctrinally, it seems only a small step from the stridently antidogmatic strains of Channing's Baltimore sermon to the naturalistic Christian Platonism of the Divinity School Address. The previous generation had undermined the authority of the Bible and come to view Jesus as a man; the next logical step was to jettison such unfortunate aspects of revealed religion as miracles and the other incredulous baggage of the historical church. "In this point of view," Emerson wrote in the Divinity School Address, "we become sensible of the first defect of historical Christianity. Historical Christianity has fallen into the error that corrupts all attempts to communicate religion. As it appears to us, and as it has appeared for ages, it is not the doctrine of the soul, but an exaggeration of the personal, the positive, the ritual." Parker stated precisely this in his 1841 sermon, "A Discourse on the Transient and Permanent in Christianity."

65. *JMN* 1:85.

66. "Thy hands are now busy with parricide," Emerson recorded in a journal entry in 1820. See *JMN* 1:218.

67. *JMN* 7:338–39.

68. *JMN* 5:58.

2

BORN TO BE EDUCATED

Every man is a wonder until you learn his studies, his associates, his
early acts & the floating opinions of his times, & then he develops
himself as naturally from a point as a river is made from rills.[1]

Ralph Waldo Emerson was born in 1803 into an elite New England family.
His father, William Emerson, had attended Harvard and, like his father
before him and his before him, had become a minister in the Congregational
church. The sudden, premature death of his father, just days before his eighth
birthday, abruptly altered Ralph's life as well as those of the rest of the Emerson family. Emerson's mother, Ruth Haskins Emerson, pregnant for the eighth
time when her husband took sick, never remarried. Together with her enig-
matic sister-in-law, Mary Moody Emerson, and with the help of other family
members, Ruth Emerson raised her children as a struggling widow with limited means. Her youngest, Mary Caroline, died before her third birthday, joining two other departed children, Phebe and John Clarke. One of the remaining
five brothers, Robert Bulkeley, four years Ralph's junior, suffered from mental retardation and other developmental disorders. Often Bulkeley did not
reside with his brothers; at times he was a danger to himself and stayed in
McLean Asylum, and at others he boarded with local farmers for whom he
worked as best he could. That left Ruth to raise her four other boys: William,
Ralph, Edward, and Charles.

The Emersons' poverty never amounted to deprivation, but it was real. It
profoundly affected all of the children, especially Ralph who always felt like
something of an outsider among the Boston elite. The First Congregational
Church, where the Emersons' father had been minister upon his death, granted
the family use of the parsonage at Chauncy Place but only until the arrival of
a new minister. For more than a year the church proprietors paid Ruth her
husband's salary of twenty-five dollars per week, after which they reached a
final settlement with their pastor's widow that provided an annual stipend of

five hundred dollars for seven years. Hardly sufficient to meet the family's needs much less to pay off William's considerable debts, these funds were augmented by the sale at auction of William Emerson's estate, the largest portion of which was his library of more than 450 volumes. The proceeds from the auction, combined with the sale of land purchased years earlier from a brother-in-law in Maine, at least covered some of the deceased minister's outstanding liabilities that totaled an astonishing twenty-five hundred dollars. The sheer size of this debt as well as the inventory of Emerson's estate amply demonstrated that until 1811 the family had lived well, and well beyond its means.[2]

The years immediately ensuing William's death proved a great struggle for the whole family. They were ameliorated in some measure by the presence of Aunt Mary, who possessed "some traits of character," Ruth wrote to a friend, "as render her peculiarly dear to me."[3] Mary proved useful too when Ruth began to take in boarders as a means of augmenting their meager income. Ruth and the family would move a dozen times in the succeeding years, and at each location Ruth's principal income came from her operation of a boardinghouse. Doubtless, the entire family understood just how much the death of their father had diminished their status in society, as family friend James Freeman had predicted. "Rev Dr. Freeman consoled my father on his deathbed," Ralph wrote in his journal some twenty-three years later, "by telling him he had not outlived his teeth, &c. & bid my mother expect now to be neglected by society."[4]

Even with the help of Aunt Mary, who "became her nephews' female stepfather after William died," Ruth struggled to find enough money to support her children.[5] The brothers' recollections amply attested to their penury. James Cabot tells the story of Ralph and Edward sharing one winter coat between them, which inevitably caused the boys to suffer "the taunts of vulgar-minded school-fellows inquiring: 'Whose turn is it to wear the coat to-day?' "[6] Ruth seldom complained of the family's straitened circumstances, sharing her troubles primarily with Aunt Mary, and then only rarely. Taking in William's successor, the Rev. John Abbot, proved so trying that she wrote Mary that "I cannot find time in your absence to do even the necessary sewing of the family with my other cares & have now 4 or 5 shirts for the children which they need, waiting to be made when you return."[7] By the fall of 1814, Ruth had given up all claims to the parsonage, perhaps as much to get away finally from the exclusive society of First Church as to escape that dismal place where her husband had died only a few years earlier. Children in tow, Ruth Emerson moved to Bennet Street and perhaps lived for some time at her father's home on Rainsford Lane.[8] She would surely have preferred to depart wartime Boston for more affordable surroundings, having never cared for

Boston society, but the children's education demanded they remain within the proximity of the Boston Public Latin School and Harvard College. Ruth concurred with Aunt Mary about the all-but-immeasurable value of higher education. The Emerson boys, Mary informed a friend, "were born to be educated."[9]

The genteel poverty that plagued the Emersons left its mark on the entire family. Aunt Mary tried to downplay the family's financial problems, writing in 1814 that "You would think from this [poverty] we are *cast down* but we are not. A low and humble state is generally without much change."[10] Their confining circumstances affected the brothers in many ways. The older brothers felt especially protective of their mother. They surely would have agreed with family friend James Cabot when he observed that "It was in truth a heavy burden that fell upon the widow in her affliction, with scanty means of support, and six children, all under ten years of age."[11] As boys and young men, the brothers worked at chores and errands to keep the household functioning. Thrown upon their own resources, they toiled together doing whatever they could to ease their mother's burdens and to improve their lives. The boys provided crucial labor to a household economy that always seemed stretched to the limit. Before and after his instruction at the Latin School preteen Ralph assisted his mother in providing for their boarders. The brothers viscerally disliked Ruth's catering to the needs of outsiders and her daily struggle to ensure sufficient income. One of Emerson's most searing memories from his youth concerned misplacing a dollar bill with which he had been entrusted to buy a new pair of shoes. Having lost the note somewhere between the house and the market, the youngster was forced to search for it in desperation among the fallen poplar leaves in the street.[12]

The great difficulty in making ends meet necessitated that the Emerson family move many times. After the War of 1812, Ruth Emerson plucked her children from their temporary lodgings in Concord only to bring them back to Boston, agreeing to take up residence in the Beacon Street home of merchant Daniel P. Parker. During his frequent trips abroad, she took care of his family, while simultaneously taking in boarders to supplement her income. One of her paying guests at this fashionable address was, according to Ralph Rusk, none other than Lemuel Shaw, the future Massachusetts chief justice. The irony of keeping a boardinghouse on Beacon Street was not lost on the family. Understandably uneasy about accepting gifts and hand-me-downs from her former peers, Ruth stoically resigned herself to the family's diminished social status; Aunt Mary, who was living with the family at this moment, was less impassive. She wrote to her friend Ann Brewer that while they were "surrounded by a Neighbourhood of the highest Class—Otis, Dexter, Sulivan, Emery, Gore,

Phillips, and Eliot," their neighbors did not deign to socialize with them. "Ladies do not like to visit where are Boarders," Mary derisively concluded.[13]

The social ramifications of their genteel poverty did not stop with the reticence of Boston's ladies to come calling. Being poor made the brothers stand apart from their peers, especially during their years at Harvard. For the Emerson brothers, William and Ralph in particular, their poverty distinguished them from their well-to-do schoolmates, making them occasionally envious, always aloof, and resolutely ambitious to prove themselves. As important was the fact that their mother's support and the family's lack of resources seem to have made the boys markedly less materialistic and self-satisfied than their fellows. Their father's premature death and their subsequent financial straits thus purged the sons of the reflexive conservatism of Brahmin Boston. The intimacy engendered by financial hardships combined with social ostracism seemed to foster at least in Ralph an elemental distrust of the Brahmin elite as well as an affinity with the millions of women and men who toiled mightily to eke out a living.

It was not that the boys did not belong among their peers in Boston or at Harvard. They were very bright, had procured a fine preparation at the Boston Latin School, and carried the proper genealogy. They were Emersons, which everyone understood meant that for several generations the males had gone to Harvard and into the Congregational clergy. In fact, William and Ralph could trace their family roots in the clergy as far back as Joseph Emerson of Mendon, whose congregation ordained him in 1667, and Peter Bulkeley, one of the original founders of Concord. Yet as much pride as the boys rightfully took in their genealogy, they more often than not had to swallow it. Their learning and lineage only got them so far. The precariousness of their finances constantly reminded them that they were at best their wealthy classmates' poor relations. When William first entered Harvard he seems to have been seduced into neglecting his studies by his wealthy but less serious classmates, or so his mother feared. She admonished him to "ever rise superior to these little things for though small indeed consume much time that might be appropriated to better purposes & far nobler pursuits." In the same letter, Ruth went on to beseech her eldest son to live up to his genealogy. "Let your whole life reflect honour on the *name* you bear."[14] In a similar vein, Ralph recalled the consequences of being poorer than his classmates, a condition that clearly made him feel inferior. "My manners & history would have been very different," he confided to his journal in 1834, "if my parents had been rich, when I was a boy at school."[15] In other places, too, Emerson attributed his distinct lack of confidence to his family's indigence.

The fact that Ruth managed to send her children to Harvard despite their poverty demonstrates more than merely a remarkable and praiseworthy devotion to education. Ruth Emerson understood that money was not an end, but only a means, and not a means to luxury. Money could, however, buy her children an education, which was an end in itself. When she wrote William that he had it "in [his] power to lay the foundation of future eminence in every thing praiseworthy & excellent," she had no intention of suggesting that he use his time at Harvard to become a man of business or to pursue material ends.[16] Ultimately, William did become a lawyer and a judge, but he first had to exile himself to distant New York City. He had initially sought to follow his father into the ministry. Only after graduate study on biblical criticism in Germany did William forsake a clerical career, his religious faith presumably having been undermined as it had been for so many earnest young men by studying with the great J. G. Eichhorn at Göttingen. Both in college and for a number of years after graduation, Ralph too suffered from a crisis of vocation. Yet it seems clear that at no time did he seriously consider a career in business or law. There is no evidence that he gave much thought to parlaying his Harvard education into great personal wealth. Quite the opposite was the case.

Emerson reflected upon his early years of relative deprivation, though he would not have called them such, in a fine essay, "Domestic Life," which he published in his 1870 collection entitled *Society and Solitude*. Originally delivered as the lecture "Home" in Providence, Rhode Island, in March of 1840, it is clear that Emerson wrote the essay with his young son Waldo gallivanting around his Concord home.[17] Deliciously distracted by his enchanting three-year-old, whose "ignorance is more charming than all knowledge, and his little sins more bewitching than any virtue," Emerson paused to reflect upon his own childhood and its importance in the development of the adult. As if keying his listeners to understand him by his own childhood recollections, Emerson quotes Milton that "childhood shows the man as morning shows the day."[18]

"Domestic Life" draws a number of important distinctions between the Emersons' experiences and those of their more fortunate Harvard classmates. Necessity taught them important lessons about values; it made them serious and studious, or at least more so than they would otherwise have been. "What is the hoop that holds them stanch?" he rhetorically asks. "It is the iron band of poverty, of necessity, of austerity, which, excluding them from the sensual enjoyments which make other boys too early old, has directed their activity in safe and right channels, and made them, despite themselves, reverers of the grand, the beautiful and the good."[19]

Typically, Emerson does not imply that he preferred straitened circumstances. Who would? He notes that children are invariably "short-sighted; . . .

they sigh for fine clothes, for rides, for the theatre, and premature freedom and dissipation, which others possess. Woe to them if their wishes were crowned!" The significance of this recollection of his own childhood rests with its relation to the overall theme of the essay. "Domestic Life" contrasts with essays like "Self-Reliance" and "Experience" in its extremely down-to-earth assessment of human values, which the author sets against the crass materialism of the well-to-do. Using the universal desire for a "household" as his point of departure, Emerson disassociates that noble end from materialist means. "I think it plain that this voice of communities and ages, 'Give us wealth, and the good household shall exist,' is vicious." Wealth more often than not proves a barrier to virtuous living. "Genius and virtue, like diamonds, are best plain-set,—set in lead, set in poverty. The greatest man in history was the poorest."[20]

Because of his pedigree, perhaps, Emerson's own childhood poverty is easily dismissed as insignificant. Intent on portraying him as an apologist for the upper classes, tainted with his father's Brahmin smugness, scholars brandish the fact that Emerson did not call for the renunciation of private property, as did a number of his socialist contemporaries, some of whom Emerson admired a great deal. Indeed, in a number of places Emerson praised wealth as a great motivator of men. The point is that Emerson steadfastly pursued loftier objectives than political economy, which he considered subsidiary to the study of ethical living. Material pursuits were dangerous, even to good ends. "'*Give us wealth.*' You ask too much," Emerson wrote. "Few have wealth but all must have a home. Men are not born rich; and in getting wealth the man is generally sacrificed, and often is sacrificed without acquiring wealth at last. Besides, that cannot be the right answer;—there are objections to wealth." Necessity and austerity were more likely than luxury to instill character.[21] Again reflecting on his own experiences, Emerson urged his audience to view wealth and poverty anew. "It begins to be seen that the poor are only they who feel poor, and poverty consists in feeling poor. The rich, as we reckon them, and among them the very rich,—in a true scale would be found very indigent and ragged." These are the lessons that Ruth inculcated in her children. Now in his thirties, Emerson had transformed boyhood insecurity into self-knowledge and spiritual depth. The truly rich can do without. Their ends are never material; "only the low habits need palaces and banquets."[22]

Another theme explored in "Domestic Life" that reflected Emerson's adolescent experiences and resonated in his later work was that of the great value of education in the life of a democratic society. Emerson believed that educational opportunities provided the critical outlet for talented youth from all economic backgrounds. Ruth and the entire Emerson family laid significant emphasis on education, even if it was not always popular with the boys. Just before his tenth birthday Ralph wrote his Aunt Mary "I have from about quater [*sic*] after 7 till 8 to play or read. I think I am rather inclined to the former."[23] A more mature Emerson highlighted his mother's devotion to their education after their father had died. "He died in 1812 and left her with six children & without property," Emerson wrote to Nathaniel Frothingham in 1853. "She kept her family together & and at once adopted the only means open to her by receiving boarders into her house & by the assistance of some excellent friends, she carried four of her five sons through Harvard College."[24] Education, and what Emerson would later call self-culture, was the crux of an open, egalitarian society. It was the great means of individual improvement and self-respect.

The four able boys all graduated from Harvard, but it was not easy. Ruth decided that Ralph would have to postpone matriculating until the family's finances improved, William's attendance being difficult enough. According to Ruth, only the intervention of Benjamin Gould, Emerson's instructor at the Latin School, with Harvard President John Thornton Kirkland enabled Ralph to join the freshman class in August of 1817. "Mr Gould called in W. room & said he had seen the President & he & himself rather advised to R. W.s going to College *this year*—The Pred.t. observed he should be his freshman, & he would try to grant him some other priviledges."[25] Like his father and brother before him, and Edward and Charles after, Ralph was off to Harvard.

By his own recollection Emerson's experience at Cambridge was at best mixed. Matriculating at the age of fourteen, he was a precocious freshman even for the early 1800s. His academic record at Harvard was no better than fair, while his personal life proved not altogether happy. He struggled to fit in, making no lifelong friends during his undergraduate years. His letters and journals (the latter of which he began in the middle of his junior year) reveal two main themes: the family's pinched economic situation and his perception of the great divide between his ambitions and his abilities. "I cannot dissemble," he wrote, "that my abilities are below my ambition."[26]

The funds that enabled Emerson to get through Harvard came from many sources. Some were relatively small, such as the Penn legacy from First Church, while others were more substantial. As the President's Freshman, Ralph's expenses for room and board were largely defrayed. He resided free of charge in Wadsworth House, the president's house, and may have received his meals there as well. His board became virtually free when in 1819 he "was appointed waiter in the Junior Hall." He earned money from tutoring work procured for him by President Kirkland and from teaching school when not at Cambridge. Ralph was particularly indebted to William, who was doing his part for the family by keeping school in Kennebunk, Maine. Understandably, the brothers' correspondence is replete with money matters. A letter addressed to William from February of 1819 is representative. "Dear William," Ralph begins,

> You speak of Mother's pecuniary exigencies at present; though pressing they are not distressful quite yet, though she is relying considerably on your assistance, for rent &c.; she has only paid Mr Bruce $50 on his last Quarter & I believe is waiting for you to pay the rest. I brought twenty dollars from Waltham day before yesterday, besides your $3.50 . . . so much for pecuniary embarrassment relief & expectation.[27]

Being poor at Harvard was no disgrace, but it had its effects upon Emerson, who plainly confessed his poverty caused him considerable embarrassment. He was glad to work as a waiter in the commons because he saved the expense of meals, but he confided to his brother, "I do not like it for which sentiments you can easily guess the reason."[28] It is hardly the case that Emerson was especially jealous of his classmates, as he never seems to have been particularly materialistic. Rather, his difficult financial situation reinforced a certain aloofness, a sense of difference that Emerson felt from the children of the well-to-do who never had to write their brothers beseeching them for money. "Dear Will I have brought your letters to Mother," he wrote in 1819, "& she is very much disappointed in not recg. the cash."[29] This gulf between himself and his classmates ensured that he would never feel himself one of those "proper Bostonians" whose life was predestined to be one of ease and easy authority.[30]

Lack of money and the family's dependence on charity proved to be only one of several factors that contributed to Ralph's awkwardness and aloofness at Harvard. Virtually the youngest in his class and already approaching six feet in height, at the age of fourteen Ralph was "nearly as tall as when he had reached maturity."[31] Former classmates remembered him as remarkably self-composed and quite distant at the same time. "Mingling shyness, awkwardness, and dignity," Ralph got on well enough with his contemporaries, but shied away from intimacy. In his sophomore year Ralph grew somewhat closer to other members of the notorious class of 1821. Moving out from under the president's nose surely helped, as did his tangential participation in the food fight and subsequent protests jocularly called "The Rebelliad." Although predictably Ralph played no part in the initial fracas, he joined other members of the class in staging a protest in solidarity with those members punished for the episode in the commons. When the entire class refused to attend chapel, the administration promptly sent them home.[32] There is no mention in the "Rebelliad" of Ralph Emerson's participation in this "very praiseworthy resistance to lawful authority," as William sarcastically wrote his brother; nor does Emerson's own commentary survive.[33] It seems likely that he was among the thirty-odd students who applied for readmission after only a week's absence. The fact that he "received the *very important intelligence* that I was appointed waiter . . . in the Junior Hall" so shortly after reinstatement is evidence that he played only a bit part in the troubles.[34] As in the "Rebelliad," for most of college Ralph was, as he put it himself, "a spectator rather than a fellow."[35]

Emerson's academic record proved almost singularly bereft of distinction. Finishing exactly in the middle of his class, he betrayed little evidence in his academic work that he would become one of his generation's most respected intellectuals. While his classmate Josiah Quincy, who would go on to become mayor of Boston, may have exaggerated when he brusquely declared Emerson "to have given no sign of the power that was fashioning itself for greatness," it is the case that Ralph almost failed mathematics and struggled mightily in the sciences.[36] Confessing to William in his sophomore year, "Mathematics I hate," Ralph seems to have performed so poorly in that subject that his old teacher and mentor, Benjamin Gould, resolved not to hire Ralph as a tutor at the Boston Latin School.[37]

Emerson's performance at Cambridge is consistent with several features of his later life. He regularly berated himself for not working with more diligence and focus and for never being very systematic in his thinking. At the time Emerson lamented his remarkable knack for reading not for his classes or examinations, but to distract himself from them. In his junior year Emerson began to keep a journal, or a series of journals, notebooks, and reading concordances, a practice that he would maintain for more than four decades. In the fall of his junior year, he chastised himself in his journal for being "idle, vagrant, stupid, & hollow."[38] At sixteen he was already being brutally honest with himself, noting that "if I do not discipline myself with diligent care I shall suffer severely from remorse & the sense of inferiority hereafter. All around me," he continued, "are industrious & will be great, I am indolent & shall be insignificant."[39] Emerson did not particularly berate himself for his decidedly unsystematic thinking; instead he seems to have accommodated himself early on to his apparent logical shortcomings as more a matter of fate than volition. That no force of will could make him into a logician or a systematic thinker actually seems to have offered the young man a certain solace. Others could refute Locke's materialism and Hume's radical skepticism—

both necessary endeavors—but he was not up to it. So much the better. He would move on to new and more interesting projects.

Emerson's reading habits proved unique. He read prodigiously, fancying unassigned literature above prescribed texts, could quote huge sections of his favorite Shakespeare sonnets and plays, and already possessed a penchant for selectively skimming what did not interest him. In short, he read for himself. These peculiar habits did not bring him renown among his peers at Harvard. In part this was because he was too self-conscious to flaunt his erudition, in part because his classmates were only so impressed with bookishness. Most telling of all, his singular reading proclivities did not translate into tangibly improved grades. Emerson assumed a genuinely modest pose when it came to his insatiable appetite for reading because he knew it to be at least in some measure a subterfuge. Reading literature and history enabled him to feel a bit less guilty about avoiding assigned subjects and required texts. This rather awkward teenager thought it no credit to himself that he read so much in those hours when he should have been studying Legendre's geometry, Hedge's impenetrable *Elements of Logick*, or the *Lectures on Rhetoric* of Hugh Blair. Years later, several of his Harvard associates recalled that "more studious members of his class began to seek him out," finding him to be "unusually thoughtful and well-read; knowing perhaps less than they about text-books, but far more about literature."[40] The poor academic performance of many of Emerson's classmates stemmed from the fact that they did not read; Emerson's from the fact that he read so much and to his own tastes and prejudices.

It seems clear that from a very young age Emerson possessed a certain comfort around books that comes only from intimacy. His utter affinity with the written word, inculcated at such an early age by his mother, father, and Aunt Mary, bred a certain self-reliance. As a precocious fourteen-year-old freshman, Emerson already found it all too easy to dismiss authoritative texts. Some books he found "vital and spermatic," whereas most others were not worth the time.[41] Remarkably, even as a teenager Emerson rarely occupied himself with working through an argument not to his liking. Rarer still were those times that he engaged in line by line refutation. He seems to have lived his entire life by the credo he affirmed in "Books," an essay he published as part of *Society and Solitude*. "Never read any but what you like."[42] Emerson considered the knowledge gleaned from books to be only of relative utility. Acquired knowledge, or secondary learning, had to be molded and reshaped by the reader or it was worthless. Even as a teenager, Emerson had the intellectual fortitude to read selectively and for his own idiosyncratic purposes.

Despite his pedestrian academic performance, particularly in his freshman year, Emerson managed to struggle through Harvard, graduating thirtieth in a class of fifty-nine. He later complained that sending one's children to Harvard was something of a gamble; one let them go and hoped for the best. Whether it was because of the relative youth of the students, because Harvard was still in transition from a seminary to a university, or because the college classes were so small, Harvard seemed to be less an institution of higher education than a boarding school for wealthy boys. The rare true intellectuals among the professorate could hardly be said to have devoted themselves to their unruly charges. Professors such as Edward Everett and George Bancroft loathed the fact that they had to be disciplinarians first and pedagogues second. Emerson recorded few highlights during his four years in Cambridge as Harvard offered few intellectual challenges.

Emerson's most vivid and positive assessments of his education date from his junior year, when he seems to have begun to take his schooling and himself more seriously.[43] This maturation also coincided with the triumphal return from study in Germany of Edward Everett and George Ticknor, both of whose lectures Emerson attended while at Harvard.[44] Having discerned what a true institution of higher learning could be, this tandem began to transform Harvard dramatically. Most of the changes they instituted came too late for Emerson, but Everett's lectures alone made a lasting impression on the teen. "I ought to have this evening a flow of thought rich, abundant, & deep," Emerson noted in his journal, "after having heard Mr Everett deliver his Introductory Lecture."[45]

As the new professor of Greek, Everett brought the Göttingen method of historical criticism of ancient texts to New England in 1819. His highly erudite critical interpretations of Homer and the later Greeks, as well as the New Testament, enthralled Emerson and his classmates. Building on the efforts of Joseph Stevens Buckminster, who as the first Dexter lecturer had introduced German higher biblical criticism to the United States, Everett combined a professorship at Harvard with his role as Congregational minister.[46] "In the pulpit," Emerson wrote of Everett years later, "he abounded in sentences, in wit, in satire, in splendid allusion, in quotation impossible to forget, in daring imagery, in parable and even in a sort of defying experiment of his own wit and skill in giving an oracular weight to Hebrew and Rabbinical words."[47] At Harvard, Everett encouraged his students to utilize the same hermeneutic whether analyzing scripture, classical literature, or mythology. He exhorted his students to adopt a less reverential stance toward their religious texts, which would inevitably result from studying the scholarship of Eichhorn, Wolf, and Heyne, whose critical-historical scholarship on the New Testament, Homer, and occidental mythology undermined the centuries-old rigid distinction between sacred and historical texts.[48] These new, critical ideas and Everett's smooth style made him and his lectures the *cause célèbre* of Emerson's years in Cambridge.[49]

Edward Everett's impact upon Ralph Emerson would be difficult to exaggerate. "There was an influence on the young people from the genius of Everett which is almost comparable to that of Pericles in Athens," Emerson remarked years later. He consumed literature and history, reading books critically and for personal growth. He chafed at having to study the required texts and the predictable interpretive strategies of the Harvard Unitarian establishment. Everett not only reintroduced Emerson to Homer, Plato, and the other Greek classics, but also encouraged a kind of critical stance that appealed to the increasingly deep thinking and self-reliant scholar that Emerson was becoming. "It was all new learning," Emerson noted, "that wonderfully took and stimulated the young men." Highly erudite, extremely popular, and only in his mid-twenties, Everett became the model intellectual for Emerson. One can only assume that Emerson was speaking of his own college efforts when he observed that "not a sentence was written in academic exercises, not a declamation attempted in the college chapel, [b]ut showed the omnipresence of his genius to youthful heads." As much as any other trait the still awkward sixteen-year-old desperately aspired to his idol's "self-command and the security of his manner." Unlike Everett, he never would possess that complete composure that comes from "pure act."[50] Years later, Emerson wrote more critically of Everett. In retrospect, Emerson observed in "Historical Notes of Life and Letters in New England" that Everett appeared to have possessed more form than substance. The several pages on Everett in this 1868 lecture are infused with a critical tone. Everett may have inspired the youth with his style, but he offered nothing singularly his own, and thus little of intellectual depth. It is faint praise for Emerson to write that Everett's "power lay in the magic of form." "When Massachusetts was full of his fame," Emerson concluded, "it was not contended that he had thrown any truths into circulation."[51]

As with so many of his peers, Emerson's Harvard experience impressed upon him the power of the spoken word. He had been intoxicated with the oratory of Edward Everett and had studied the craft of declamation with diligence in the classes of Edward Tyrrell Channing. He took a certain personal pride in the fact that gifted oratory was an art that had belonged to the Congregational clergy, and that members of his family had been among its greatest practitioners.[52] One of Emerson's childhood friends, William Henry Furness, stated as much, declaring that "those days may be distinguished as the era of rhetoric; we boys went into ecstasies over a happy turn of expression or a brilliant figure of speech."[53] Caught up in Boston's infatuation with the spoken word, Emerson promised himself that he would eventually make use of his talent for eloquence, even to the point of confessing to Moncure Conway that his ambition was to become a professor of rhetoric.[54]

Emerson ultimately came to a similarly negative conclusion about other elements of his Harvard education, most notably his courses in religion. He learned a great deal, but his studies left him still searching for truth, for something vital and usable. The majority of the upper-class curriculum featured the study of moral philosophy.[55] Taught by Levi Frisbie, the first Alford Professor, Hollis Professor Henry Ware, Levi Hedge, and Andrews Norton, among others, these subjects reflected Harvard's recent past as a seminary. They included the examination of religious doctrines, study of the Old and New Testaments, the review of ethical philosophy through the works of theologians such as Bishop Butler and William Paley, as well as close study of the critique of materialism in the works of Dugald Stewart, Francis Hutchinson, and others of the so-called Scottish school. Emerson was particularly drawn to Butler's *Analogy* and Stewart's two-volume *Dissertation*.

As unsatisfying as it seemed at the time, the Unitarian training in ethical philosophy that Emerson received at Harvard proved critical to his intellectual development, more important perhaps than his later reading of German idealism.[56] The idealist ontology of his mature work was for him a decidedly peripheral issue. Like the ethical philosophy he studied at Harvard, his own interests were eminently ethical. For Emerson, the issue was how to live. Like his Harvard professors who sought to construct a "unique and integrated theological synthesis," as Sydney Ahlstrom noted, Emerson struggled to create a moral philosophy that "encompassed the whole study of human nature."[57] As Protestants who had largely reconciled themselves to the Enlightenment, the Unitarians concerned themselves almost exclusively with the search for a post-Humean foundation for morality.[58] "Without supernatural religion," they asked, are morality and social order possible?[59] Emerson parted company with his Harvard teachers more in relation to personality and political sensibilities than to philosophical outlook. "I am not sure that the educated class ever ascend to the idea of Virtue; or that they desire truth," he wrote in his journal years later. "They want safety, utility, decorum."[60]

Emerson's most mature work at Harvard, for which he earned some modest recognition, took up issues of ethical philosophy. He won second place in the Bowdoin essay competition in consecutive years. The subjects of his essays reflected interests Emerson pursued throughout his life. He submitted his first essay on "The Character of Socrates" in July of 1819 and followed it up with "The Present State of Ethical Philosophy" the ensuing year. In his sophomore year, Emerson listed André Dacier's *Dialogues of Plato* as one of the books he had read and thoroughly enjoyed; shortly thereafter he wrote to his brother about composing an essay on Socrates. As for many who read the Platonic dialogues, Socrates became for Emerson an idol whose "moral superiority" demanded admiration. Whether or not the young Emerson specifically sought to model himself on his Athenian hero, his Bowdoin essay reveals aspirations along that line.[61]

Emerson's 1819 Socrates is closer to Xenophon's wise old man, comparable to Benjamin Franklin, than to Plato's peerless seeker of truth. The more mythical and ideal reading would come thirty-one years later in *Representative Men*, where he writes that "Socrates and Plato are the double star which the most powerful instruments will not entirely separate."[62] Here Socrates is "the perfect man," whose idealist philosophy deserves praise for being "a source of good sense and of sublime practical morality." For Emerson, Socrates was a national hero who "desired to restore his countrymen" to greatness by exhorting them to improve themselves. Socrates embodied self-sacrifice, rejecting Athens' enticement of political office because "he would not descend treacherously to flatter the [demos]." He was famously abstemious, so dismissive of bodily pleasures that even the beautiful and wicked Alcibiades failed to seduce him. Socrates "endeavored to subdue his corporeal wants so far as to make them merely subservient to the mental advantage, yet," Emerson significantly adds, offering a preview of what would be a central argument in *Nature*, "never carrying it to anything like the excess of Indian superstition which worships God by outraging nature."[63]

Most important to the author's appreciation of the character of Socrates was the Athenian's wholehearted dedication to his calling. Socrates was first and foremost a pedagogue, who "devoted himself entirely to the instruction of the young, astonishing them with a strange system of doctrines which inculcated the love of poverty, the forgiveness of injuries, with other virtues equally unknown and unpracticed." Most remarkable of all, Emerson elaborated on the singularity of Socrates' character and mind—both of which were "eminently calculated to instruct"—in terms uncannily similar to those subsequently used by Emerson's acquaintances to describe him. From his Harvard classmates to Margaret Fuller and even his wife Lidian,[64] observations abound of Emerson's peculiarly reserved character.[65] They declared of the Concord sage precisely what he wrote of his Athenian hero, that his "didactic disposition always rendered him rather a teacher than the companion of his friends."[66]

In addition to the Bowdoin essays, he also contended for a Boylston prize in declamation that included an award of thirty dollars. Delighted with his victory but even more enthralled by the prospect of what his mother might do with this modest windfall, Ralph, now sixteen, brought the prize money directly home to Ruth. He subsequently noted his disappointment that the money could not go to buying Ruth a new shawl as he had hoped, but rather went straight away to pay the baker's bill.[67]

The family's ever-pressing pecuniary difficulties hung like a pallor over Emerson's entire Harvard career. Emerson's college years were no different than the other times since their father's decease; times were tough, especially in the aftermath of the Panic of 1819. There seems little doubt that in addition to reinforcing his aloofness and sense of social distance from his peers, the family's circumstances stoked Emerson's ambitions, which burned deep within. By all estimates he was not the brightest of the brothers. His father thought William showed more promise, while Ralph's maternal grandfather assessed Edward and Charles more highly. "He admired their scholarly tastes and methods," David Haskins quotes his father as saying. "In particular he cherished great expectations from the brilliant oratorical powers of the two young brothers."[68] His classmates and teachers at Harvard seem to have underestimated him as well. One apocryphal story that Emerson related later in his life was when the class valedictorian, Robert Barnwell, "put his hand on the back of my head" and pronounced that his "bump of ambition . . . was very very small."[69] In spite of others' estimations, or perhaps because of them, the young Emerson felt he had much to prove. This internal ambition would remain unfulfilled for several years after college, as the family depended upon Ralph for support while Edward in his turn went to Harvard. During those years, when his classmates went on to "great things," Ralph would be confined to teaching school.

One winter day in the middle of his senior year Emerson fled the confines of Harvard Yard in search of fresh air. This was not unique; Emerson made many and frequent journeys into the adjacent meadows of Mount Auburn during his tenure at Cambridge, especially when he sought to avoid the drudgery of studying the same dull texts. After this particular December foray, Emerson entered remarkably prophetic lines in his journal:

> I claim & clasp a moment's respite from this irksome school to saunter in the feilds [*sic*] of my own wayward thought. The afternoon was gloomy & preparing to snow—dull, ugly weather. But when I came out from the hot, steaming, stove-ed, stinking, dirty, a "b"-spelling school room I almost soared & mounted the atmosphere at breathing the free magnificent air, the noble breath of life. It was a delightful exhilaration; but it soon passed off.[70]

These lines can be read as an apt prefigurement of Ralph's experience in the years after graduation. He was exhilarated to be approaching the end of his college career, as eager as the rest of his classmates to escape from the "school room." Anticipating his eighteenth birthday, he now had a reasonable grasp of his abilities and some mastery over his weaknesses. "My talents are popular," he opined, "[and] are fitted to enable me to claim a place in the inclinations & sympathy of men." Ambitious in the extreme, though he knew not precisely what for, Emerson's delightful exhilaration concerning his prospects "soon passed off," as had his momentary thrill of bursting out of the recitation room into the open air.[71]

Emerson had few positive details to report in his journal about his 1821 Harvard commencement. He played little part in the actual exercises, only being selected class poet after a fifth of his class had declined the honor. On his resume were two second-place finishes in the Bowdoin prize competition and one Boylston prize for declamation, from which he had won a total of fifty-five dollars. He could be proud that all but $150 of the cost of his entire Harvard career he had either earned himself or had been provided by the charity of others. Less tangibly, Emerson had utilized the preceding four years to read copiously in literature and history. He had worked his way, at times with difficulty, through the ancients and the more contemporary philosophy of Hobbes, Hume, Locke, and the writers of the Scottish Common Sense school. He confessed that he would never be a systematic thinker nor "ever hope to write a Butler's Analogy or an Essay of Hume,"[72] his talents being more literary and poetical than philosophical in nature. He aspired to be a poet or a writer.[73] At the time of his graduation, Emerson was greatly ashamed of his mediocre academic record. He confessed to being "Mortified by my own ill fate or ill conduct," which had resulted in his garnering few honors and little recognition. Only after a decade of maturation could he look back more favorably upon his Harvard experience. "I was the true philosopher in college," he concluded years later, "and Mr Farrar and Mr. Hedge and Dr Ware the false."[74]

In 1821 the Emersons were as poor as ever, and now with Edward at Harvard, Ralph set his sights on providing for his mother and brothers. When William departed for Europe to pursue his Doctor of Divinity at Göttingen and Charles subsequently matriculated at Harvard, Ralph was thrust into the role—with Ruth—of being the family's chief breadwinner. He willingly assumed his place in the "family galley," as Edward had called it, just as William had three years earlier. "There are harder crosses to bear than poverty," he confidently declared. His ambitions on hold, Emerson resigned himself to supporting his family by teaching school, which he had been doing during his breaks at Harvard. He had not particularly liked it then, and he never warmed to the profession. Ralph began by assisting his brother, who two years earlier had opened a school for young ladies in their mother's Federal Street residence in Boston. By 1823 Ralph had taken over the entire operation, so that William could go to Europe to pursue his graduate studies. Instructing young ladies proved particularly trying for him. "I was nineteen," Emerson later confessed, "had grown up without sisters, and, in my solitary and secluded way of living, had no acquaintance with girls. I still recall my terrors at entering the school."[75] Even after three years of teaching, Emerson concluded that he was "a hopeless school-master," whose teaching was "partial and external," and whose outward demeanor reflected a nagging sense of insecurity in social situations.[76]

For much of his early life, Emerson spent his free time reading. His years keeping school were no exception. One of his father's possessions that the family had propitiously withheld from auction was his share in Boston's lending library, which was conveniently located virtually across the street from Emerson's school. Emerson's reading—"sinful strolling from book to book"—included literature, history, theology, and philosophy.[77] His eclectic list of borrowings included histories by Gibbon, Sismondi, and Lemaire, as well as works by More, Milton, Bacon, Burke, Voltaire, and Molière. Among his countrymen, Emerson read Franklin, Washington Irving, and James Fenimore Cooper, praising *Pioneers* highly. In a letter to friend, he commended the *North American Review* as being "full of wit & literature" and worthy of perusal.[78] His voracious appetite for books of all types diminished only when his eyes began to fail him in the spring of 1825.

The young schoolteacher's interest in the Scottish Common Sense school continued unabated, as he mentions reading the work of Dugald Stewart, Thomas Reid, James Mackintosh, and Adam Smith. It is not difficult to understand Emerson's passion for these philosophers. They spoke directly to his penchant for a philosophy that could be understood on its own commonsensical terms. Emerson read philosophy as he read everything else—not as an academic or a specialist but as a generalist and for its utility. He thoroughly concurred with the Common Sense philosophers, who professed that practical issues touching on how one should live were the vital questions of philosophy. Emerson took heart in their eschewing long discourses on the fine points of ontology and disputes over the validity of Cartesian dualism. Although he taught from Hume's history of England, which he highly esteemed, he was greatly disquieted by the "Scotch Goliath," whose profoundly disturbing challenge to natural religion Emerson's friends sought (in vain) to refute.[79] Noting that his own "reasoning faculty is proportionately weak," Emerson depended on others to provide him with the necessary ammunition to take on Hume.[80] "One good book I advise you to read, if you have not, with all convenient celerity," he advised his friend John Boynton Hill, "—Stewart's last Dissertation—one of the most useful octavos extant. It saves you the toil of turning over a hundred tomes in which the philosophy of the Mind, since the Revival of Letters, is locked up."[81] If Stewart was satisfied with the self-evident status of intuition, then so was Emerson.

Greatly dissatisfied with keeping school, Emerson resolved to bring this portion of his professional life to an end. While still teaching in the autumn of 1824 he consoled himself in several ways. His hard work had paid dividends, his schoolmastering having earned "two or three thousand dollars," while his own expenses had not exceeded a few hundred dollars annually.[82] Even more importantly, his teaching purgatory constituted payment in kind to William. Just as William had looked after the family and vitally contributed to the purse while Ralph attended Harvard, so the younger brother in turn bankrolled Ruth and the younger brothers during William's stay in Göttingen. Similarly, he enabled Edward and Charles to attend to their schooling, as William had enabled him to do a few years earlier. "I can thank heaven," he concluded after he closed his school, "I can say none of my house is worse for me."[83] Ralph took particular pride in the fact that both Edward and Charles ranked at the head of their respective Harvard classes. At his lowest moments, he could also console himself with the fact that his father and his father's father before him used keeping school as a stepping-stone toward their true vocation within the Congregational church. After three years of teaching, for which "the instructor is little wiser," his family was on relatively secure financial footing, William was pursuing his doctorate in Germany, and Edward and Charles were making their marks in Cambridge. It was now time to get on with his own professional life. Emerson resolved to follow his father and his male forebears into the ministry.[84]

NOTES

1. *JMN* 5:30.

2. Cited in Phyllis Cole, *Mary Moody Emerson and the Origins of Transcendentalism: A Family History* (New York, 1998), 140; see also Ralph L. Rusk, *The Life of Ralph Waldo Emerson* (New York, 1949), 30.

3. Ruth Haskins Emerson to Phebe Emerson Ripley, 1/27/12, as cited in Rusk, *Life*, 31.

4. *JMN* 5:30.

5. Cole, *Mary Moody Emerson*, 139.

6. James Eliot Cabot, *Memoir of Ralph Waldo Emerson* (Cambridge, 1887), 29.

7. Ruth Haskins Emerson to Mary Moody Emerson, 7/20/13, as cited in Rusk, *Life,* 36.

8. David Greene Haskins, *Ralph Waldo Emerson: His Maternal Ancestors* (Boston, 1887), 83–85.

9. Emerson's comments about Aunt Mary's usage of this phrase are in *JMN* 9:239.

10. Mary Moody Emerson to Phebe Emerson Ripley, 9/20/14, as cited in Rusk, *Life*, 41.

11. Cabot, *Memoir*, 27.

12. Cited in Rusk, *Life*, 55.

13. Nancy Craig Simmons, ed., *The Selected Letters of Mary Moody Emerson* (Athens, Ga., 1993), 93, as cited in Cole, *Mary Moody Emerson*, 144–45.

14. Ruth Haskins Emerson to William Emerson, 10/13/14, as cited in Rusk, *Life*, 41–42.

15. *JMN* 4:263.

16. Ruth Haskins Emerson to William Emerson, 10/13/14, as cited in Rusk, *Life*, 42.

17. Emerson to Ruth Haskins Emerson, 3/28/40, *Letters* 2:266–67.

18. "Domestic Life," *Works* 7:101, 103.

19. See *Works* 7:117 and *JMN* 5:438.

20. *Works* 7:117, 112–13.

21. *Works* 7:111.

22. *Works* 7:115.

23. Emerson to Mary Moody Emerson, 4/16/13, as cited in Cabot, *Memoir*, 36.

24. Emerson to Nathaniel L. Frothingham, 12/3/53, *Letters* 4:408.

25. Ruth Haskins Emerson to Mary Moody Emerson, 8/28/17, as cited in Rusk, *Life*, 62.

26. *JMN* 2:238.

27. Emerson to William Emerson, 2/14/19, *Letters* 1:77.

28. Emerson to William Emerson, 2/15/19, *Letters* 1:78.

29. Emerson to William Emerson, 2/20/19, *Letters* 1:79.

30. This is Cleveland Amory's phrase from *The Proper Bostonians* (New York, 1947).

31. Rusk, *Life,* 66.

32. Official records are at Houghton Library, *Records of the College Faculty* 9:168–80.

33. William Emerson to Ruth Haskins Emerson, 11/29/18, *Letters* 1:74.

34. Emerson to William Emerson, 11/15/19, *Letters* 1:78; italics original.

35. Cited in Rusk, *Life*, 72.

36. Josiah Quincy IV, *Figures of the Past, from the Leaves of Old Journals* (Boston, 1883; rep., 1926), 17–18. Ralph Rusk claims that Emerson did not enroll in his natural science course because of the cost of materials. On Quincy, see Matthew Crocker, *The Magic of the Many: Josiah Quincy and the Rise of Mass Politics in Boston, 1800–1840* (Amherst, 1999).

37. Emerson to William Emerson, 4/1/19, *Letters* 1:80. Cabot, among others, suggests that higher academic standing in his class would have resulted in an ushership. See Cabot, *Memoir*, 1:72. For his part, Emerson wrote William that he did not "think it necessary to understand Mathematics & Greek thoroughly, to be a good, useful, or even *great* man." For good measure he added: "Aunt Mary would certainly tell you so." Emerson to William Emerson, 7/20/18, *Letters* 1:67.

38. *JMN* 1:39.

39. *JMN* 1:39.

40. William Bancroft Hill, "Emerson's College Days," *The Literary World*, 5/22/80, as cited in Rusk, *Life*, 67.

41. Emerson, "Books," *Works* 7:188.

42. Emerson, "Books," *Works* 7:188.

43. Scholars are apt to conclude that Emerson began to work more seriously in his junior year because he began his journal keeping at this time. Accordingly, there is direct evidence of his reading and thinking for the first time.

44. Emerson also came to admire George Bancroft upon his return from Göttingen in 1822, referring to him in a letter to John Hill as "an infant Hercules." See Emerson to Hill, 1/3/23, *Letters* 1:127.

45. *JMN* 1:12.

46. On Buckminster and the Dexter lectureship, see Jerry Wayne Brown, *The Rise of Biblical Criticism in America, 1800–1870: The New England Scholars* (Middletown, Conn., 1969).

47. "Historical Notes of Life and Letters in New England," *Works* 10:314.

48. P. R. Frothingham, *Edward Everett: Orator and Statesman* (Boston, 1925), ch. 3.

49. The nourishment of secular high culture among the Boston Brahmins had begun in earnest a generation earlier with the efforts of Ralph's father, William Emerson, and the Anthology Society he had been so instrumental in founding. In the pages of the *Monthly Anthology and Boston Review*, the Brahmins had asserted that "when any theological work passes under our examination, it will only be in the regular survey of the literature of our country." The Anthologists' endeavors foreshadowed the breakdown of the separation between sacred and secular high culture, as well as orthodox Congregationalists' conviction that the Brahmins had catastrophically undermined religiosity in the process. In many ways, Everett's Harvard lectures proved the high-water mark of this trend within what was by 1820 called the Unitarian establishment. "Editors' Address," *Monthly Anthology and Boston Review* 2 (1805), 678.

50. All quotations in this paragraph are from "Historical Notes," *Works* 10:313–15; "pure act" is what Mencken called Theodore Roosevelt.

51. "Historical Notes," *Works* 10:316. He surely had Everett in mind as a negative reference when he declared in his 1837 Harvard Phi Beta Kappa address, "The American Scholar," that "each age must write its own books." Neither Everett nor any other Cambridge resident had done that.

52. Emerson would surely have excluded his father, who in his *History of the First*

Church of Boston had cast aspersion of some of his own new light ancestors. See Amy Schrager Lang, *Prophetic Woman: Anne Hutchinson and the Problem of Dissent in the Literature of New England* (Berkeley, 1987), 112–16.

53. Cited in Cabot, *Memoir*, 44.

54. Cited in Cabot, *Memoir*, 72.

55. Daniel Walker Howe, *The Unitarian Conscience: Harvard Moral Philosophy, 1805–1861* (Cambridge, 1970).

56. Among the Emerson scholars to make this point of emphasis, the latest is David Robinson in *Apostle of Culture: Emerson as Preacher and Lecturer* (Philadelphia, 1982).

57. Sidney Ahlstrom, "Theology in America: A Historical Survey," in *The Shaping of American Religion*, ed. J. W. Smith and A. L. Jamison (Princeton, 1961), 1:253; Howe, *Unitarian Conscience*, 2.

58. William Ellery Channing's "God is spirit" is quite similar to Emerson's idealism.

59. Howe, *Unitarian Conscience*, 31.

60. *JMN* 7:104.

61. Emerson, "The Character of Socrates," in *Two Unpublished Essays: The Character of Socrates and The Present State of Ethical Science* (Boston, 1895), 19.

62. "Plato; Or, The Philosopher," *Collected Works* 4:39–40.

63. Emerson, "The Character of Socrates," 34, 25.

64. Her name was Lydia, but Emerson almost always referred to her as his "Lidian."

65. Emerson most clearly confesses his diffidence toward even close friends in a famous letter to Margaret Fuller in 1840: "Can one be glad of an affection which he knows not how to return?" See *Letters* 2:351.

66. Emerson, "The Character of Socrates," 25, 16.

67. Quoted in Cabot, *Memoir*, 56.

68. Haskins, *Emerson: His Maternal Ancestors*, 81.

69. *JMN* 7:169.

70. *JMN* 1:46–47.

71. *JMN* 1:41, 47.

72. *JMN* 2:238. Interestingly, Emerson in time would write essays that might be considered in the vein of Hume's.

73. Stanley Cavell seems to have Emerson wrong when he points to the similarities between him and Ludwig Wittgenstein.

74. Cited in Rusk, *Life*, 87–88.

75. Cited in Cabot, *Memoir*, 70.

76. In Cabot, *Memoir*, 72; Emerson refers to helping his brother "lift the truncheon against the fair-haired daughters of this raw city" in a letter to John B. Hill, 2/12/22, *Letters* 1:106.

77. *JMN* 2:332.

78. Emerson to John B. Hill, 2/28/23, *Letters* 1:131.

79. Emerson to Mary Moody Emerson, 10/16/23, *Letters* 1:138.
80. *JMN* 2:238.
81. Emerson to John B. Hill, 11/12/22, *Letters* 1:125.
82. *JMN* 2:332.
83. *JMN* 2:332; see also Emerson to William Emerson, 1/18/25, *Letters* 1:158–59.
84. Cited in Rusk, *Life*, 108.

3

THE PROBLEM OF VOCATION

The call of our calling is the loudest call. There are so many worthless lives, apparently, that to advance a good cause by telling one
anecdote or doing one great act seems a worthy reason for living.[1]

Finding a vocation that is at once remunerative and personally fulfilling
presents a perennial problem for young people. This proved especially
the case for young men of Emerson's generation whose career choices were
limited. For those who sought to utilize their high cultural training to secure a
livelihood, the problem of vocation could seem unsolvable. Looking back on
the era from the perspective of middle age, Henry James wrote of "the terrible
paucity of alternatives" for young men coming of age in antebellum America.[2]
In an earlier time, the four Emerson boys might well have followed their father
into the Congregational ministry, which was essentially the family profession.
For generations, learned and eloquent young men like William, Ralph,
Edward, and Charles had traded their Harvard training for a call from one of
New England's Congregational churches. To be sure, the older brothers did
for a time pursue clerical careers. With his own fateful decision to become a
minister clearly in mind, Emerson in 1838 offered an admonition to a gathering of Dartmouth seniors who were about to embark on their careers. "The
hour of that choice," he warned them, "is the crisis of your history."[3]

For the Emerson brothers, their pinched economic circumstances made
the problem of vocation all the more immediate and portentous. Since the
death of their father, the family's relative deprivation served as a dramatic
reminder that finding personal fulfillment in their careers was only one of the
challenges confronting them. Ruth's struggles, Bulkeley's inability to provide
for himself, and the family's history of illness brought home the probability
that one or more of the boys would be called upon to support their mother,
and perhaps others in the immediate family. In fact, for decades Ralph would
provide for his mother and materially assist his brothers.

Economic considerations may well have been the primary motive for Edward and Charles's decision to study the law. Brilliant, personable, and yet destined for tragic ends, the two younger brothers seemingly effortlessly cruised through Harvard, where their records were as exemplary as Ralph's had been mediocre. Edward, whom Ralph declared "lived & acted & spoke with preternatural energy," not only finished first in his Harvard class, but was "smitten to the bowels with ambition."[4] At his 1824 Harvard commencement, where he gave the valedictory address with the deific Lafayette gracing the dais, Edward seemed to have triumphed in the world in a way that his older brother had only imagined. Fresh from his conquests at Harvard, Edward wasted no time in accepting Daniel Webster's offer to join his Boston law practice.[5] According to contemporaries, Charles, the youngest of the brothers, resembled Edward intellectually and socially. The two younger brothers were by most accounts more classically handsome than Ralph or William; they also possessed more energetic, even magnetic, personalities, and were seemingly destined to accomplish great things. Like Edward, Charles early decided to study for the law instead of the ministry. He migrated from an outstanding undergraduate career at Harvard, where he once confessed, "I see none whom my vanity acknowledges as more intelligent than myself,"[6] to the law offices of Charles Upsham and then on to the newly established Harvard Law School.

Ironically, the early and striking success of the two younger brothers augured poorly for their futures. Unlike Ralph, whose reflexive caution and aloofness enabled him to conserve his limited physical and emotional resources, Edward and Charles dissipated themselves as they charged triumphantly through their teens and into their twenties. Illness and emotional distress plagued both brothers during their short lives. Like so many of their era, they suffered from tuberculosis. Neither Edward nor Charles found solace or success in their chosen vocations. Exhausted and depressed, Edward suffered a mental collapse in May of 1828, from which he never fully recovered. On October 1, 1834, Edward Bliss Emerson died, five months short of his thirtieth birthday. Charles fared no better, dying "instantly after returning from a ride with mother" at William's New York home on May 9, 1836.[7] He too never lived to see thirty.

William, who lived into his sixties, ultimately became a successful lawyer and judge in New York. His reasons for pursuing a legal career are more complex than those of his youngest brothers. Unlike Edward and Charles, and like Ralph, William had seemed destined to become a Congregational minister—even if his own minister, Nathaniel Frothingham, as Aunt Mary reported, believed him to be "ignorant of the difficulties of a clerical profession."[8] At the age of twenty-four, and a few years out of Harvard, William resolved to follow in the path of Boston's young intellectual hero, Edward Everett. Thus he set sail for Europe and graduate studies at the great center of religious learning in the German city of Göttingen. Less than two years later, he was on his way back to New England lacking a Ph.D. in theology only because he declined to pay the required sixty-dollar fee.[9] As for so many of his generation, graduate study in Göttingen decidedly undermined his Christian convictions. From his correspondence with Ralph, it seems clear that William experienced something of a crisis of faith during his time abroad. Challenged and excited by his studies, he wrote to a friend that he could not "avoid tracing much of this [enthusiasm] to the books and lectures of Eichhorn."[10] William's renewed ardor for careful, critical study of sacred texts was not matched by an enlivened spiritual sentiment. As his intellectual curiosity waxed, his religious faith waned. In a letter to his brother in January of 1825, William predicted his inevitable decision to forgo his clerical aspirations upon his return to New England. His time at Göttingen had convinced him that "every candid theologian after careful study will find himself wide from the traditionary opinions of the bulk of his parishioners."[11] The young American confessed his doubts to Goethe in an interview with the great German poet at his Weimar home in September of 1824. When the author of *Faust* and *The Sorrows of Young Werther* insisted that an effective minister need not necessarily possess an overwhelming personal faith and that private belief should be distinct from public profession, Emerson, at the moment still an earnest young Göttingen graduate student, recoiled in shocked disbelief at the prospect of such dangerous dissembling.[12] It seemed the height of mendacity to so much as consider a ministerial career based on anything less than complete personal conviction. Later, in the midst of a raging gale during his return passage to Boston, William repudiated what he considered to be the great German's cynicism; he "could not go to the bottom in peace with the intention in his heart of following the advice Goethe had given him." At that precise moment, he later told Ralph, he "renounced the ministry."[13] When he arrived home, he informed his family that he had resolved to move to New York City to become a lawyer.

William's decision to renounce a ministerial calling proved a great blow to the family. That the eldest brother felt his decision to be a momentous one is most amply demonstrated by the fact he fled New England in favor of New York City. It seems as if only by relocating to what his younger brother called "that obstreperous Babylon" could he escape the family's unfulfilled expectations and make a fresh start in law.[14] Of the entire Emerson clan, no one was more dismayed by William's vocational decision, and that of Edward and Charles as well, than Aunt Mary. Not only had she displayed the greatest personal religious fervor in the family; she had also devoted herself as much to the spiritual education of the boys as to anything else in her life. Always consistent in flaunting contemporary convention and in disparaging New England's increasing materialism, Mary dismissed as unworthy the mundane drives for secular success and material gain that she believed induced William, Edward, and Charles to abandon promising careers in the ministry. Mary needed no convincing that the Emerson boys were destined to higher pursuits than the law. A generation older than her nephews, Mary fervently believed, anachronistically, that to be a minister of the Standing Order was to reach the top rung of New England society, joining the ranks of Shepherd and Cotton, of the Mathers, Wises, and Edwards. She had to look no further than her father's heroic stand at Concord in 1775 and her own brother's respected career at Boston's venerable First Congregational Church to prove her case. For the Emersons, Moodys, Bulkeleys, and Blisses, vocational eminence in New England entailed a career in the Congregational clergy. When Mary envisioned Ralph or one of the other brothers as ministers, she saw them as part of New England's most highly respected and cherished vocation. "The kind Aunt whose cares instructed my youth (& whom may God reward) told me oft of the virtues of her & mine ancestors," Emerson wrote in 1825. "They have been clergymen for generations & the piety of all & the eloquence of many is yet praised in the churches." The boys had been called to be ministers, a station from which Mary may have been alone in expecting greatness. When she urged Ralph to enter the ministry immediately, she believed he would simultaneously rejuvenate Unitarian Congregationalism while achieving personal greatness. Convinced that the two were inextricably intertwined, she reasoned that Ralph was destined to revive New England's flagging faith. Aunt Mary profoundly influenced her nephew's religious education; equally, she was instrumental in helping him to suspend his disbelief that he might attain greatness through the traditional vocation of Congregational cleric.[15]

Unlike Aunt Mary, who was gravely disappointed by William's vocational change of heart and its foundation in religious dubiety, Ralph seems to have readily accepted his older brother's decision against the ministry. He intuitively grasped William's explanation of his spiritual reversal, as he would shortly face the analogous problem during his tenure as minister of Boston's Second Congregational Church. "Have you settled the question," William asked his brother in 1825, that all highly educated clerics must address when faced with the great gulf between his convictions and those of his parishioners, "whether he shall sacrifice his influence or his conscience?"[16]

Nowhere in his writings does Ralph reveal his attitude about the younger brothers' decisions to become lawyers. Several times over the years, however, it seems that he noted in his journals that his brothers lacked a certain spiritual depth commensurate with their genius. Their intellectual prowess at such an early age and their remarkable academic success had come too easily. Accordingly, Emerson worried that his brothers faced the great peril of gifted young men such as themselves, that of seeking popular acclaim at the price of personal integrity. He feared that his younger brothers might be driving themselves too hard, too fast without enough thought as to their ultimate destination. In 1825 as he was preparing to enroll in divinity school, Emerson reflected on his brothers' talents and personalities. "Thus one of my house is a person of squared & methodical conduct," he confided. "Another on whose virtues I shall chiefly insist is an accomplished gentleman of a restless worldly ambition who will not let me dream out my fine spun reveries but ever and anon jogs me and laughs aloud at my metaphysical sloth."[17] Ralph's critical and all-too-precise insights about Edward and Charles made him all the more devastated by their tragic demise. "So falls one pile more of hope for this life," Ralph lamented upon Edward's death. "I see I am bereaved of a part of myself."[18]

Never having considered the law as a vocation, Ralph had grave reservations about becoming a minister. Yet he was no more sanguine about any other vocational possibilities that New England of the 1820s presented him. In the spring of 1824 he had already resolved to close his school, thus bringing to an end a lackluster teaching career that he had always considered a vocational purgatory. He confessed in his journal that the other professions he could think of pursuing did not seem particularly suited to his peculiar talents:

> Now the profession of law demands a good deal of personal address, an impregnable confidence in one's own powers, upon all occasions expected & unexpected, & a logical mode of thinking & speaking—which I do not possess & may not reasonably hope to attain. Medicine also makes large demands upon the practitioner for a seducing Mannerism. And I have no taste for the pestle & mortar, for Bell on the bones or Hunter or Celsus.

The ideal career for this aspiring Emerson might have been as a professor of rhetoric at Harvard. But, as he well knew, his undistinguished academic performance in the college all but precluded this vocational possibility for the foreseeable future. Even an ushership at Boston Latin School had seemed beyond his grasp in 1821. Years later, he asked, "Why has never the poorest college offered me a professorship of rhetoric?"[19] He confessed to his friend Moncure Conway that he would have relished such an opportunity. Having thus written off professional careers in the law and medicine, and seeing no immediate opportunity in academia such as it was, Emerson virtually backed his way into the ministry.

Perhaps even more than Aunt Mary, Emerson amply perceived the alarming signs in the religious attitudes and practices among the elite of eastern Massachusetts. "Boston or Brattle Street Christianity," he derisively noted years later, "is a compound force or the best diagonal line that can be drawn between Jesus Christ and Abbot Lawrence." Unitarians still bought their pews, regularly attended services on Sundays, and basked in the reflected glow of the polished sermons of their cherished clerical intellectuals. Yet, in the third decade of the nineteenth century, the denomination was hardly growing, conversions were drastically decreasing, especially among the male population, and parishioners were looking less often to their churches and ministers for guidance and enlightenment.

Similarly, the ministry seemed no longer to attract the most interesting or committed intellectuals. And even those it did draw, such as Edward Everett, spent much of their time either lecturing at Harvard or in other public arenas.[20] Although Emerson found a great deal to admire in William Ellery Channing, who was "preaching sublime sermons every Sunday," he offered scant praise for any other Unitarians in his journals and letters.[21] His journal entries while enrolled in divinity school barely mask his evident disdain for his Harvard peers, with the sole exception of Frederic Henry Hedge, the son of Alford Professor Levi Hedge and in time one of Emerson's closest associates in the ministry. His contempt continued unabated during his years as an approbated minister, leading Emerson to cite with approval Harriet Martineau's caustic observation that "Mr Ware is sanctimonious, Mr Gannett popish, [and other] Unitarians in a twilight of bigotry."[22] His dismissive attitude toward, among others, his own Concord minister, Barzillai Frost, constituted the subtext of his attack on his Unitarian brethren in the Harvard Divinity School Address of 1838. Utterly ambitious "to do good in a golden way," Emerson was all too conscious that he was not enrolling in the divinity school to join a charismatic elite.[23]

The most dynamic preachers in Boston were not Unitarians. They were their orthodox opponents, who like Lyman Beecher reserved their most scathing attacks for the Unitarians, whose ministries they considered apostasy. It is no small irony that Beecher ministered to the newly formed Hanover Street church at precisely the moment that Emerson was embarking on the same vocation across the Charles River.[24] Emerson admired the energy and dynamism of the orthodox Trinitarianism, as he did of Methodism. In 1829 Emerson began to attend services at the Seaman's Bethel in Boston's seedy North End, so that he might hear the bombastic preaching of Edward Taylor, "that living Methodist [and] the Poet of the Church" upon whom it was said Herman Melville modeled Father Mapple in *Moby Dick*.[25] Emerson valued pulpit eloquence highly but found it emanating all too rarely from Boston's churches, and almost never from those going by the name Unitarian. "The Unitarian ministers here are young men," Beecher wrote to his colleague, the equally energetic Nathaniel Taylor of Connecticut, "and most of them feeble."[26] Emerson could only concur.

Aunt Mary had suggested that her nephew consider attending Andover Theological Seminary, which the orthodox had founded in 1808 in opposition to the Unitarian takeover of Harvard, but there is no evidence that Emerson gave Andover serious consideration. He had only Harvard in mind. Much like his father, who as editor of the *Monthly Anthology* had welcomed sharp criticism of Andover and its "Associate's Creed," Emerson identified the Andover Seminary, and orthodoxy in general with dogmatic Calvinism and a spirit of intolerance. On both counts he found Beecher and his colleagues wanting. He respected their vital energy, which he compared favorably with that of his Milquetoast colleagues, but the doctrines of Calvinism proved too much for his catholic tastes and doctrinal latitudinarianism. A child of the Enlightenment and schooled in Scottish Common Sense philosophy, Emerson dismissed orthodoxy as at best hopelessly anachronistic and at worst the babble of pseudointellectuals. "Calvinism suited Ptolomaism," Emerson concluded in 1832:

> The irresistible effect of Copernican Astronomy has been to make the great scheme for the salvation of man absolutely incredible. Hence great geniuses who studied the mechanism of the heavens became unbelievers in the popular faith: Newton became a Unitarian. Laplace in a Catholic country became an infidel, substituting Necessity for God but a self-intelligent necessity is God. Thus Astronomy proves theism but disproves dogmatic theology.[27]

Whatever the weaknesses of Unitarianism, Emerson could not countenance orthodoxy, or any "Religion that is afraid of science."[28]

For two decades Boston's Brahmin ministers had assiduously avoided an open fight with their erstwhile orthodox colleagues. Downplaying the doctrinal differences between the parties, the Brahmins reluctantly adopted the name Unitarian only in 1819 and then took up the challenge only when the orthodoxy party cast aspersion upon their personal integrity and character. In the first decades of the nineteenth century, the schismatics seemed to be in the orthodox camp. Led by the vitriolic minister of Charlestown, Jedidiah Morse, the orthodox made their top priority the exposure of Brahmin heterodoxy. In this way they hoped simultaneously to revive their own waning prestige as well as to restore the vital piety of the commonwealth. The pamphlet wars and the momentous *Baker* v. *Fales* court decision of 1820 forced the Unitarians' hand. At the beginning of the third decade of the century, they changed their tactics in order to deal more forcefully with the manifest bifurcation of the Congregational ranks. Cognizant that the almost two-centuries-old Standing Order of the Massachusetts Congregational clergy was moribund and that disestablishment was only a few years away, the Unitarians began to create their own denominational institutions. This included the formation of the Harvard Divinity School, where Emerson enrolled in the middle class, and the founding in 1825—on Emerson's twenty-second birthday—of the American Unitarian Association. The fact that the crisis of the Standing Order had damaged the power and prestige of the Congregational clergy was not lost on Emerson. He repeatedly lamented the party spirit among his clerical brethren. "I suppose it is not wise, not being natural, to belong to any religious party," Emerson remarked in his journals. "In the Bible you are not directed to be a Unitarian or a Calvinist or an Episcopalian. Now if a man is wise, he will not only not profess himself to be a Unitarian, but he will say to himself I am not a member of that or of any party. I am God's child, a disciple of Christ or in the eye of God a fellow disciple with Christ."[29]

Fearful of being allied too closely with any party, Emerson nevertheless understood that he was in fact joining the Unitarian denomination by enrolling at Harvard. In distinct contrast with the orthodox, he most assuredly preferred its learned, rational stance, its embrace of science and the Enlightenment, and its revulsion at anything that smacked of creedal uniformity. There can be little doubt that Emerson had consciously used the orthodox as a foil when writing his first published essay, "Thoughts on the Religion of the Middle Ages," for the *Christian Disciple* in 1822.[30] Particularly in the countryside, the orthodox party stood for ignorance and a vulgar anti-intellectualism for which Emerson had nothing but contempt. Emerson embraced the high culture of the Unitarianism that his own father had helped to incubate. On this level, Harvard served Emerson perfectly, for the Unitarians had incorporated the study of science, philosophy, and classical literature into what had only recently been a glorified seminary. Simultaneously, then, Emerson understood that the Unitarians professed a greater respect for science, art, and literature, but the orthodox undeniably possessed more fire, more vitality. If only he could stand above the parties, he might be able to mix together the spirit of orthodoxy with the erudition of Unitarianism. "*Alii disputent, ego mirabor*" (Let others dispute, I will marvel), Emerson quotes St. Augustine. "It shall be my speech to the Calvinist & the Unitarian."[31] He envisioned himself as the peacemaker.

Emerson's decision to enter the ministry proved momentous. Like all his important resolutions, he deliberated a great deal on this profound vocational choice. He hoped that joining the Congregational-Unitarian clergy would offer him the opportunity to be more than just one more settled minister. From the first he harbored far greater ambitions than merely to imitate his father or any of his contemporaries. "I am he who nourished brilliant visions of future grandeur," he admitted a year after finishing Harvard College. "My infant imagination was idolatrous of glory, & thought itself no mean pretender to the honours of those who stood highest in the community, and dared even to contend for fame with those who are hallowed by time & the approbation of ages."[32] Spurred by his boundless ambition, he aspired to achieve greatness by repairing the schism in the Congregational church. He hoped to reinvigorate New England piety and instill a faith commensurate with that of his Puritan ancestors by combining the orthodox's street eloquence with the Unitarians' rational marriage of science, philosophy, literature, and ethics. "I inherit from my sire a formality of manner & speech [typical of the Unitarians], but I derive from him or his patriotic parent a passionate love for the strains of eloquence. I burn after that '*aliquid immensum infinitumque*' which Cicero desired."[33]

His most ambitious hopes for the ministry notwithstanding, Emerson did not miss the profound personal irony of his decision to become a Unitarian preacher. He understood that his particular talents, which to that point had not been tested, were at least equal to the demands of the Unitarian ministry. "The preaching most in vogue at the present day depends chiefly on imagination for its success," he noted in his journal, "and asks those accomplishments which I believe are most within my grasp."[34] But therein lay part of the irony, for Emerson realized that becoming a Unitarian minister, such as the profession was, might bring him stability, a handsome income, and even some local renown, but it would never tax him to his limits. Other talents that he possessed in abundance might be superfluous to the minister's regular duties and would atrophy from disuse. Having decided to embark upon this vocation, a decision that seemed to have the mark of inevitability, Emerson fully understood that he might be foreclosing other, more challenging opportunities. After listing his reasons for becoming a minister, Emerson realized that he was not setting his sights overly high. "I have set down little which can gratify my vanity."[35]

Emerson noted another irony of his move back to Harvard in the winter of 1825. As he approached his twenty-second birthday, this ninth in an ancestral line of ministers had already come to a fundamental realization about himself. He might not be a rebel, but he was no conformist either. Intellectually self-reliant long before he uttered his famous doctrine, he harbored profound doubts about whether he could follow in the seemingly predetermined path of his forefathers and even remotely conceive of such a choice as a means toward self-fulfillment. To this point in his brief life, Emerson had never faced a greater dilemma. As he decided to close his school and turn toward the ministry in April of 1824, Emerson confronted this issue squarely. "I am beginning my professional studies," he wrote; "and I *deliberately* dedicate my time, my talent, & my hopes to the Church."[36] In his use of an adverb now famous in American judicial history for its ambiguity, Emerson clearly meant "deliberately" as a transparent indicator of the measured, even cautious, nature of his vocational choice. Far from throwing himself into a career that was likely to bring him unmitigated personal satisfaction, Emerson entered the ministry with his eyes wide open. "I should be loth to reflect at a remote period," he wrote in his journals, "that I took so solemn a step in my existence without some careful examination of my past & present life."[37]

From the first, then, Emerson understood that fulfillment in the ministry would entail his altering the profession to preserve his integrity. Anticipating later his observation about politics that "Good men must not obey the laws too well," Emerson was not about to conform to his calling too much.[38] That he had his doubts about the ministry and that he was determined to continue to go his own way as he entered divinity school is clear from two events surrounding his preparation for the ministry. The first relates to his association with William Ellery Channing, whose Dudleian Lecture of 1824 Emerson called his "model," and the second concerns Emerson's decidedly unique course of study while ostensibly enrolled in the divinity school.[39] Both issues reveal his autodidactic style and irrepressible intellectual independence.

Once Emerson had decided upon a ministerial career, he immediately sought guidance from the two people whose religious sentiments he most respected: Aunt Mary and Dr. Channing. He had conducted a spirited correspondence with Aunt Mary for many years; now, with Emerson about to commence formal preparation for the ministry, Aunt Mary's letters took on a vital importance. He beseeched her for answers to "a catalogue of curious questions" ranging from theodicy and the relationship of Platonism and Christianity to Hume's "definition of a miracle as 'a violation of a law of nature.' "[40] On spiritual and philosophical issues Aunt Mary was Emerson's essential interlocutor. Though she offered her searching nephew few pat answers, she spurred his philosophical investigations more than any of his contemporaries. Mary's relentless certitude proved a critical counterpoise to Emerson's intractable dubiety.

Like Aunt Mary, Channing provided Emerson with something he obtained nowhere else, for Federal Street's beloved minister was his model preacher. Writing Edward a few years into his studies, Emerson suggested that had it not been for Channing he might have given up on the Unitarian ministry altogether. "Glad of Dr. Channing, as some amends for the dullness, I fear I can't say degeneracy, of the pulpit in the whole country."[41] Once he had decided upon the ministry, Emerson sought out Channing for something akin to a personal tutorial. The family's precarious finances never far from his thoughts, Emerson had practical and financial considerations in mind when he approached Channing. He could ill afford to spend the time and money that the three-year Harvard Divinity curriculum required of its students. Studying under Channing for some time while still teaching school, Emerson reasoned, might well obviate the need to enroll at Harvard for the full three years. Explaining to William why he had decided against going abroad, Emerson wrote "in a few months I shall probably be at Cambridge & attempt to enter the *middle* Class, which if practicable will be an economy of time not to be despised by a hard handed American who reckons acquisitions by dollars & cents not by learning & skill." According to this calculus, Harvard was "the cheapest stall where education can be bought."[42]

Channing did not altogether warm to the idea of Emerson becoming a minister, at least not at the outset.[43] He gave his would-be pupil a list of inspirational readings and sent him on his way. As Emerson rather brusquely noted, Channing's somewhat terse inventory of books to be studied was remarkable for its brevity and seeming superficiality. Seeking to inspire Emerson more than prepare him for the professional aspects of the ministry, Channing suggested Emerson immerse himself in a set of spiritual works with which Emerson was either already familiar or in which he was just not particularly interested.[44] In either case, Emerson paid little heed to his tutor's advice. Later, Emerson wrote off Channing's diffidence as the result of his incapacity "of taking another person's point of view, or of communicating himself freely in private conversation."[45] More plausibly, Channing and Emerson understood each other very well. Channing discerned Emerson's misgivings about pursuing a career in divinity. What the young man needed was precisely what the good doctor had prescribed: inspirational works to encourage some form of rudimentary conviction that he sensed Emerson palpably lacked. Emerson admitted as much in a letter to Mary. "I ramble among doubts to which my reason offers no solution."[46]

For his part, the twenty-one-year-old Emerson likely had not sought out Channing with such lofty hopes as to be moved by inspirational reading or dialogue. Resolving to prepare for the ministry was his choice; Emerson was not asking Channing's opinion or advice. What he wanted from him was the means to skip a year of his required study. During a subsequent visit together, the two men must have come to some understanding. Throughout November and December of 1824 Emerson frequently called on Channing, who had given his charge a second list of readings. This much more substantive syllabus, which included recent treatises of German higher criticism and detailed biblical study, was not really to Emerson's liking either, but it served its purpose. Emerson set about working his way through his assignment with about as much determination as he could offer any project that was not of his own creation. He certainly understood that Channing's syllabus constituted the substance of the current Harvard curriculum such as it was. By February of 1825, Emerson was ready to enroll at the divinity school.

As Emerson had envisioned a year earlier when he had solicited Channing's help, the Harvard theological faculty—all three of them—waived one year of the required three-year curriculum, allowing Emerson to enter the middle class on February 16, 1825.[47] This proved only the first of several instances in which Emerson essentially set his own course of study. Having graduated from the college less than four years earlier, he was not particularly sanguine about what the divinity school and its faculty could offer him. Emerson surely had himself in mind when he wrote in his journal that Solomon "was no sickly student immured in a library & reading men thro' the spectacles of books . . . , but a man whose curiosity & temper made him an indefatigable pursuer of happiness."[48] One of the most expansive readers and thinkers of his generation, Emerson felt utterly constrained by Harvard's walls and its insular, uninspired curriculum.

When his eyes began to fail only a month into his Cambridge stay, Emerson could neither read nor take notes. The faculty, in the person of Andrews Norton, again granted him a special dispensation. Rather than withdraw from school altogether, Emerson could attend lectures while excusing himself from recitation. Because of his poor eyesight and his repeated opening and closing of schools in order to ensure the family's solvency, he seems to have spent just enough time at Divinity Hall to maintain at least the appearance that he was enrolled. The hours he did spend at Cambridge proved neither salubrious nor particularly inspirational. Living in 14 Divinity Hall in order to save money proved a disaster. The room's perpetual dampness was extremely unhealthy and doubtless contributed to his tubercular condition. As for the intellectual life of the school, Emerson had very little positive to write about his peers, who engaged in "cheap extemporaneous draggletail dialogue that takes place in our evening companies even among men of letters & ambition from candlelight till the bell strikes nine & breaks up the company."[49] At this point in his life, Emerson by no means preferred solitude to society, particularly considering that it was all but impossible for him to read for any length of time. The problem was not with companionship or conversation per se, but with the present company, as Emerson made clear in a sermon entitled "Conversation," which he first delivered in October of 1829. "Fine conversation is very rare," the young minister lamented in this curious address. To engage in meaningful dialogue, Emerson cautioned, "remember that it is the truth and not you that wins. . . ."[50] For the most part, Emerson avoided intimate association with his Harvard peers. "The day is gone by," he abruptly concluded, "when the useless & the frivolous should command my respect."[51]

Having "lost the use of my eye for study,"[52] Emerson abandoned his formal studies at Cambridge for almost a year. He took up teaching again, first in Chelmsford, then in Roxbury where he reopened Edward's school, and finally in Cambridge. When he closed the Cambridge school in October of 1826, he said his final farewell to the teaching profession. To add to his problem with eyesight, which was only marginally alleviated by several operations performed by "Dr. Reynolds," Emerson began to suffer from a rheumatic condition in his hip.[53] Relieved of the strain of regular study, Emerson's vision seemed to improve somewhat. For the most part refraining from letter writing and his habitual journal scribbling, Emerson reported to Aunt Mary that "My eyes are well comparatively, my limbs are diseased with rheumatism."[54] By the fall of 1826 Emerson was weak and complaining of chest pains, which by November were sufficiently severe that he borrowed seventy dollars from his Uncle Ripley and departed for Charleston, South Carolina. Throughout these physical trials, all of which were part of the family's tuberculosis bug, Emerson retained both his spirited determination to become a minister and his own sense of humor. It was an essential tonic to remain "garrulous and silly," he wrote William in September of 1826.

> Among my other scarecrows to fill gaps of conversation, are my lung complaints. You must know in my vehement desire to preach I have recently taken into my bosom certain terrors not for my hip which does valiantly, nor for my eyes which deserve all commendation, but for my lungs without whose aid I cannot speak, and which scare me & thro me scare our poor mother's sympathies with stricture & jenesaisquoisities.[55]

Determined to fulfill his goal of becoming a minister despite his ailments, Emerson read a trial sermon before the Middlesex Association of Ministers on October 10 and was duly approbated, or licensed, to preach. As momentous as this milestone was, Emerson downplayed the event, perhaps because he understood that the fact his uncle Samuel Ripley and grandfather Ezra Ripley were members of the committee made his approval a formality only. "In the fall, I propose to be *approbated*, to have the privilege, tho' not at present the purpose, of preaching but at intervals," Emerson had written Aunt Mary the previous August. "I do not now find in me any objections to this step.—Tis a queer life, and the only humour proper to it seems quiet astonishment."[56] No member of the Middlesex Association examined Emerson as to his beliefs, the Unitarians having long ago eschewed the kind of doctrinal rigidity that necessitated a full vetting of candidates. "If they had examined me strictly," Emerson remarked to a friend, "they would not have let me preach at all."[57]

On the following Sunday morning, October 15, Emerson delivered his first sermon from the pulpit of Samuel Ripley's Waltham church. A month later, he presented the same sermon, "Pray without Ceasing," to a gathering at Boston's First Congregational Church from the pulpit his father had commanded some fifteen years earlier. Emerson nowhere stated whether this Boston homecoming of sorts had a dramatic impact upon him. He rarely mentioned his father in his journals and found no reason to do so on this occasion. It is no small irony, however, that in order to preserve his own writings at this time, Emerson reused his father's worn sermon binders that he had saved. Of course, this necessitated the young preacher's trashing the manuscript sermons of his father that the binders contained. For a person who so consciously preserved so much, not least of which were Aunt Mary's exquisite Almanacks, the symbolic significance of destroying his father's hand-written sermons while embarking upon the identical vocation is hard to miss—or deny.

Both in its origins and content Emerson's "Pray without Ceasing" sermon could never have been mistaken for one of his father's.[58] Its author claimed to have conceived of it while working on his Uncle William Ladd's Newton farm the preceding summer. Emerson's son, Edward, noted that the premise of the sermon, whose title Emerson recorded in his journal in June of 1826, stemmed from a rewarding interchange in which the candidate minister had engaged with "a Methodist labourer, named Tarbox, as they worked in a hay-field."[59] Emerson felt a distinct satisfaction at spinning his first sermon from a source so close to the land, literally, and so distant from Divinity Hall. In subsequent years, Emerson the essayist would praise the "language of the street" which was "always strong."[60] In "Pray without Ceasing" Emerson had not yet attained his mature voice, but it is clear that he was already dismissive of that stilted sermonic style favored by the Brahmins.[61] "I preach half of every Sunday," he wrote Aunt Mary in 1827. "When I attended church on the other half of a Sunday . . . I said to myself [of the preacher] . . . all his communications to men are unskilful plagiarisms from the common stock of tho't & knowledge & he is, of course, flat & tiresome."[62] The style of his first sermons was immature, containing those very rhetorical questions and hackneyed conventions that he disparaged in other ministers' sermons; it also contained some hints of the author's searching for that more earthy, homegrown style that he so highly praises a few years later. In his 1859 lecture "Art and Criticism," Emerson reminded his audience what it took him years to learn: "The key to every country [is] command of the language of the common people." Surely Henry David Thoreau and Walt Whitman heartily concurred. Emerson took special delight in the words of a fellow stagecoach passenger leaving Waltham the following day. "Young man, you'll never preach a better sermon than that."[63]

Though not devoid of hardship, the year 1826 had been Emerson's happiest. As the leaves turned and the New England weather grew cooler, the increasingly self-reliant and confident young minister was at once relieved and excited. Emerson had become the rock of the family, providing his mother and brothers with more than just money. He had taken over his brother's school when Edward's health had given out; he had seen after Bulkeley, whose mental condition had deteriorated significantly in the last year; and he had helped the family through William's vocational crisis. As for his professional life, this year had marked a turning point. The reluctant teacher had closed his last school; he had methodically worked his way toward the ministry, making it through his second stint at Harvard, where he would shortly be granted a master's degree and elected to Phi Beta Kappa; most importantly, Emerson had been approbated to preach and had delivered a series of well-received sermons in and around Boston. His prospects appeared auspicious indeed.

As usual, Emerson found himself not entirely satisfied. The family was far from secure and he was particularly worried about Edward, whose health had forced him to seek relief abroad. William, having resolved to make his way in New York, was in dire financial straits and would remain without much of a law practice for many years to come. Emerson's own poor health proved a concern, too. When "a certain stricture on the right side of the chest" made it almost impossible for him to preach, Emerson had no choice but to attend to his perilous physical state.[64] On November 24, he boarded the *Clematis* bound for South Carolina in the hope of regaining his failing health.

Emerson's months in the South, particularly his convalescence in St. Augustine, Florida, proved a great boon. Not only did he recover his health, a process that he measured in his slow but steady weight gain, but he took intellectual advantage of his first trip outside of the parochial confines of his New England home. Exposed for the first time to Spaniards, slavery, and southern manners, as well as to Catholic Mass and atheism, Emerson gained a better perspective on the world and his place within it. He reaped the benefits of hours and hours of solitude, which from this trip forward he would prize dearly, as well as from the stimulating society of Achille Murat, one of the most colorful characters on the continent. All of these disparate events combined to make the winter of 1826–27 a profound learning experience and an ideal complement to years of book learning and Harvard lectures. By the time Emerson returned to New England the following summer, he had recovered his health, such as it was, and had grown in self-confidence.

Emerson's friendship with Achille Murat turned out to be the most important intellectual stimulus of his southern retreat. "A new event is added to the quiet history of my life," begins a journal entry. "I have connected myself by friendship to a man . . . with as ardent a love of truth as that which animates me, with a mind surpassing mine in the variety of its research, & sharpened & strengthened to an energy for *action*, to which I have no pretension by advantages of birth & practical connexion with mankind beyond almost all men in the world."[65] A nephew of Napoleon, and formerly the crown prince of Naples, Murat cut quite a figure on the coast of Florida. He had been forced into exile with the execution of his father and demise of his uncle. At twenty-six, Murat was only two years older than his new Unitarian friend; yet he was much more a man of the world, whose social grace Emerson would have liked to emulate. Wishing he could forgo "the ambition to shine in the frivolous assemblies of men," Emerson noted with measured envy that "whilst [Murat] taxes my powers in his philosophic speculations [he] can excel the coxcombs, & that, *con amore*, in the fluency of nonsense."[66]

Murat was unlike anyone Emerson had met in his life. He was "a consistent Atheist," an elitist, and ardently proslavery. Emerson had never had to face so squarely in his insular New England world the subtle arguments put forth by this handsome, highly intelligent political refugee. Later to write of the American South that it was "the finest edifice raised by man," Murat fervently maintained that true civilization, great men, and high art could only be nourished in a caste society in which slave labor freed men like himself for higher pursuits.[67] Only aristocracies produced the artifacts of human greatness, Murat assured his doubtful young friend during one of their marathon conversations. Convinced that Murat's "soul is noble, & his virtue . . . is sublime," Emerson sought to explain his opposing views and in doing so to clarify his thoughts.[68] He seems to have failed to win the argument, but it is clear that he did not lose it either; he won the grudging respect of Murat, who would later write that Emerson and his Unitarian beliefs were "pure, elegant, and free from every species of ceremony or superstition."[69]

The conflict between aristocracy and democracy about which the two men "talked incessantly" proved to be one of the great problems to which Emerson would return time and again.[70] Like Alexis de Tocqueville, who would shortly make his own excursion through the United States, Emerson believed that republics constituted the only just form of government. Accordingly, he could never endorse aristocracy or any type of regime in which some persons by blood, birth, or blemish were considered superior or inferior to others. Emerson's populist sympathies made aristocracy anathema in any form because of its inherent injustice. The more vexing problem rested with Murat's assertions about the relationship between republican society and culture. As he would ponder the same question as put to him by William Wordsworth, whom Emerson quotes as worrying that the United States "lack a class of men of leisure—in short of gentlemen to give a tone of honor to the community," so he contemplated Murat's assertion that aristocracies fostered high culture and greatness in a way that republics never could.[71] On this issue Emerson had no definitive answer. American democracy, as Emerson called it, was too young to suggest one; without certitude, Emerson could only steadfastly retain his optimistic vision that some day the United States would boast a high culture commensurate with its material promise. Mulling over this very issue a few years earlier, Emerson had posed the question in his journal. "But you have no literature. It is admitted we have none. But we have what is better. We have a government and a national spirit that is better than poems or histories & these have a premature ripeness that is incompatible with the rapid production of the latter."[72] Emerson often ruminated on Murat's objections to democracy and the atheist's conviction that it failed to be conducive to what is noblest in humanity. In the short run, Emerson would search for the nation's first true poets while himself calling for an indigenous literature. Eventually, he would come to define the role of intellectuals like himself in a democracy to be to foster an abiding interest in high culture among the people. He would strive to bring about the very human excellence that Murat claimed impossible in the United States. Murat's critical assessment of the place of excellence in a democracy spurred Emerson's thoughts on what would become a lifelong interest. For this, he was profoundly grateful. "I blessed my stars for my fine companion," Emerson wrote to William in the spring of 1827.[73]

Emerson especially admired Murat's diverse and eclectic tastes. In the following months and years when Emerson would contrast Murat with his Unitarian colleagues, he would wince at the latter's insularity. "I like to have a man's knowledge comprehend more than one class of topics, one row of shelves," he wrote. "I like a man who likes to see a fine barn as well as a good tragedy."[74] His varied discussions with Murat, in which he impressed his aristocratic friend with his own broad erudition and tastes, validated Emerson's lifelong habit of "sinful strolling from book to book."[75] Unlike his atheist friend, Emerson's religious faith never wavered; yet Emerson harbored a great respect for Murat, "this intrepid doubter," precisely because of his skepticism. Like Socrates and Montaigne, both of whom Emerson repeatedly read throughout his life, Murat, as with all skeptics, nobly set out to discover the underlying reality about himself and his society. For Emerson, doubt was pandemic; truly rare were those men like Murat who single-mindedly sought after truth.

An increasingly self-confident Emerson returned home in late spring of 1827. He had accomplished many things while away. He had gained weight and his health had improved. Cognizant of the grave troubles that dogged his younger brothers, Edward in particular, Emerson was slowly coming to embrace his unique personality. Those very traits of which he had long been so critical he now valorized more highly; his tendency toward solitude, his puerile silliness, and his lack of enforced diligence now appeared to have their compensations. "When I consider the constitutional calamity of my family which in its falling upon Edward has buried at once so many towering hopes," he confided to his journal,

> with whatever reason I have little apprehension of my own liability to the same evil. I have so much mixture of silliness in my intellectual frame that I think Providence has tempered me against this. My brother lived & acted & spoke with preternatural energy. My own manner is sluggish; my speech sometimes flippant, sometimes embarrassed & ragged; my actions (if I may say so) are of a passive kind. Edward had always great power of face. I have none. I laugh; I blush; I look ill tempered; against my will & against my interest. But all this imperfection as it appears to me . . . is a ballast—as things go—is a defence.[76]

At once, then, Emerson understood that for the sake of his health he had consciously to pace himself and that his own peculiar personality equipped him to do just that.

Emerson had lost none of his deep-seated ambition during his sojourn. In fact, it seems that in his solitude he promised himself to be great if he could. "I believe myself to be a moral agent of an indestructible nature," he resolved at the beginning of the new year, "& designed to stand in sublime relations to God & my fellow men; to contribute in my proper enjoyments to the general welfare."[77] He hoped to find greatness in the church, in his chosen vocation. In his conversations with Achille Murat, Emerson had gone to great pains to portray Unitarianism in the best possible light, which he evidently succeeded in doing. In his history of the United States, Murat offered an effusive, positive assessment of Emerson's faith. Accordingly, upon his return the young minister came face-to-face with the very institution he had defended in the ideal. It was his job to make Unitarianism live up to his exhortations before Murat and, more importantly, up to his own lofty expectations. As far as his health allowed, he devoted the next several years to just that project.

With conviction and tolerably good health, Emerson set about helping his countrymen improve themselves and their society through the means and opportunities presented to him as minister of the Gospel. Even before he arrived home, Edward had written that First Church sought him as a temporary replacement for its settled minister, Nathaniel Frothingham, who was off to Europe for the summer. This was a promising sign; as long as his health held out, Emerson the minister would have at least some opportunity to move his fellow citizens. After visiting William in New York, Emerson returned to New England in time to preach before his mother and family at Concord on June 10, where he delivered his sermon "Setting a Good Example."[78] For the next twenty-five straight Sundays, Emerson read a sermon or two in one of Massachusetts's Unitarian houses of worship. The majority of Sundays throughout the summer found Emerson in his father's old pulpit at First Church in Boston. In the fall the Unitarian Association officially licensed him to be a supply preacher, available to deliver sermons on a temporary basis in any pulpit in the area. Licensure came with a salary of ten dollars per week.[79] He traveled from New Bedford, Massachusetts, to the Connecticut Valley and back to Boston, preaching from a growing collection of original sermons that by the end of 1827 exceeded a dozen. Emerson's last sermon of the year, number thirteen, "The Nativity," he delivered in Concord, New Hampshire, before his future bride, Ellen Louisa Tucker, on Christmas Day.

The summer and fall of 1827 had been heady months for Emerson. True enough, he was not yet a shining star in the Unitarian firmament, but at the age of twenty-four he had obtained his bachelor's and master's degrees from Harvard, had been licensed to preach, and had delivered sermons from some of the most prestigious pulpits in New England. His repertoire of sermons was growing, as was his reputation. Watertown, Massachusetts, minister Convers Francis, who would become one of Emerson's lifelong associates, declared his sermons to be "distinguished by a great felicity of thought & style, by rich moral eloquence, & by a fresh & fervent earnestness."[80] When Boston's Second Congregational Church asked him to supply its pulpit while waiting to see if its ordained minister, Henry Ware Jr., would recover his health, Emerson must have known that it was just a matter of time until he would be called to one of the leading Unitarian pulpits. In the meantime, Emerson kept busy traveling throughout New England, writing sermons, and continuing his work as a supply preacher. Between his first sermon at his Uncle Ripley's Waltham church the previous October and his ordination at Second Church in March of 1829, Emerson drafted thirty original sermons and delivered one or more of them to Massachusetts' congregations nearly two hundred times.

Emerson seems to have liked his work as a supply preacher. Admittedly, busy as he was, supply preaching did not pay particularly well, as he remained some three hundred dollars in debt to Ezra Ripley and others. For the moment, at least, neither his mother nor his brothers were in immediate need of his material assistance, and Emerson himself had never been profligate. Residing in Divinity Hall at Harvard, his living expenses were negligible. Being unattached had distinct advantages. In his present position as supply preacher, Emerson found time to compose sermons, persisted in his omnivorous reading, which if anything had grown even more varied, and, most critically, continued to nurse himself back to health. The relatively undemanding work of supply preaching had enabled Emerson to recuperate markedly since the previous June when he had worried in a letter to William that at times he was considering "total abdication of the profession on the score of ill health."[81] By February Emerson was still far from robust. "It is a long battle this of mine betwixt life & death & tis wholly uncertain to whom the game belongs," he lamented to his brother. "So I never write when I can walk or especially when I can laugh."[82]

Emerson's health improved with the warmer weather. In March William wrote that his younger brother "is getting stronger & better—He is so busy in getting health, wisdom & sermons, that he writes no letters."[83] In the spring and summer of 1828, Emerson's recuperation had progressed sufficiently for him to consider some rather dramatic changes in his life. His deliberately independent lifestyle underwent a significant transformation as he became attached both professionally and personally. Upon his twenty-fifth birthday, Emerson could reflect with no small satisfaction upon his situation. Inwardly, he was growing in confidence and maturity as he consciously developed what he termed his "intellectual Voice."[84] Outwardly, he was gaining a reputation for pulpit eloquence and personal decorum that made him all but assured of being called to one of the top Unitarian churches. Emerson was "the most popular preacher among the candidates," Sarah Ripley reported to Aunt Mary, "and all he wants is health to be fixed at once in Boston."[85]

Emerson did not have to wait long for his chance. In June he agreed to a promising offer from Boston's Second Church when it became clear that Ware had become too sick to perform his duties. "I have engaged to supply his pulpit," he wrote to William, adding that he understood Ware to be "very ill."[86] Second Church retained his services "until he should give notice to the contrary," with the stipulation of a weekly salary of fifteen dollars.[87] Emerson delivered his first sermon, his favorite, "On Showing Piety at Home," on the morning of July 13. Throughout the summer and fall Emerson preached in place of Ware, who by that time had recovered somewhat, but whose precarious health had made his return to his pulpit exceedingly remote. When Ware moved on to Harvard as the first Professor of Pulpit Eloquence and Pastoral Care, the way was open for Emerson to succeed him at Second Church.

The pastorate of Boston's venerable Second Church was a high honor, one on which Emerson had set his sights for at least a year. In the winter of 1828–29 he had all the more reason to accept the call, having undertaken a monumental step in his personal life. Emerson had become engaged. The same young man who had confided in his journals of his singular lack of love, or perhaps even the capacity for that higher emotion, had fallen deeply in love with Ellen Tucker. Only a year before first meeting Ellen, he had compared himself with the solitary Robinson Crusoe, declaring that he was obliged to "apprise the reader that I am a bachelor & to the best of my belief have never been in love."[88] Emerson wrote that Ellen was "very beautiful by universal consent,"[89] while Charles did his older brother one better, conceiving of her comeliness as "an Ideal that, if I were a Platonist, I should believe to have been one of the Forms of Beauty in the Universal Mind."[90] Only seventeen at the time of their engagement, by all accounts Ellen was beautiful and possessed of an exquisite and charming personality. To his brothers Emerson expressed admiration for Ellen's poetry, praised her character and her tenderness, and confessed "finally I love her."[91] They married at the Concord, New Hampshire, home of her mother and stepfather on September 30, 1829. "Cannot a married man write," Emerson noted exuberantly to his brother after the wedding, "& say that tis excellent to double his being?"[92]

There can be little doubt that Emerson had his mind set on becoming the settled pastor of Boston's Second Congregational Church. In the preceding months he had declined offers from the Unitarian Church at Brighton, Massachusetts—"one should preach Bucolics there," he wrote to William—as well as from two other unnamed pulpits, and had informed Ellen's stepfather, William Kent of Concord, New Hampshire, that he would not consider anything greater than occasional supply preaching at the newly formed Unitarian church there.[93] Once it became clear that Henry Ware would not return to his pastorate, Emerson expected to be offered the post. When the offer was not immediately forthcoming, Emerson decided in consultation with his grandfather Ezra Ripley to bring some pressure to bear on the situation. In a strategic retreat, Emerson informed the congregation that he would preach his last sermon as supply preacher "at the end of November." Writing to his brother concerning his "professional affairs" in December of 1828, Emerson made reference to his discreet, considered tactics:

> I have preached a good while at Mr Ware's. I was on no definite agreement as to time. It is well understood Mr Ware w[oul]d shortly resign & go to Cambridge. I did not think it very delicate to hang on longer; if the parish was to be regarded as open for candidates I was monopolizing. . . . Why I should come away is in plain daylight.[94]

After the Congregation "made a fuss," it formally voted on January 11, 1829, seventy-four to five, to make Emerson the new minister.[95] His official title of colleague pastor promised a generous salary "fixed at the sum of twelve hundred dollars per annum," which would be increased to eighteen hundred dollars, the current salary of Henry Ware, upon the final retirement of the senior pastor.[96] On the thirtieth of January Emerson accepted the invitation, and two months later he was ordained as junior minister of the Second Congregational Church of Boston.

Both of Emerson's new and presumably lifelong relationships, his ordination in March and his marriage in September, proved short lived. Ellen's tubercular condition, which became acute during the couple's brief courtship, and her tragic death overshadowed Emerson's career at the Second Church. It is impossible to separate his great personal sufferings from his experience as a settled minister. His marriage and Ellen's death, as well as the ultimate settlement of her considerable estate, had a great impact upon his brief and eventful relationship with his congregation.

Ellen's tragic death after only fifteen months of marriage had a profound effect upon Emerson, who simultaneously had to cope with the physical and psychological problems of Edward and Bulkeley. Like so many of their generation, the Tucker and Emerson families suffered under the ubiquitous specter of tuberculosis. Ellen had manifested the disease that struck Emerson's father and Edward and Charles as well as her own mother and sister, before their engagement. She suffered severely during the newlyweds' brief months together. Ironically, Ellen seems to have endured the greatest hardships when the couple were together as a result of her heightened emotional state, as they were deeply in love. Predictably, their short-lived marriage revolved around Ellen's failing health, which made it impossible for them to settle in Boston.[97] They resided there for less than a year of their marriage and not more than five months consecutively. Upon her death early in the morning of February 8, 1831, Emerson composed himself long enough to write a single letter; fittingly it was to Aunt Mary, to whom he always looked for comfort and guidance during trying times. "My angel is gone to heaven this morning & I am alone in the world & strangely happy," he noted with brutal honesty. "Her lungs shall no more be torn nor her head scalded by her blood nor her whole life suffer from the warfare between the force & delicacy of her soul & the weakness of her frame."[98] Charles sent word of Ellen's death to William and reported that "Waldo is well & bears well his incalculable loss."[99]

From February 1831, Emerson was alone in the world yet "strangely happy." The loss of his young wife and first love was difficult to accept. Death and disease became the dominant metaphors in much of his writing, both in journals and in sermons; Emerson seemed to be "one over whom the waters have gone," Charles informed William.[100] Yet, as with the devastating loss of his son Waldo a little more than a decade later, Emerson forced himself to accept death as an unavoidable part of a life that in no way should be wasted in mourning or inactivity. In the months between Ellen's death and his departure for Europe, he made a daily pilgrimage to her grave at the Tucker family tomb in Roxbury. On one of those visits, he opened her casket as if to affirm that, with terrible loss as with everything else, nothing could substitute for direct personal experience.[101] The impact of Ellen's death on the young minister cannot be separated from the basic import of their falling in love. For Emerson, both love and death were novel experiences that proved critical to his development. The Emersons' single-minded commitment to education had made him an intellectual; the family's endemic financial struggles had deepened Emerson's social awareness, but had done little to convince him of his personal and emotional depth. Ellen had changed all that, and the whirlwind of love, courtship, marriage, illness, and death transformed Emerson. Six feet tall and barely 150 pounds, Emerson had recognized for years that his relative emotional shallowness was woefully inferior to his intellectual range and expansive imagination. His relationship with Ellen created in Emerson an emotional depth commensurate with his awesome intellect.

It is difficult to assess the impact of Emerson's marriage upon his professional life. Paradoxically, it proved great and negligible at the same time. As with all newlyweds, Emerson was faced with a plethora of novel financial and personal responsibilities, which he could best meet by becoming a settled minister with a guaranteed salary. With his wife in tow, he was ready to pursue the steady work entailed in ordination and in ministering to a large Boston congregation. The young man who until his nuptials had lived as an aloof bachelor in Divinity Hall at Cambridge, and who understood his own vital need for solitude, was suddenly confronted with tremendous community and institutional responsibilities. Yet to attribute his acceptance of Second Church's invitation to his new domestic responsibilities is illogical. With or without Ellen he had planned to make the same fateful step. His professional training and personal ambition dictated the move. At the same time, Ellen's death and his inheriting her substantial estate enabled him to resign from Second Church and break those same institutional bonds. Indeed, the Tucker inheritance facilitated his quitting the church altogether. Furthermore, the personal crisis brought on by Ellen's death added urgency to his growing sense of professional frustration. However, the premature death of his wealthy wife was no more than a necessary condition for his decision to resign. The deeper causes of his profound frustration and unhappiness with his station at Second Church proved to be social and vocational. From the first, Emerson had harbored reservations about the Unitarian ministry, and his brief stay at Second Church did nothing to assuage them. Married or single, rich or poor, Emerson was profoundly dissatisfied with the ministry.

Emerson's vocational crisis played itself out during his three-year tenure at Second Church. Yet the seeds of discontent with his chosen vocation can be traced as far back as his decision to enroll at Harvard Divinity School almost a decade earlier. Emerson had "deliberately" embarked on his career, cognizant that all was not well with the Unitarian clergy. Channing was a gifted preacher and Everett possessed eloquence, but they were exceptions among clerics "in danger of becoming wards and pensioners of the so-called producing classes."[102] For the most part, Emerson believed in the 1820s what he would write in "The Sovereignty of Ethics" many decades later: "Luther would cut off his hand sooner than write theses against the pope, if he suspected that he was bringing on with all his might the pale negations of Boston Unitarianism."[103] From his days at Harvard to his ordination at Second Church, Emerson understood that for him to find professional satisfaction as a minister, Unitarianism would have to change and he would be the instrument to effect the transformation. He sought to rewrite "the old story," as he termed it; "once we had wooden chalices and golden priests, now we have golden chalices and wooden priests."[104] Despite his wife's illness and sorrowful death, Emerson had ample opportunity at Second Church to ascertain if he could make the ministry fit his ambitions. Ultimately, he concluded that it could not.

Emerson resigned himself to a career in the ministry because he could imagine no other suitable venue for his talents and ambitions. Once he decided upon that means, however, he sought with all the strength he could muster to tailor it to his lofty objectives, as his letter of acceptance and his first sermon before his congregation made evident. After confessing his lack of conviction in his abilities and his present "weakness" due to Ellen's illness, the candidate deftly altered the tone of his letter, turning outward to challenge his new congregation. "But, brethren, whilst I distrust my powers," he wrote to the church society, "I must speak firmly of my purposes."[105] He elaborated on these purposes in his inaugural sermon on "The Christian Minister," which he delivered on March 15, the Sunday after his ordination. "[H]eard Waldo preach his first sermons to his own people," wrote Edward, who with other Emerson and Tucker family members was present at Second Church. "They were excellently good. . . . What Paul said to the great & powerful of the world, he said to the wise of this world—I am not ashamed of the gospel of Christ."[106]

Emerson's own aspirations and the traditional duties of a Christian minister were by no means isomorphic. As the role of the Unitarian minister evolved in the third and fourth decades of the nineteenth century, the minister's duties included a marked emphasis on pastoral care in addition to traditional preaching. This evolution was best exemplified in the career of Henry Ware, Emerson's predecessor at Second Church and for the first months of his tenure his senior colleague. When Ware retired from Second Church, where he had been much loved for his tender, personal involvement with the congregation, he became the first Professor of Pulpit Eloquence and Pastoral Care at Harvard Divinity School. The establishment of this new chair signaled that the Unitarian clerical leadership sought to lay a new stress upon those ministerial duties above and beyond the delivery of sermons. Emerson's aloofness and general dislike of pastoral duties contrasted sharply with this pastoral trend. His uneasy manner and lack of solicitousness toward his flock could not have been farther from that of Henry Ware, as members of his congregation did not fail to inform him.

Emerson articulated what he considered the duties of a Christian minister in his inaugural sermons; remarkably, they virtually collapsed to singularity—preaching. When it came to the minister's additional duties, which he was understandably reticent about articulating before his congregation, the junior minister doubted his aptitude for pastoral care. Supremely confident in his pulpit abilities, Emerson elaborated his conviction that preaching "must be manly and flexible and free beyond all the examples of the times before us."[107] Characterized by an "indefinite charm of simplicity and wisdom," his pulpit eloquence led one appreciative parishioner to predict that he would "make another Channing."[108] Already self-reliant in the extreme, Emerson was determined from the first to conduct his professional life in the manner that he and he alone considered appropriate. The Unitarians who attended these first sermons could hardly miss the point, one to which he repeatedly returned in subsequent sermons. Insisting on "freedom in my preaching," Emerson warned his audience that he intended to institute changes in the services and in the sermon particularly:

The world was wrong and the pulpit has not set it right. It seems to me that our usage of preaching is too straitened. It does not apply itself to all the good and evil that is in the human bosom. . . . I shall not be so much afraid of innovation as to scruple about introducing new forms of address, new modes of illustration, and varied allusions into the pulpit, when I believe they can be introduced with advantage. I shall not certainly reject them simply because they are new. I must not be crippled in the exercise of my profession.[109]

Comparing himself to Paul in the sermon, it is almost as if Emerson was admonishing his proud congregants that they might find his performance of some aspects of his clerical duties distasteful. "And where he went," Emerson noted with approval, "he heard the hisses of the world."[110] He anticipated a fate comparable to that of the Apostle to the Gentiles.

The choice of Paul's "declaration with a valiant heart" from Romans 1:16 for his inaugural sermon suggests an interesting element of irony. The subject of the sermon was not really Paul's responsibilities or the duties of the preacher, but those of the converted or, in Emerson's case, of the congregation before him. Instead of emphasizing his own responsibilities, as might be presumed in an inaugural sermon entitled "The Christian Minister," Emerson in fact detailed what he expected of his flock. For years, he had criticized the Unitarians, clergy and congregant alike, for their complacency and lack of religious fervor, and he was not about to desist now that he had a captive audience. "We are Christians by the same title as we are New England men, that herein we were born and reared." There could be no more important element of the minister's calling than to reverse this disturbing complacency, which had engendered "the grossest ignorance and the most injurious prejudices in regard to that which I love and honour."[111] He hoped that he was up to the challenge, "that the cause in whose strength I come, will give power to my weakness."[112] Of this, however, he was not entirely confident.

After warning his audience, whom he compared to "the world whose pride [Paul] insulted," about interfering with his innovative preaching and challenging them to begin to take their religion more seriously, Emerson concluded the afternoon sermon on a note of optimism.[113] Using repetitive syntax to bring his message to a dramatic climax, Emerson set the stage for his thirty-month experiment as minister of Boston's Second Church. "We will talk of the resurrection of the dead," he began earnestly.

We will call to mind the words of the Friend of the human race to his elder disciples, "Yet a little while and ye shall see me." We will think of the love he bore us. We will comfort one another by the thought of the benevolence of God which having encompassed us with so many blessings here, may surely be trusted with our future welfare. We will talk of the new heavens and the new earth, till the earth shall fade before the magnificence of the growing vision. Across the darkness so long dreaded of the valley of death, we will behold the Mount of our Hope lifting its everlasting summits into light. And though our flesh fail and our heart fail we will rejoice in the Lord, we will glory in the God of our salvation.[114]

Eyes wide open, Emerson went into his work as ordained minister hoping to transform the denomination and convinced that anything short of reformation signaled failure. "It is a sad and meagre commendation of a Christian minister," Emerson declared in terms that prefigured his revolutionary 1838 Divinity School Address, "when the departing whisper to each other the praises of his manner, his language, and his voice and congratulate themselves on a skillful emphasis, or a musical period, and then go away and remember the service no more. Believe me, brethren," he dramatically concluded, "if this is the top of my success, I have failed miserably of my end."[115] It took him only three years to conclude that his ministry was bankrupt.

The roots of Emerson's disaffection with his post relate to two basic problems with the pastoral office at Second Church. First, Emerson harbored impossibly lofty ambitions, which in a letter to Henry Ware he had himself confessed "were very high," particularly concerning how his preaching might spark in his parishioners some sort of regeneration, the precise characteristics of which he could never articulate.[116] "God's greatest gift is a Teacher," Emerson ruefully noted to his Aunt Mary, cognizant that as junior pastor, or teacher, at Second Church, he seemed to accomplish very little.[117] Expecting to move his people with every sermon, Emerson fretted over the preparation of each one. "I fear nothing now except the preparation of sermons," he confided to Ezra Ripley. "The prospect of one each week, for an indefinite time to come is almost terrifick."[118]

The second issue related to Emerson's singular lack of social skills. He was dreadfully ill at ease performing the pastoral duties incumbent upon a minister, as he well knew. His awkwardness quickly became legendary. Ralph Rusk relates how an embarrassed Emerson, distracted and fumbling for words, was asked to leave the deathbed of one of his parishioners by the dying man himself.[119] Because he was so ill-suited for these duties, he considered a great waste the inordinate amount of time he was obliged to devote to pastoral care. "I am labouring abundantly in my vocation so have little time," he wrote to William only a month into his tenure.[120] Emerson was never a man to abide wasted time and effort; with Ellen's death he became that much more disgusted with trifles, manners, and social custom. Effective preaching proved insufficient to offset the routine and ritual aspects of the ministry that Emerson increasingly despised. "The activity which is the duty of a Christian minister in the discharge of his office, is of two kinds, preacher and pastor, and often in some measure incompatible," he lamented a year into his ministry.[121]

Evidence of Emerson's growing disaffection with his pastorate practically leapt off the pages of his sermons. In one of his most biting discourses, "Trifles," Emerson began by asserting that the great benefits of city life "are purchased by some considerable disadvantages. One of the evils of social life is its tendency to give importance to trifles." This evil manifested itself in regarding too highly "other's opinion," becoming seduced by "fashion," and worrying over "'What will people think?'" Emerson felt that his ministrations had little effect on his worldly-wise congregation. "There is nothing so absurd or insignificant," he warned, "but you shall find men of respectable powers who are agitated and piqued about it."[122] At the time of his first anniversary at Second Church, Emerson delivered another caustic sermon entitled "The Ministry: Year's Retrospect," in which he blamed both himself and his flock for failing to live up to the minister's initial high expectations. He looked back on "the sanguine hope of the past year" with "the deepest regret at failure."[123] Always aware of his own shortcomings, Emerson in this sermon admonished his congregation for not enabling him to do his job. His ministry was not being served. "You have chosen me to aid in its public functions. I conceive it then becomes yours to make me as useful to you as possible by bringing hither a devout temper and hearing with what candor you can."[124] His admonitions notwithstanding, the next months did not show marked improvement. Church membership actually declined slightly in each of Emerson's years as minister, a fact that Henry Ware attributed to Emerson's innovative preaching style. In a few well-intentioned letters Ware offered his junior colleague some unsolicited advice. He should make more direct scriptural references, as parishioners had come to expect them, and attempt to refrain from using, as Emerson noted in a reply, "a mode of illustration rather bolder than the usage of our preaching warrants."[125]

Emerson's ministry seemed to be plagued with problems. Ware and others criticized his preaching, which Emerson believed to be his strongest suit. The congregation made note of its minister's ineptitude at performing his pastoral duties. Parishioners complained that Emerson dismissed those duties too readily, a rebuke that prompted the minister to offer a public excuse: "Obviously then the minister who makes it an important aim to convey instruction must often stay at home in search of it when his parishioners may think he would be more usefully employed in cultivating an acquaintance with them."[126] Emerson took to heart these admonitions, Henry Ware's in particular. Yet, always self-reliant in the extreme, Emerson found precious little in his congregants' proffered advice that he could follow in good conscience. Not long after Ellen's death, with this litany of professional problems weighing upon his conscience, Emerson began to consider resigning his office.

The immediate occasion of Emerson's decision to quit the ministry was a disagreement concerning the sacrament of the Lord's Supper. The issues involved in the dispute proved to be precisely those that had soured Emerson on his vocation since his ordination. The actual disagreement over the Lord's Supper, about which Emerson even delivered a sermon—his only published sermon for years—the minister might have classified under the issue of "trifles." Had he not been looking for a pretext to leave Second Church, he likely would have dismissed the entire issue. As it was, the Lord's Supper controversy afforded him as good a vehicle as any other to elaborate his more global complaints.[127] His experiment as a settled preacher of the Gospel had been a failure. The Lord's Supper sermon constituted one of Emerson's rare attempts at public exculpation.[128] His congregation deserved an explanation, which Emerson stated bluntly. "It is my desire, in the office of a Christian minister, to do nothing which I cannot do with my whole heart."[129]

The Lord's Supper was one of the central sacraments of the Christian faith. Unitarians believed it to be designed by Jesus to be held sacred for eternity: "This is my body which is broken for you. Take; eat." They were not about to give it up to assuage the scruples of their twenty-eight-year-old minister, particularly insofar as "certain of the most influential men in the Church," according to Charles, adamantly adhered "to the ordinance."[130] Contrary to Emerson's expectations, the congregation, loath to break with its struggling pastor, sought to reach some sort of reasonable compromise. "His people don't like to let him go away from them," Charles informed William. "At present the disposition is to make arrangements so as to keep him."[131] Emerson knew better; there could be no compromise when the Lord's Supper was pretext merely. "The hour of decision" had come the previous summer in the White Mountains of New Hampshire.[132] He had already resolved to resign.

The disagreement between the congregation and its young pastor over the Lord's Supper contained in microcosm Emerson's problems with the ministry generally. This sacrament, like the ritual prayers that punctuated the service and the numerous strictures concerning what should and should not go into his sermons, inverted Emerson's sense of what constituted true faith. "We ought to be cautious," he warned, "in taking even the best ascertained opinions and practices of the primitive church for our own."[133] Emerson praised the Society of Friends because, he argued, the Quakers surpassed the Unitarians in trusting inner conviction over outward ritual. Emerson could no longer brook accepting any doctrine or participating in any ritual "on grounds of mere authority."[134] He had tried to nudge his congregation in that direction in many of his sermons. "The soul stands alone with God," he had declared to little avail for three years.[135]

> I seem to lose the substance in seeking the shadow. That for which Paul lived and died so gloriously; that for which Jesus gave himself to be crucified; the end that animated the thousand martyrs and heroes who have followed his steps, was to redeem us from a formal religion, and teach us to seek our well-being in the formation of the soul. The whole world was full of idols and ordinances.[136]

While in the wilds of New Hampshire, Emerson had tried to find a middle ground between his convictions and the wishes of his congregation. He fretted over being too puritanical and petty, confessing that he knew "very well that it is a bad sign in a man to be too conscientious, & stick at gnats." The issue should not be that he considered his congregation in error. Always unhesitating in his honesty, Emerson concluded that he could not in good faith "go habitually to an institution which they esteem holiest with indifference & dislike."[137] Such duplicitous conduct might maintain peace but was beneath his dignity. By summer's end he despaired of making a significant impact upon his denomination, or at least the possibility of achieving it from the pulpit of Second Church in Boston.

On a more mundane level, Emerson had several significant reasons for choosing the issue of the Lord's Supper to make his break with Second Church. "There remain some practical objections to the ordinance," he told his well-heeled congregation.[138] The Lord's Supper was a divisive sacrament, separating the putatively saved from the uncertain. Emerson never liked this artificial distinction that no human could rightly make, in many ways preferring "intrepid doubters" to devout communicants.[139] He adamantly objected to "the unfavorable relation in which it places that numerous class of persons who abstain from it merely from disinclination to the rite."[140] Sometime during the weeks and months when his resignation hung fire, Emerson borrowed from Charles a copy of William Sewel's sympathetic two-volume history of the Quakers.[141] With his own vocational problems never far from his mind, Emerson took solace in his examination of the career of George Fox. He favorably copied into his journal a number of striking details related to the martyr's fight against the established church, citing specifically Fox's "indignation" concerning the fact that "Rails had been built about the communion table."[142]

Like Fox, Emerson could not sanction the type of social discrimination that sacraments like the Lord's Supper perpetuated. In the ensuing years, Emerson looked to Quakers such as Mary Rotch and Deborah Brayton of New Bedford, Massachusetts, and Henry Thoreau's friend Daniel Ricketson for advice and inspiration on the very issues where he felt that the Unitarians faltered so egregiously. The Unitarian's social conservatism and exclusiveness always repulsed Emerson.

Emerson's reservations concerning the Lord's Supper were similar to those he expressed about the role of public prayer. Whether it was delivering prayers during the exercises on Sundays or at funerals and weddings, the pastor often found himself at a loss for words. He loathed hackneyed phrases, which were the rote elements of most prayers and the stock and trade of many of his colleagues. When New Bedford, Massachusetts, sought Emerson to become its pastor—without having to administer the Lord's Supper—Emerson turned to his reticence about public prayer. He demanded that he not be obliged to offer up any prayers except when he felt inspired to do so. The New Bedford congregation demurred and decided against the union. That Emerson took issue with the use of ritual prayer was altogether appropriate, because it brought him full circle, back to the very first sermon he had ever written at his Uncle Ladd's Roxbury farm. Entitled "Pray without Ceasing," it was Emerson's first attempt to boil away ritual and dogma to get to the marrow of Unitarian divinity. Ritual incantations "are not prayers, but mockeries of prayers," he had exhorted in the fall of 1826. "But the true prayers are the daily, hourly, momentary desires, that come without impediment, without fear, into the soul and bear testimony each instant to its shifting character."[143] One hundred and sixty-one sermons later, he expressed identical sentiments.

Emerson sent his letter of resignation to his congregation on September 11, 1832. Plagued by a severe case of diarrhea, Emerson preached sporadically at Second Church through the late summer and fall of 1832. On October 21, he delivered his final sermon to the congregation as their settled minister. Appropriately titled "The Genuine Man," the sermon served as a fitting culmination to Emerson's ministry. "It is the essence of truth of character that a man should follow his own thought," Emerson concluded, "that he should not be accustomed to adapt his motives or modes of action from any other but should follow the leading of his own mind like a little child."[144] A week later, Second Church voted to accept their embattled minister's resignation. "On the acceptance of the pastor's letter," Emerson entered without commentary in his journal, "Ayes 30; Nays 20; blanks 4."[145] He gave no indication that he was aware that he would never again be the settled minister of any congregation. Aunt Mary thought he had made a great mistake. Other family members were more confused than shocked. Charles, who at this time was closest to his brother, thought that the resignation represented nothing more than a hiatus, writing to William, "I think he will gather a parish of his own by & by."[146] Emerson felt a nagging disappointment that he had failed to transform Unitarianism from his position as an ordained minister of the Gospel, and he would continue to feel a certain loyalty to those individuals in his parish who had supported him and been moved by his ministrations. On the other hand, he had no regrets about giving up the blandishments that came with the office. Still a young man and from a family that had kept company with poverty, Emerson calmly dismissed his social rank, institutional affiliations, the Unitarian clerical brotherhood, his estimable salary, and the vocation for which he had trained. Resigning his pastorate was an intrepid decision.

Emerson's tenure at Second Church could hardy be termed a success. Not only did he ultimately resign the office, but he also sharply criticized Unitarianism as "an effete superannuated Christianity."[147] By 1838 Emerson was so disgusted with Unitarianism's "pale negations" that he publicly rebuked his erstwhile colleagues in the now famous Divinity School Address. Taken together, his dissatisfaction with his charges and his pastorate, his resignation from Second Church, and the diminution of his subsequent supply preaching, as well as his Divinity School Address, attest to the vocational impasse of an ambitious, peripatetic, public-spirited, and brilliant individual profoundly frustrated with his untenable situation. Emerson craved a relevance and an impact that his ministry utterly failed to provide.

Emerson was hardly despondent in the weeks and months leading up to his break. Even if he was unsure about precisely what he would do next, quitting his office was nonetheless the proper course of action. "As fast as any man becomes great, that is, thinks, he becomes a new party," Emerson had written in his journal the previous summer. "Socrates, Aristotle, Calvin, Luther, Abelard, what are these but names of parties? Which is to say, as fast as we use our own eyes, we quit these parties or Unthinking Corporations & join ourselves to God in an unpartaken relation."[148] Now, at the age of twenty-nine, with his experience at Second Church behind him, Emerson was free to begin imagining what kind of vocation he would pursue next.

NOTES

1. Epigraph is from *JMN* 4:252.
2. Henry James, "Emerson," *Partial Portraits* (1888; rep., Westport, Conn., 1970), 7.

3. "Literary Ethics," *Collected Works* 1:115.

4. *JMN* 3:137; *Letters* 1:149; see also Edward Emerson, *Emerson in Concord* (Cambridge, 1888), 51.

5. Already a man of renown, Webster took in the precocious Emerson "as well on account of your own merits, & Mr Everett's wishes, as from a sincere regard for the memory of your excellent father, whom I had the pleasure, in some little degree to know, and from whom I rec'd when quite a young man, tokens of kindness." Daniel Webster to Edward Bliss Emerson, 12/5/24, as cited in Ralph L. Rusk, *The Life of Ralph Waldo Emerson* (New York, 1949), 112.

6. Charles Chauncy Emerson to Mary Moody Emerson, 10/11/25, Emerson Family Papers, Massachusetts Historical Society.

7. Emerson to Lidian Jackson Emerson, 5/11/36, *Letters* 2:18.

8. Mary Moody Emerson to Emerson, 4/23/23, in *The Selected Letters of Mary Moody Emerson,* ed. Nancy Craig Simmons (Athens, Ga., 1993), 171.

9. Already losing his faith, William chose not to obtain his terminal degree, convinced that the sixty-dollar fee might be better spent in some other fashion. The diploma was "not worth the whistle," he noted laconically to Aunt Mary.

10. Karen Kalinevitch, "Ralph Waldo Emerson's Older Brother: The Letters and Journal of William Emerson" (Ph.D. diss., University of Tenn., 1982), 123. Emerson mentions "Eichorn" in a letter to William on 10/17/28; see *Letters* 1:249–50.

11. Cited in *Letters* 1:352n.

12. William seemed to misunderstand utterly that Goethe, a statist in politics, could not care less about the young American's qualms of individual conscience.

13. Cited in Rusk, *Life*, 113.

14. Emerson to William Emerson, 1/18/34, *Letters* 1:404.

15. Most of the able, ambitious young men of the preceding decades had eschewed clerical careers. Even in John Adams's day, the law or business seemed to promise greater opportunity than the Congregational church for the colony's enterprising youth. Adams himself had gone to Harvard to study for the ministry only to change his mind while in Cambridge. Whatever Mary's hopes, even she was largely disappointed by the dry preaching she endured in Boston's churches. Desiring inspiration, Mary scorned the Unitarian preachers who, like her deceased brother, tended to divorce themselves from the vital piety that had for so long imbued Congregationalism with its energy and eloquence.

16. William Emerson to Emerson, 1/25/34, *Letters* 1:352n.

17. *JMN* 2:316. Edward Waldo Emerson states that his father was describing his brothers William and Edward respectively. See *Journal* 2:42 n1,2. The latter description reminds this author more of Charles than Edward.

18. *JMN* 4:325.

19. Cited in F. O. Mattheissen, *American Renaissance: Art and Expression in the Age of Emerson and Whitman* (New York, 1841), 18.

20. The most brilliant of Emerson's ministerial colleagues was surely Theodore Parker. His abbreviated career proved exceedingly challenging and in many ways dissatisfying.

21. Emerson to Mary Moody Emerson, 10/16/23, *Letters* 1:138.

22. *JMN* 5:47.

23. *JMN* 2:221.

24. See Mary Cayton, *Emerson's Emergence: Self and Society in Emerson's Boston* (Chapel Hill, N.C., 1989), ch. 2.

25. *JMN* 4:381.

26. Beecher to Taylor, as reprinted in Lyman Beecher, *The Autobiography of Lyman Beecher*, ed. Barbara Cross (Cambridge, 1961), 1:402.

27. *JMN* 4:26 (so Emerson reasoned in May of 1832).

28. *JMN* 3:239.

29. *JMN* 3:259.

30. See *Christian Disciple*, 24 (Nov.–Dec., 1822), 401–8.

31. *JMN* 3:193.

32. *JMN* 1:133.

33. *JMN* 2:239; the English translation is "something awesome and infinite."

34. *JMN* 2:238.

35. *JMN* 2:238.

36. *JMN* 2:237 (Sabbath). Italics added.

37. *JMN* 2:237.

38. "Politics," *Collected Works* 3:122.

39. *JMN* 2:238.

40. Emerson to Mary Moody Emerson, *Letters,* 1:137; *JMN* 2:402.

41. See Lenthiel H. Downs, "Emerson and Dr. Channing: Two Men of Boston," *New England Quarterly* 20 (1947), 525.

42. Emerson to William Emerson, 11/18/24, *Letters* 1:152.

43. See Downs, "Emerson and Dr. Channing," 524–26.

44. Robert Richardson, *Emerson: The Mind on Fire* (Berkeley, 1995), 55.

45. James Elliot Cabot, *Memoir of Ralph Waldo Emerson,* 2 vols. (Cambridge, 1887), 102.

46. Emerson to Mary Moody Emerson, *Letters* 1:137.

47. Rusk, *Life*, 110.

48. *JMN* 2:310–11.

49. *JMN* 3:64.

50. *Young Emerson Speaks,* 64, 65.

51. *JMN* 2:317.

52. Rusk, *Life*, 111.

53. Cofounder of the Massachusetts Charitable Eye and Ear Infirmary, Edward Reynolds became famous for this procedure which provided at least temporary relief from the pressure build-up behind the cornea. See Evelyn Barish, *Emerson: The Roots of Prophecy* (Princeton, 1989), 178–79.

54. Emerson to Mary Moody Emerson, Cambridge, 4/6/26, *Letters* 1:168.

55. Emerson to William Emerson, Cambridge, 9/29/26, *Letters* 1:176–77.

56. Emerson to Mary Moody Emerson, *Letters* 1:170.

57. Cited in Franklin Benjamin Sanborn, *Ralph Waldo Emerson* (Boston, 1901), 20.

58. Style may be a different matter, at least according to Robert Richardson, who claims that Emerson's early sermons could hardly be distinguished from those of his father. See Richardson, *Mind on Fire*, 90.

59. Edward Emerson's remarks are in *Journal* 2:98n; *JMN* 3:28.

60. *JMN* 7:374.

61. See Philip Gura's *The Wisdom of Words: Language, Theology, and Literature in the New England Renaissance* (Middletown, Conn., 1981), ch. 3, for a discussion of Emerson's distinctive tropes.

62. Emerson to Mary Moody Emerson, 8/17/27, *Letters* 1:207.

63. *Journal* 2:98n.

64. Emerson to William Emerson, 1/6/27, *Letters* 1:184.

65. *JMN* 3:77.

66. *JMN* 3:78.

67. Achille Murat, *The United States of North America* (London, 1833), iv.

68. *JMN* 3:77.

69. Murat, *United States*, 125.

70. Emerson to William Emerson, 3/15/27, *Letters* 1:194.

71. *JMN* 4:222.

72. *JMN* 2:256.

73. Emerson to William Emerson, 3/15/27, *Letters* 1:194.

74. *JMN* 3:137–38.

75. *JMN* 2:332.

76. *JMN* 3:137.

77. *JMN* 3:72.

78. Emerson's sermon record is located in *Young Emerson Speaks*, 263–71.

79. Supply preachers were paid fifteen dollars in Boston.

80. Guy R. Woodall, "The Journals of Convers Francis (2)," *SAR*, ed. Joel Myerson (New York, 1981), 245.

81. Emerson to William Emerson, 6/24/27, *Letters* 1:201.

82. Emerson to William Emerson, 2/18/28, *Letters* 1:227.

83. Cited in Albert J. von Frank, *An Emerson Chronology* (New York, 1994), 28.

84. *JMN* 3:26.

85. James B. Thayer, *Reverend Samuel Ripley of Waltham* (Cambridge, 1897; microfilm), 40–41.

86. Emerson to William Emerson, 6/30/28, *Letters* 1:236.

87. *Proprietors Records* of the Second Congregational Church, Massachusetts Historical Society, as cited in *Letters* 1:236 n49.

88. *JMN* 3:99.

89. Emerson to William Emerson, 12/24/28, *Letters* 1:256.

90. Quoted in David G. Haskins, *Ralph Waldo Emerson: His Maternal Ancestors* (Boston, 1887), 111.

91. Emerson to William Emerson, 1/28/29, *Letters* 1:259.

92. Emerson to William Emerson, 10/21/29, *Letters* 1:285.

93. Emerson to William Emerson, 4/30/28, *Letters* 1:234.

94. Emerson to William Emerson, 12/14/28, *Letters* 1:253.

95. The vote was in fact virtually unanimous, as three of the five votes against Emerson were cast by the single owner of three pews. Emerson, who missed nothing, wrote as much to William. See Emerson to William Emerson, 1/28/29, *Letters* 1:260; citation is in Emerson to William Emerson, 12/14/28, *Letters* 1:253.

96. *Proprietors Records* of the Second Congregational Church, as cited in *Letters* 1:260, n4.

97. Emerson had his own health problems, his rheumatic hip plaguing him at least through December 1830. See *Letters* 1:287–88.

98. Emerson to Mary Moody Emerson, 2/8/31, *Letters* 1:318.

99. Charles Chauncy Emerson to William Emerson, 2/8/31, *Letters* 1:318n; for Emerson's description of the days of Ellen's demise, see *JMN* 3:227–28.

100. Charles Chauncy Emerson to William Emerson, 2/8/31, *Letters* 1:318n.

101. Emerson records the event in his journals on March 29, 1832; see *JMN* 4:7; Richardson sees this as the critical event in Emerson's early life.

102. "The Preacher," *Works* 10:221.

103. "Sovereignty of Ethics," *Works* 10:196.

104. "The Preacher," *Works* 10:221.

105. Emerson to Second Church and Society in Boston, 1/30/29, *Letters* 1:260–61.

106. Cited in von Frank, *Chronology*, 38.

107. *Young Emerson Speaks*, 27.

108. Cited in Rusk, *Life*, 139.

109. *Young Emerson Speaks*, 28.

110. *Young Emerson Speaks*, 22.

111. *Young Emerson Speaks*, 23.

112. *Young Emerson Speaks*, 34.

113. *Young Emerson Speaks*, 22.

114. *Young Emerson Speaks*, 34–35.

115. *Young Emerson Speaks*, 30.

116. Emerson to Henry Ware, 7/1/29, *Letters* 1:273.

117. Emerson to Mary Moody Emerson, 5/17/33, *Letters* 1:375.

118. Emerson to Ezra Ripley, 7/1/29, *Letters* 1:376.

119. Rusk, *Life*, 140.

120. Emerson to William Emerson, 4/25/29, *Letters* 1:270.

121. *Young Emerson Speaks*, 70.

122. *Young Emerson Speaks*, 46–48.

123. *Young Emerson Speaks*, 67.

124. *Young Emerson Speaks*, 73.

125. Emerson to Henry Ware, 12/30/28, *Letters* 1:257.

126. *Young Emerson Speaks*, 70.

127. Scholars generally agree that Emerson used the Lord's Supper largely as a pre-

text to resign. In this they are only partially correct. The Lord's Supper was a subterfuge in some measure, but not necessarily to break with Second Church. Emerson used it to elaborate his changing spiritual commitments, as he was rejecting formalism. The Lord's Supper symbolized that larger fight.

128. It is worth noting that Emerson regretted ever having delivered his Lord's Supper sermon, much less publishing it. He claimed that he did not reread it for many years. Even then, he thought better of publicly explaining his actions. They could speak for themselves.

129. "The Lord's Supper," *Works* 11:28.

130. Charles Chauncy Emerson to William Emerson, 9/18/32, *Letters* 1:355n.

131. Charles Chauncy Emerson to William Emerson, 9/26/32, *Letters* 1:356n

132. *JMN* 4:30.

133. "The Lord's Supper," *Works* 11:21, 21.

134. "The Lord's Supper," *Works* 11:21, 17.

135. "The Lord's Supper," *Works* 11:23.

136. "The Lord's Supper," *Works* 11:26–27.

137. *JMN* 4:30.

138. "The Lord's Supper," *Works* 11:27.

139. Emerson's term for Achille Murat.

140. "The Lord's Supper," *Works* 11:27.

141. See William Sewel, *The History of the Rise, Increase, and Progress of the Christian People Called Quakers*, 3rd ed., 2 vols. (Philadelphia, 1823).

142. *JMN* 4:31.

143. Compare with Theodore Parker's famous sermon *A Discourse on the Transient and Permanent in Christianity* (Boston, 1841).

144. *Young Emerson Speaks*, 184. It is not entirely clear that Emerson did not deliver his final sermon that Sunday, according to von Frank who cites a letter from Charles to William dated November 2. See von Frank, *Chronology*, 73–74.

145. *JMN* 4:54.

146. Charles Chauncy Emerson to William Emerson, 9/18/32, *Letters* 1:355n.

147. *JMN* 4:27.

148. *JMN* 3:259.

4

UNITARIANISM AND
ITS DISCONTENTS

I wish to be a true & free man, & therefore would not be a woman,
or a king, or a clergyman, each of which classes in the present order
of things is a slave.[1]

After his resignation from Second Church in the fall of 1832 Emerson
found himself blessed with, as he put it, "a terrible freedom."[2] Free from
institutional attachments, he had no job, little money, and the perennial concern for the welfare of his mother and brothers. The prospect of receiving a
sizable settlement from Ellen's estate promised to relieve him of some financial anxieties, although, according to his brother, even the receipt of the first
of several disbursements in 1834 failed to alleviate altogether the family's
financial exigencies. "Therefore for the present," Charles wrote William, "we
seem pretty nearly as poor as ever only Waldo does without a Profession."[3]
Emerson seemed unfazed by the loss of a steady income. "We can get used to
being poor for the first men & happiest men of the earth have been," he
explained to his older brother with a tinge of irony; the brothers had endured
financial difficulties for years. Emerson was decidedly grateful for the even-
tual settlement of the Tucker estate, which enabled him to purchase Coolidge
Castle, a rambling but down-at-the-heels homestead in Concord, where the
family had its roots. In the course of the next decade his growing income provided the wherewithal to stave off the insecurity that had dogged the family
since his childhood.

The far more intractable problem remained: what Emerson—a widower
by his thirtieth birthday—would do with himself. After resigning from Second
Church, Emerson persevered as a minister of the Gospel, working as he had
before his ordination as a supply preacher throughout eastern Massachusetts.
He did not regret giving up his settled pastorate; nor did he express reservations about the doctrinal and social antipathy toward his putative denomina-

tion that had contributed to his resignation. His journals are replete with the growing conviction that Unitarianism was nothing more than "an effete super-annuated Christianity" and that his calling, like that of the great Quaker George Fox, was to preach "out of doors."[4] Nothing in these years prompted Emerson to reconsider what he had written while contemplating his departure from Second Church: that "in order to be a good minister it was necessary to leave the ministry. The profession is antiquated. In an altered age, we worship in the dead forms of our forefathers."[5]

Emerson continued to attend church, write sermons, and preach in and around Boston, albeit on his own terms, for several more years. Until his final separation from the Unitarian establishment in 1838, Sundays invariably found Emerson at one of his colleagues' churches, usually in the pulpit delivering one of his idiosyncratic and beautiful sermons much as he had done before being ordained. His Harvard Divinity School Address, delivered on July 15, 1838, which marked Emerson's Rubicon, was a forty-minute summation of more than a decade's worth of accumulated disgust with the "dead forms of our forefathers."[6] Bearing intimate witness to the steady erosion of true faith, as he saw it, compelled Emerson to admonish publicly the leaders of his denomination. As the accretion of his personal maturation over the past decade—"all true greatness must come from internal growth," he had written at the time of his resignation—the address proved to be Emerson's ultimate expression of his commitment to "go alone."[7] Whether he knew it or not, from that summer evening forward he was *persona non grata* among most Unitarians.

Emerson's escape from his settled pastorate and his ensuing travels in Europe convinced him that whatever his religious convictions, he would forever desire some type of ministry. Traveling abroad and subsequently settling down in Concord confirmed what had been gestating inside during his unfulfilling years as the pastor of Second Church. Preaching to the same congregations of self-satisfied parishioners without much prospect of changing people's lives could not possibly slake his ambition to undertake some greater task, to do something vital and challenging. Ambition demanded finding a novel, more formidable task.

Emerson searched in these months and years for a means to combine his Cartesian "first philosophy"—his term for the inner search for man's moral nature—with an evolving egalitarian vision.[8] This highly personal quest for utility and meaning took on distinctly political overtones during his trip abroad. Emerson achieved something of an epiphany.[9] He came to the realization that his personal disenchantment with Unitarianism was inseparable from his more vague, yet no less genuine, disgust with the social and political elitism of his Brahmin inheritance. Observing firsthand Europe's hierarchical, tradition-bound, and fundamentally inegalitarian ethos helped convince Emerson that his vocational problems were as much political as personal. The very democratic openness of the United States that so disturbed the Unitarians became for Emerson the nation's great and imminent destiny. He promised himself that upon his return to New England he would find the means to utilize his unique talents to further those national ideals. By the time of the Divinity School Address and his first successes in public lecturing, Emerson had come to envision a novel ministry in which he might address the entire United States.[10]

The last months of 1832 proved very trying for Emerson. Having resigned from his pastorate and with little to occupy him, the twenty-nine-year-old former ordained minister suffered from something akin to depression. Plagued by chronic diarrhea Emerson seemed, according to Charles, enervated and exhausted. "Waldo is sick again," Charles informed William, "very much dispirited—& talking of the South, the West Indies & other projects."[11] In order to resurrect his flagging health and sinking spirits, he resolved to go abroad. His 1827 trip to the South at another turning point in his career had rejuvenated him in both body and mind. Intrigued by a romantic "purpureal vision of Naples and Italy," Emerson resolved to take his older brother's advice and set out for Europe in search of a more salubrious climate for his health and some adventure for his spirit. On Christmas Day of 1832, exactly five years after he had first met Ellen, Emerson departed New England aboard the brig *Jasper* for Europe in search of answers to the questions that dogged him.

Emerson's transoceanic voyage, which began inauspiciously with a ten-day gale that trapped the passengers below deck, proved to be the ideal tonic for his health. By the time he had reached Rome in March, Emerson could boast to his Aunt Mary that although he "went away from home a wasted peevish invalid," he was "now in better health than I remember to have enjoyed since I was in college."[12] The ocean crossing afforded him several weeks of leisure. Reading little, he had ample time to observe the workings of the brig and to marvel at the captain and his mates, about whom he wrote admiringly. He praised the seaman, "the man of his hands," who stoically braved an existence that for the most part confined him to a "prison with the chance of being drowned."[13] Emerson's admiration of the sailors' self-assured carriage echoed a theme he had developed in a recent sermon in which he extolled the value of common blessings and common duties. The *Jasper*'s hands deserved commendation for "infusing great principles into plain and vulgar actions"; they served as fine examples of "the power of giving interest and respectability to the meannest offices."[14] In his typically unassuming way, Emerson favorably compared the sailors' manifold, practical talents with his own limited abilities. "I learn in the sunshine to get an altitude & the latitude," he humorously noted, "but am a dull scholar as ever in real figures. Seldom I suppose was a more inapt learner of arithmetic, astronomy, geography, political economy than I am as I daily find to my cost. It were to brag much if I should there end the catalogue of my defects."[15] In this topside rumination Emerson lightheartedly explored one of the themes that occupied him throughout his voluntary exile. He was determined to resolve what precisely his peculiar talents were and how he could apply them, like the sailor, toward eminently practical ends.

Cornelius Ellis, the sturdy captain of the *Jasper,* piqued Emerson's interest and admiration. The passenger noted approvingly the ship's master's multifarious talents, which he strikingly juxtaposed to his own relative effeminacy. "Honour evermore aboard ship to the man of action,—to the brain in the hand," he declared.

> Here is our stout master worth a thousand philosophers—a man who can strike a porpoise, & make oil out of his blubber, & steak out of his meat; who can thump a mutineer into obedience in two minutes; who can bleed his sick sailor, & mend the box of his pump; who can ride out the roughest storm on the American coast, & more than all, with the sun & a three cornered bit of wood, & a chart, can find his way from Boston across 3000 miles of stormy water into a little gut of inland sea 9 miles wide with as much precision as if led by a clue.[16]

The captain proved a man of ideas as well. Emerson found compelling Ellis's thoughts about the history of seafaring and his stories of naval heroes, as well as his parochial notions about what might generously be termed *world politics.* He recorded with interest the master's chauvinistic assertions of New World preeminence. "The Captain believes in the superiority of the American to every other countryman. 'You will see,' he says, 'when you get out here how they manage in Europe; they do everything by main strength & ignorance.' "[17] On his way to the Old World for the first time, Emerson was eager to make precisely this comparison for himself.

The twin themes of personal prospects and American uniqueness dominated Emerson's thoughts throughout his European odyssey. As he made his way through Naples, Rome, Florence, Paris, and Geneva and on to England and Scotland, just what he was going to do when he returned to his "own little town" was never far from his thoughts.[18] Emerson intuited that the resolution of his vocational dilemma was intimately tied to his deepest reflections about his relation to his region and nation. He had fled New England not only to regain his failing health, but to discover the larger meaning of his own country and his place within it. He sought to reorient himself, "the plain old Adam," in relation to Europe and its history in much the way he had recalibrated his religious faith during the previous years.[19] "Perpetually we must East ourselves, or we get into irrecoverable error," he noted in his journal.[20] By going east, to Europe, Emerson made the most of his reconnoitering. On one level, his European travelogue served as the basis of a number of public lectures, including his 1835 series on English literature.[21] On a far deeper level, Emerson's profound personal experiences while abroad inspired a new vocation. This national poet-preacher resolved, as he surveyed the Old World, to explain to Americans the meaning of New.

In many ways, Emerson's trek through Europe did not so much alter his thinking as substantiate what he had been pondering over for the previous decade. "Do you know," he explained to Charles from Paris, "that my European experience has only confirmed & clinched the old laws wherewith I was wont to begin & end my parables."[22] His excursion through Europe, nevertheless, immeasurably deepened and solidified those convictions in a way that no amount of book learning could have. They fantastically confirmed the multitude of thoughts and ideas about history, philosophy, science, society, and himself that he had amassed during the previous decades. Emerson's core convictions and values were congealing, making him infinitely more self-reliant, self-assured, and secure in his nationality. "I collect nothing," a lone journal entry in Venice begins,

> that can be touched or tasted or smelled, neither cameo, painting, nor medallion; nothing in my trunk but old clothes, but I value much the growing picture which the ages have painted & which I reverently survey. It is wonderful how much we see in five months, in how a short time we learn what it has taken so many ages to teach.[23]

"Travelling is a poor profession," Emerson explained to his friend George Adams Sampson, but "it may be good medicine."[24] For Emerson, at the age of twenty-nine, it was the perfect prescription.

Foremost in Emerson's thoughts was religion. His excursion presented an ideal opportunity to reflect upon his singular and increasingly controversial religious beliefs as well as the more global issue of the place of Christianity in the West. Committed in his own life to locating the sacred in the day-to-day, Emerson admired the mundane and centuries-old traditions evoked in much of the daily life of ordinary Europeans. He was so enthralled by the almost sublime quiescence of a Capuchin monastery in Syracuse that he "told the Padre that I would stay there always if he would give me a chamber."[25] When the father offered his own "little neat room," Emerson demurred, "my friend's whipcords" hanging by the bedside perhaps contributing to his sudden change of heart.[26] As appealing as the contemplative life of a monk might have been to Emerson, he seemed acutely aware of the need for society as well as solitude. A few weeks later in Venice, he confessed as much. "But would it not be cowardly to flee out of society & live in the woods?"[27] The aloof and ever-awkward Emerson hungered to put his knowledge and talents to use in a way similar to the self-assured sailors he had surveyed aboard the *Jasper*.[28] Emerson took a similar delight in the unadorned churches and chapels that were so much a part of the European peasant's daily life. That the beautifully frescoed churches of Malta, for example, never locked their gates drew Emerson's effusive praise. "How beautiful to have the church always open," noted the admiring American, "so that every tired wayfaring man may come in & be soothed by all that art can suggest of a better world when he is weary with this."[29]

Equal to Emerson's admiration of the plainness of the provincial Catholicism he witnessed in Malta and Sicily was his disdain for the excess of pomp and extravagance he witnessed at the Vatican a few weeks later.[30] For one who so greatly admired Quaker simplicity to warm to the opulence and display of the Vatican was all but impossible; that Emerson's stay in Rome coincided with the Papal ceremonies of Easter week made the contrast that much more overwhelming. Emerson observed the Palm Sunday ceremonies in the Sistine Chapel, noting how "the Cardinals came in one after another, each wearing a purple robe, and ermine cape, & a small red cap to cover the tonsure." Intrigued by the splendor, he could not help marveling at the overblown obeisance to hierarchy that characterized the ritual. "A priest attended each one to adjust the robes of their Eminences,"[31] Emerson added with a certain humorous detachment. After taking down paragraphs of acute observations of scarlet robes, copes of gold cloth, bishop's mitres, and immaculate attendants, the young Unitarian concluded that "there is no true majesty in all this millinery & imbecility,"[32] in the end offering a highly critical assessment of the elaborate proceedings, albeit in the most sympathetic language he could muster. "It was hard to recognize in this ceremony the gentle Son of Man who sat upon an ass amidst the rejoicings of his fickle countrymen."[33] To "the eye of an Indian," the exquisitely frescoed cathedrals of Rome and Florence were superhuman works of artistic achievement, which ultimately did little to foster religion.[34] "But one act of benevolence is better than a cathedral," Emerson concluded.[35] As he recounted to Thomas Carlyle several weeks later, he preferred the "wholesomeness of [the] Calvinism" of the English peasant to the overwrought rituals of Continental Catholicism.[36]

Emerson's firsthand observation of Catholicism in Italy inevitably reinforced his anti-institutional bias. For all his admiration of the piety of the peasants and monks, he reflected far more upon the great gulf between their heartfelt desire for true religion and the institutional and hierarchical edifice of the Catholic Church and all formal religion. "The errors of traditional Christianity as it now exists, the popular faith of many millions," he wrote in his journal in Paris, "need to be removed to let men see the divine beauty of moral truth."

> I feel myself pledged if health & opportunity be granted me to demonstrate that all necessary truth is its own evidence; that no doctrine of God need appeal to a book; that Christianity is wrongly received by all such as take it for a system of doctrines,—its stress being upon moral truth; it is a rule of life not a rule of faith. And how men can toil & scratch so hard for things so dry, lifeless, unsightly as these famous dogmas when the divine beauty of the truths to which they are related lies behind them, how they can make such a fuss about the case & never open it to see the jewel—is strange, is pitiful.[37]

Emerson pledged himself to articulate this fervent elemental belief as soon as he returned to the United States and his own countrymen.

Moving on to northern Europe, Emerson attended several Unitarian services in France, England, and Scotland. In Paris, he went "to the Faubourg St Martin to hear the Abbé Châtel."[38] Born in 1795, Ferdinand Toussaint François Châtel was "a Unitarian but more radical than any body in America who takes that name," as well as something of a celebrity. The founder of the Église Catholique Française, Châtel had gained notoriety at least in part for introducing novel costumes and an odd mixture of martial and choral music into the Unitarian services. At the time of Emerson's visit, as the New Englander noted in his journal, Châtel was staggering under the burden of "an annual rent of 40,000 francs." Emerson "was interested in his enterprize for there is always something pathetic in a new church struggling for sympathy & support."[39] There can be little doubt that he was thinking about himself and the prospects for a similar undertaking in the United States. He wondered whether his struggle to create "a new theatre, a new art" would suffer from the same vast difficulties.[40]

After delivering at least one sermon on almost every Sunday for the previous five years, Emerson must have been greatly relieved not to have to preach while abroad. He delivered the only sermon of his many months exploring Europe in Edinburgh, Scotland. At the request of Alexander Ireland, who would arrange Emerson's 1848 lecture tour and publish a memorial of his friend in 1883, Emerson preached to his congregation at Unitarian Chapel on August 18, 1833. Ireland effusively praised the New Englander's inspired meditations and prayers for "the consummate beauty of the language in which they were clothed." He admired "the calm dignity of his bearing, the absence of any oratorical effort, and the singular directness and simplicity of his manner, free from the least shadow of dogmatic assumption." This was a fitting commentary about a man who so consistently eschewed the formality and pomposity of religion on both sides of the Atlantic. Ireland declared that "nothing like it had ever been heard" in Scotland.[41]

After Emerson took leave of Ireland and the Unitarian Chapel, he made his way up the Forth in search of the home of Thomas and Jane Carlyle. Already famous as an author and critic, Carlyle was one of the four or five individuals whom Emerson had initially set out to discover while in Europe. "I thank the great God," Emerson entered in his journal while awaiting his passage back to the United States, "[who] has shown me the men I wished to see—Landor, Coleridge, Carlyle, Wordsworth."[42] Emerson broached religion with each man, but found them "all deficient all these four—in different degrees but all deficient—in insight into religious truth."[43] During his twenty-four hours with the Carlyles at Dunscore, "a white day in my years" he called it, Emerson made a lifelong friend and a most highly valued correspondent.[44] Walking "amid wild & desolate heathery hills," the two men had time to discuss issues ranging from German idealism to American politics.[45] To Emerson, the conversations that were far and away the most consequential dealt upon the topic of religion, Calvinism in particular. The Scot's views did not sit well with Emerson, who noted that "Carlyle almost grudges the poor peasant his Calvinism."[46] Emerson of course was no Calvinist—"I have practical difficulties myself"—but understood Carlyle to be assaulting Calvinism as just one example of the silly popular notions, even superstitions, so doggedly clutched by the English peasant.[47] Emerson shied away from such caustic criticism, thinking it better to "speak lightly of usages which I omit."[48] What Carlyle styled superstition Emerson called the genuine religious faith of a people in search of greater knowledge and understanding. As for the Boston Unitarians, from what Carlyle had heard and read, he considered them to be "a tame limitary people" who unfortunately were "incapable of depth of sentiment."[49] Emerson confessed that when it came to the effete, self-satisfied aspect of the Unitarians, he and Carlyle shared a similar disgust. Five years later, Emerson would incorporate Carlyle's words into his address before the graduating class of the Harvard Divinity School.

While lingering in Liverpool—"I perish waiting," he wrote—Emerson sought to bring together his observations about religion in England and on the Continent.[50] Concerning the religious views of Carlyle, Wordsworth, and Coleridge, Emerson wrote, "the great men of England are singularly ignorant of religion."[51] So very anxious to return home, Emerson all but discarded his inarticulate "hope of communicating religious light to benighted Europe." He would focus on Americans.[52] "Back again to myself," he wrote in language foreshadowing the Divinity School Address,

> I believe that the error of the religionists lies in this, that they do not know the extent or the harmony or depth of their moral nature, that they are cling-ing to little, positive, verbal, formal versions of the moral law & very imper-fect versions too, while the infinite laws, the laws of the Law, the great circling truths whose only adequate symbol is the material laws, the astron-omy, &c, are all unobserved, & sneered at when spoken of, as frigid & insufficient. I call Calvinism such an imperfect version of the moral law. Unitarianism is another, & every form of Christian and of Pagan faith in the hands of incapable teachers is such a version. On the contrary in the hands of a true Teacher, the falsehoods, the pitifulnesses, the sectarianisms of each are dropped & the sublimity & the depth of the Original is pene-trated & exhibited to men.[53]

Waiting impatiently to return home, Emerson now believed more than ever that he was that teacher. He would return to America to articulate the moral truth beneath the superficiality and formalism of the great religions; this "One bottom," he called it.[54]

Emerson's months of European exploration altered his political views more profoundly than his religious ones, which were well developed before he had set out. His politics, on the other hand, were far more amorphous and unformed, primarily because Emerson believed the subject to be subsidiary to religion and culture, both of which related more to the individual than to soci-ety as a whole. Always self-reliant in the extreme, Emerson had been uncom-fortable with the self-satisfied Whiggishness of his parents, teachers, and colleagues. Yet he had not formulated sufficiently his own tenets by the time of his trip abroad in 1833. As he witnessed the great social, economic, and political disparity between the Old World and the New, he began to think more deeply about politics and its impact upon society. The Emerson family's pen-ury and social dislocation had long ago softened his inherited Federalist-Whig elitism, with which he had never been comfortable, although it had not softened to the point of making the emerging Democratic Party or party politics palatable. His months abroad altered the entire debate. No longer was it Federalists and Republicans, Whigs and Democrats, but Europe and the United States, aristocracy and democracy. Emerson's use of the word "democracy" began to change. Where formerly he had used the term almost derisively in reference to the posturing of party hacks looking for votes, he now deployed it in a less strictly political sense. By the spring of 1833 democracy came to mean something more broadly social. Never one to insist on essentialist definitions, Emerson now defined democracy as the inverse of aristocracy and the tradition-bound inequalities he witnessed in Europe. Democracy became virtually a synecdoche for the United States, or at least for what Emerson understood to be best about the nation. He repeatedly championed Americans' passion for equality and their utter belief in their inherent self-worth and innate capacities, as well as their elemental distrust of hierarchical convention. By the time he returned to New England, Emerson was filled with a patriotic pride in the promise held out by the nation's dedication to equality. He deployed that protean term *democracy* as a shorthand for this uniquely New World disposition. "The simple untitled unofficed citizen," Emerson noted in his journals, "is more formidable & more pleasing than any dignitary whose condition & etiquette only makes him more vulnerable & more helpless."[55]

Much as Alexis de Tocqueville had crossed the Atlantic from east to west to discover the future of Continental politics, so Emerson only months later came to understand his sense of the Americans' political promise by means of an Atlantic voyage in the opposite direction. Both men would go on to reflect in comparative terms upon the nature of American institutions and the type of individual they actualized. The most important repercussion of Emerson's trip, then, as well as Tocqueville's, turned on his new understanding of the unique features of the Americans inculcated by a society dedicated to equality. The social divisions of European society startled and repulsed Emerson, just as the politics and poverty of the place had given a lesson of their own. All in all, it was "very melancholy" to explore the grandest art and most celebrated architecture in the midst of a "declining church & impoverished country."[56] In his most revealing assessment of the European society in which he had been traveling, Emerson referred to himself as "a freeman among slaves":

> I thought of the singular position of the American traveller in Italy. It is like that of a being of another planet who invisibly visits the earth. He is a protected witness. He sees what is that boasted liberty of manners—free of all puritan starch—& sees what it is worth—how surely it pays its tax. He comes a freeman among slaves. He learns that old saws are true which is a great thing.[57]

Confessing that he had given little thought to "old saws," Emerson had by the end of July completely reversed field. That those truisms were true he now considered "a great thing." Finished with the Continent, a self-possessed Emerson was as secure as he would ever be in his twin convictions concerning Americans' "boasted liberty of manners" and his ironically universal and utterly American "earnest assertion of moral truth."

Emerson had plenty of time to contrast Europe and the United States while he waited in Liverpool for passage home. Calling his European excursion "this last schoolroom in which he has pleased to instruct me," he found himself optimistically adopting a democratized version of what might best be characterized as a Christianized Platonism, the amorphous and sanguine faith that he would espouse for years to come.[58] The United States was proof, or it would be, that "all men are convertible" in the right environment and with the right teacher.[59] Pivotal to Emerson's growing egalitarian faith was his belief in the inherent ability of all men to learn. Like Shaftesbury and the other Cambridge Platonists, Emerson had taken to heart Plato's argument in the *Meno*, parts of which he had copied into his first journal while a teenager at Harvard. Socrates demonstrated to Meno that by asking the right questions even a slave with no previous knowledge could complete a mathematical proof. Similarly, Emerson believed that all persons could uncover in themselves a common set of ethical precepts.[60] This belief lay at the very center of his embrace of his homeland and its political institutions.[61] Conversely, aristocracy was Europe's unnatural means to oppress the common man. A king, prince, or nobleman was no better than any other person who lived for moral truth, be he poor or rich, noble or peasant. "The Great King: How is he greater than I, if he be not more just?"[62] One only judged a person by "detaching the man from his exteriors," something that Europeans seemed utterly unable to do.[63] By no means was Emerson adopting a leveling philosophy in which all were identical; he remained disdainful of those who failed to take the proper steps toward a genuine education and who did not take themselves seriously. His sense of equality was not one in which the king became a mere mortal but in which the common man became a king.

Emerson directly identified his growing self-reliance with the fact that he was American. Exhausted from what he called the perils of travel, Emerson took particular delight in departing Liverpool and the land of aristocracy. "This morn," Emerson joyfully noted on September 4, 1833, "I saw the last lump of England receding without the least regret."[64] Having been abroad for the better part of a year, Emerson was so elated to be getting home that he could not contain his emotions in prose. On the morning of his thirteenth day at sea Emerson composed a poetic tribute to his homeland. "America, my country, can the mind/Embrace in its affections realms so vast/. . ./A land without nobility or wigs or debt/No castles no Cathedrals no kings."[65] Sounding his most patriotic, Emerson declared, "I am thankful that I am an American as I am thankful that I am a man."[66]

Back in his homeland after his nine-month odyssey, Emerson wasted no time in seeking to explain in public his expansive political nationalism. "I am very glad my travelling is done," he wrote to William. "A man not old feels himself too old to be a vagabond. The people at their work, the people whose vocations I interrupt by my letters of introduction accuse me by their looks for leaving my business to hinder theirs."[67] Superficially, little had changed since Emerson had rashly departed Boston some ten months earlier. A widower, Emerson found himself penniless, unemployed, and without a home. His reputation for pulpit eloquence immediately drew him back to the church; he preached his first sermon before the month was out. More intriguing, within two days of his return, he began to take steps toward preaching beyond the pulpit, having "engaged to deliver the introductory Lecture to the Natural History Society in November."[68] Nevertheless, as promising as these opportunities were, lecturing was not a profession and supply preaching could be no more than a temporary expedient. Emerson's vocational tribulations had not abated.

His penury promised to be alleviated with the final distribution of the Tucker estate, but the death of Ellen's sister, Margaret, and continued legal haggling delayed a final resolution for months.[69] When the first installment of $11,600 arrived in May, Emerson had more money than anyone in the immediate family had possessed at any point in his memory. The annual income from Ellen's estate enabled Emerson to pay his debts, help Charles pay some of his own and assist his mother, as well as assume responsibility for Bulkeley. Emerson seemed unfazed that the money did not go far; the annual income, according to Charles, "will scarce support both Mother and Waldo," much less Bulkeley.[70] He hoped that the Tucker settlement when combined with his own earnings, however he might apply himself, would suffice to keep the family debt free. If things went well, he might be able to purchase for his mother and brothers that home of their own that had eluded them since their father's death. Beyond that, Emerson gave little thought to his personal economy. Single and with almost no expenses to speak of, he could easily scrape by on the most meager of incomes.

The great difference between Emerson's sense of "terrible freedom" before his trip and his sanguine state after his return would be hard to overestimate.[71] Many months away fostered "the return of my own spirits & faith," enabling him to come to terms with the death of Ellen and the strong emotions it had stirred as well as with his hasty resignation from Second Church.[72] Confident that relinquishing his pastorate had been imperative, Emerson resumed his old life with his characteristic optimism greatly strengthened. "Hope," Emerson explained, "is the true heroism & the true wisdom."[73] The examples of Wordsworth, Coleridge, and Carlyle proved especially important; even if their disavowal of religion had struck the young American as unfortunate, he had been inspired by their personal examples. Each of them in some way played the role of social critic outside of the confines of a religious establishment. Emerson envisioned himself playing precisely such a role in the United States.

Nowhere was the confluence of maturity and vocational aspiration more evident than in Emerson's journal writing, which from the fall of 1833 began to take on a new seriousness, order, and urgency. Emerson seems to have realized that his notes and observations, which had long been the basis for his sermons and had become the center of his intellectual world while alone in Europe, would now take on even greater importance as he forged a new career. He called his journal his "Savings Bank" into which he put the thought "fractions . . . that shall be made integers by their addition."[74] He deliberately lettered them in alphabetical order starting from "A" on December 11, 1833, when he finished the last of the journals he had begun abroad. From this point, he paid more attention to dating his entries, indexed them with great care, and altogether made them more immediately useful.[75] Many of the journal entries dating from these first months and years back from Europe formed the substance of Emerson's most important essays and lectures.

Emerson's optimism upon his return to the United States proved well founded. The pattern of supply preaching and occasional lecturing he fell into in the fall and winter of 1833–34 satisfied him highly. "I please myself with contemplating the felicity of my present situation," he wrote in his journal. "It seems to me singularly free & it invites me to every virtue & to great improvement."[76] From New Bedford and Boston in Massachusetts and Bangor in Maine to New York City, Emerson preached to delighted congregations, several of which beseeched him to become their minister. His public lectures, though few, provided an important supplement to his sermons, affording him a critical outlet for his more social and political cogitations. With little time to contemplate what calling he might next pursue, Emerson was in fact creating a most congenial, if nontraditional, profession for himself. "May it last," he wrote.[77]

Fresh from Europe and brimming with optimism, Emerson still confronted the problem of vocation. "The call of our calling is the loudest call," he confided to his journal in December.[78] In his first sermon, "Religion and

Society," delivered less than three weeks after his return, Emerson intimated what his calling might be.

> The greatest gift of God is a Teacher and teaching is the perpetual end and office of all things. Teaching, instruction, is the main design that shines through the sky and earth. It is the end of youth, of growth, of play, of studies, of punishment, of pleasure, of misfortunes, of sickness, of contests, of connexions, of professions—the purpose of all—all teach us something, yes, even sin and death—and that lesson is the reason of their coming.[79]

Composed just days after his return to Boston, this sermon clearly reflected Emerson's growing conviction that if he were to achieve greatness it would be through some sort of teaching. Like Jesus, "the apostle of moral nature," Emerson pledged himself to teach "by word and act."[80] Emerson hoped to take the traditional somberness and bearing of the clergy, the eloquence of the pulpit, and the subject matter of the sermon, free them from churchly dogma and ritual, and create a secular ministry of ethics, idealism, and practical knowledge. Several years later, he would call on other intellectuals to follow him in order to create themselves as "Scholars out of the church."[81] But for the moment, achieving such a ministry was a tall order for a thirty-year-old.

Emerson composed "Religion and Society" specifically for his former congregation.[82] It is an altogether upbeat sermon that begins with the pastor noting that returning home is "one of the keenest enjoyments of human life." After genuinely declaring his delight at his homecoming—"I cannot tell you, my friends of this religious society, with how much pleasure I see you again and learn of your virtues"—Emerson sounded a theme similar to earlier sermons that had raised eyebrows among the congregation at Second Church. The responsibility for development and enlightenment rests only secondarily with the teacher. Christ himself "affirms the fact that the essential condition of teaching is a ripe pupil," Emerson admonished the parishioners. "No teacher can teach without the hearty cooperation of the scholar." Merely attending church and silently assenting to old doctrines in stale formulae would not do. Emerson's lofty goal, the "communication of moral truth," demanded much more.[83]

Emerson preached nearly every Sunday either in Boston or somewhere else in New England after his return to the United States. He continued to compose sermons, though not at his former rate, and rework older ones. Congregations eagerly sought him out. Not surprisingly, Emerson found supply preaching preferable to a settled ministry. The pastoral obligations of a regular ministry intruded into his hours of study and writing; members of the congregation made demands on his time that, even unfulfilled, made Emerson uneasy; and ministering to the same congregation week after week inevitably engendered Emerson's displeasure. How could it not? He seemed to put so much more into the relationship than did most of his charges. Supply preaching had none of these disadvantages. More importantly, without pastoral duties and the other incidental obligations that fell to a settled minister, Emerson could preserve the precarious balance of society and solitude that proved critical to his intellectual well-being. When church societies came calling, hoping to entice Emerson out of retirement, as it were, Emerson demurred. As his opportunities beyond the pulpit multiplied, he moved farther and farther from the traditional clerical vocation for which he had been ostensibly trained. It would still be some time before he could fully express his disenchantment with the Unitarian establishment. The hopeful teacher had not yet encountered his appropriate ministry.

While supplying the New Bedford pulpit of his cousin Orville Dewey, Emerson fortuitously became acquainted with some remarkable Quaker women, who had joined the Unitarian church a decade earlier after being expelled from the Quaker meeting. Emerson's many weeks in this sleepy whaling village did not constitute his first encounter with the Society of Friends, as he had already acquired something of a spiritual affinity with the Quakers through his reading about George Fox and William Penn. The former's life and martyrdom had inspired Emerson during the agonizing months of controversy at Second Church, even as Emerson made use of Quaker principles in the Lord's Supper controversy.[84] Now he had the opportunity to discuss the "Inner Light" and other Quaker ideas with his hostess, Deborah Brayton, as well as Mary Rotch, New Bedford's most famous dissenter. Rotch's spirited defense of the liberal views of Mary Newhall of Lynn had precipitated the crisis that resulted in their expulsion years earlier. Emerson found much to admire in "the sublime religion of Miss Rotch," who by all accounts was a woman of steadfast convictions.[85] "If she had said yea and the whole world had thundered in her ear nay," Emerson concluded, "she would still have said yea."[86] Rotch's "assurance of higher direction" moved Emerson greatly. After one of their discussions, in which Rotch's notions had "mingled with my sad thoughts," Emerson achieved something of an epiphany.

> Can you believe, Waldo Emerson, that you may relieve yourself of this perpetual perplexity of choosing? & by putting your ear close to the soul, learn always the true way. I cannot but remark how perfectly this agrees with the Daimon of Socrates, even in that story which I once thought anomalous, of the direction as to the choice of two roads. And with the grand Unalterable-

ness of Fichte's morality. Hold up this lamp & look back at the best passages of your life. Once there was *choice* in the mode, but *obedience* in the thing. In general there has been a pretty quiet obedience *in the main*, but much recusancy *in the particular*.[87]

The supreme example of Mary Rotch, holding steadfast to her convictions over and against all others, proved far more inspirational than all his recent readings in Plutarch, Fichte, Plato, and the great philosophers. His discussions with this avatar of self-reliance convinced him to redouble his efforts to follow George Fox's example: "What I am in words, I am the same in life."[88]

Emerson respected the consistency of Quaker belief. Unlike the elitist Unitarians of Boston, Quakers such as Mary Rotch had come to terms with the social implications of Christianity. They espoused a far more inclusive and democratic American society that meshed nicely with his recent thinking. Nothing could have served as a starker contrast to European Catholicism than the simple ministrations of the New Bedford Quakers. While reading about George Fox a few years earlier, Emerson had recognized in the notion of the "Inner Light" an excellent articulation of the fundamental principle of the individualism he believed to be at the heart of Christianity. Though they might not recognize it or act upon it, all persons contained something of the divine within them. The Quakers called it "Inner Light," Adam Smith called it a "moral sense," but by any name it was that universal trait around which Emerson constructed his vision of a just society. Emerson and those who would in time compose his Transcendentalist circle preferred to call this universal quality "Reason," following the German idealist terminology. "Reason is the highest faculty of the soul—what we mean often by the soul itself," Emerson explained to his brother Edward. "Beasts have some understanding but no Reason. Reason is potentially perfect in every man."[89] Mankind might have only one common trait, but that one—Reason, or the moral faculty—promised a great deal. That one part of the divine present in all men justified Emerson's budding optimism in the potential for society as a whole.

The Quakers, according to Emerson, were the only true Protestants, the only people who took literally Luther's blandishment about a "priesthood of all believers." Whereas Unitarians and other Protestant denominations sustained elaborate hierarchies and insisted upon the need for mediational institutions and sacred texts, the Quakers eschewed all that on the basis of their respect for the qualifications of each individual. For a minister like Emerson, who had resigned his pastorate over the ritual of the Lord's Supper and who would shortly decline another because of his reticence concerning the rote use of public prayer, the Quaker beliefs offered a great succor. Even at the dinner table Emerson balked at participating in such a banal ritual as saying grace. "A trivial and interesting point in connections with [Emerson family] dinners," recalled David Haskins, "was the form my cousin used in saying grace before meat. It surpassed even 'episcopal brevity.' The few but sufficient words were, 'We acknowledge the Giver.' "[90] As Emerson argued in his lecture on George Fox, delivered later in the year, the Quakers presented what he considered to be the model of true Christianity. Any religion based on something other than an internal search for goodness or Fox's notion of the "God within" was so much artificial convention.[91] After his separation from the Unitarian church in 1838, Emerson was reticent about classifying his beliefs by name or himself by specific denomination. When the cousin noted above as observing his manner of saying grace asked how he would define his religious sentiments, Emerson responded "with great deliberateness, and longer pauses between his words than usual, 'I am more of a Quaker than anything else. I believe in the "still small voice," and that voice is Christ within us.' "[92]

Fresh from his trip abroad, Emerson found in his conversations with the New Bedford Quakers a critical justification for his growing sense of the American promise. The notion of the "Inner Light," or that "still small voice," was a sufficient basis not only for a religion without ritual, but the foundation for a polity in which "all men take part." For all its monuments to individual artistic achievement, European society with its peasant squalor and extremes of wealth and poverty had repulsed Emerson. These extremes and the suffering they entailed struck Emerson, as it did many of the Americans who traveled to the Continent, as the greatest single difference between Europe and the United States. Upon his return home, his interest in politics—at least as subject of deep contemplation—blossomed as it took on a decidedly more egalitarian aspect. The ideas of Mary Rotch and the Quakers of New Bedford among Orville Dewey's congregation helped Emerson precipitate out of his disparate thoughts a universalizing political idealism. Emerson expressed the kernel of his evolving thought in his lecture on Fox and the Society of Friends. The Inner Light, he explained to his audience of non-Quakers, "is the most republican principle. . . . It is above all the dogmas of the world the seed of Revolutions. Down topple before this enormous assertion of spiritual right, all the tyrannies, all the hierarchies, all the artificial ranks of the earth."[93]

The first opportunity Emerson had to express his maturing social vision came serendipitously. Only a few weeks after moving to Concord, Emerson was asked to prepare an address to mark the bicentennial of this singularly famous village some "seventeen miles from Boston."[94] In the Concord Bicentennial Address, delivered on September 12, 1835, Emerson first formulated his political principles for public consumption. For years, he had pontificated about, poked fun at, and parodied the defects of the American political system and the dismal characters that inhabited its lowly realms. But journal entries and playful letters were of an entirely different magnitude from a public address. That he was responsible for offering a public assessment of great and significant events, such as the Battle of Concord—"the shot heard round the world," Emerson declared for posterity—to women and men, some of whom had fought for liberty on the very spot, raised the stakes immeasurably. In the solemnity of the moment, Emerson elevated the history of Concord to the history of the American nation. It was a history not without its misery, pathos, and evil, as Emerson called "disgraceful" the outrages Concord's early inhabitants committed against the Indians. When it came to their indigenous neighbors, writes Emerson, the Puritan "heart of charity, of humanity, was stone."[95] Nevertheless, Indian–white relations were but a single sad chapter in a majestic story.

The "Historical Discourse" at Concord, which the town published, offered Emerson the ideal opportunity to articulate what he believed to be the crucial differences between the Old World and the New. "The British government has recently presented to the several public libraries of this country, copies of a splendid edition of the Domesday Book, and other ancient Records of England," he alerted his audience. "I cannot but think that it would be a suitable acknowledgement of this national munificence, if the records of one of our towns,—of this town, for example,—should be printed, and presented to the governments of Europe, . . . to the continental nations as a lesson of humanity and love."[96] The address contained the distillation of Emerson's recent thinking while touring Europe about the nature of American society comparable, albeit to a lesser extent, to Tocqueville's observations of his trip through the United States in *Democracy in America*, at least insofar as both critics believed that Americans represented something vitally neoteric. As the occasion demanded, Emerson concluded with a stirring patriotic flourish. The people of Concord were religious from the first; for the most part they dealt fairly with the Indians; they were frontiersmen who expected, and received, little assistance from the government in Boston; they established a local government that enjoyed the power of the purse, so they could lay and collect their own taxes. Most importantly, to meet their needs they established the revolutionary engine of American democracy: the town meeting. When the people embraced this novel institution, "the great secret of political science was uncovered," the orator declared.

New England villagers discovered in the town meeting "how to give every individual his fair weight in the government, without any disorder from numbers."[97] Here in this minor innovation that was as numerous as the towns of New England was the native seed of just government.

> In a town-meeting, the roots of society were reached. Here the rich gave counsel, but the poor also; and moreover, the just and the unjust. He is ill-informed who expects, on running down the town records for two hundred years, to find a church of saints, a metropolis of patriots, enacting whole-some and creditable laws. The constitution of the towns forbid it. In this open democracy, every opinion had utterance; every objection, every fact, every acre of land, every bushel of rye, its entire weight. The moderator was the passive mouth-piece, and the vote of the town, like the vane on the turret overhead, free for every wind to turn, and always turned by the last and strongest breath. In these assemblies, the public weal, the call of inter-est, duty, religion, were heard; and every local feeling, every private grudge, every suggestion of petulance and ignorance, were not less faithfully pro-duced. Wrath and love came up to town-meeting in company. By the law of 1641, every man,—freeman or not,—inhabitant or not,—might introduce any business into a public meeting.[98]

Significantly, the speaker was not interested in evaluating the merits of the laws or even the specific actions taken by the local government. Emerson assiduously avoided personifying the town meeting. Like all government, it was as fallible as the individuals who comprised it. The issue before him was not a good government, but a just one. "It is the consequence of this institu-tion," the town meeting, Emerson concluded,

> that not a school-house, a public pew, a bridge, a pound, a mill-dam, hath been set up, or pulled down, or altered, or bought, or sold, without the whole population of this town having a voice in the affair. A general con-tentment is the result. And the people truly feel that they are lords of the soil. In every winding road, in every stone fence, in the smokes of the poor-house chimney, in the clock on the church, they read their own power, and consider, at leisure, the wisdom and error of their judgments.[99]

The instantaneous ends of government, wise or foolish, gave the speaker no pause. For Emerson the state was only "a poor good beast who means the best."[100]

The collateral consequences of this infant institution engrossed Emerson. The fact that "in Concord are five hundred rateable polls, and every one has an equal vote" was impressive.[101] This rudimentary equality might or might not result in good laws and passable roads and maintained bridges, but they were merely immediate material concerns. The more important collateral consequences related to the fact that, as Emerson put it, "the people truly feel they are lords of the soil," that they "read their own power" in their material progress, in their roads, chimneys, fences, and meeting houses.[102] It mattered not at all that any one person's power was small, just so long as it was not weaker than that of his neighbor. The right and responsibility to participate in government, to have a say as well as a stake, fascinated Emerson. The revolutionary element of the town meeting rested with its power to make individuals take themselves more seriously. For Emerson, the poet-preacher, government, legislation, and taxation were subsidiary to culture and cultivation of individual self-respect. Insofar as participation in the town meeting fostered self-respect it was the greatest invention of his native New England. It encouraged people to act responsibly.

By the fall of 1835 Emerson's political vision was coalescing. The promise of the town meeting, the Quaker notion of an inner light, and the Liberal Platonic view of a universal "Reason" present in everyone came together in a highly optimistic conception what he called the nation's great "republican principle." Writing in his journal he declared that "Democracy/Freedom has its root in the Sacred truth that every man hath in him the divine Reason or that though few men since the creation of the world live according to the dictates of Reason, yet all men are created capable of doing so. That is the equality & the only equality of all men."[103] No rigorous political theorist, no one understood better than he his lack of that analytic capacity necessary to construct a coherent political philosophy.[104] Yet, as amorphous as his thinking was, it served his purpose well. Emerson by 1835 had firmly come to identify self-government and moral equality with the United States and its future resplendence.

The day after he delivered his tribute to Concord's first two centuries, Emerson set off for Plymouth, Massachusetts, where he was to be married the following day. He had written his "Historical Discourse" under the influence of his budding romance with Lydia Jackson, the highly intelligent and reserved woman whom he had met in February or March of the previous year when he had delivered several public lectures in her native Plymouth. The relationship had progressed rapidly, and by January they were engaged. The groom prevailed upon Lidian, as he called her, to move to Concord, where he had purchased the spacious, if dilapidated home of John J. Coolidge.[105] It was an irony not lost on his second wife that the money to pay for their home came from a settlement of the estate of the first. Nevertheless, Coolidge Castle, renamed Bush, on the Boston Road became the Emerson homestead for the next half century. From the fall of 1835, Bush was home to Emerson's mother, Ruth, his brother Charles, and an assortment of friends and visitors. By the time Margaret Fuller began to call Emerson the sage of Concord and Henry Thoreau had made the pond at Walden (located on Emerson's land) his outpost against an encroaching modern world, Bush had become the Mecca for idealists, eccentrics, cranks, and other would-be poet-philosophers. More importantly, for Emerson, who had known only boarding and temporary lodgings, Bush became his home.

Marrying Lidian and establishing himself in Concord brought a stability to Emerson's life that it had conspicuously lacked. At Bush he enjoyed society on essentially his own terms, began the family that had eluded him in his marriage to Ellen, and instituted a highly productive routine of work and reflection. At Concord, with his wife, mother, and friends surrounding him, Emerson commenced the most productive phase of his life. In addition to his supply preaching, which he continued throughout the 1830s, Emerson branched out in more literary directions. One public lecture in 1833 became six in 1834 and mushroomed to at least twenty-nine in 1835. By the year of his marriage and move to Concord, Emerson was creating an alternative vocation that utilized the American tradition of pulpit oratory while splitting it off from its traditional mooring in the church.[106] The following year, Emerson published *Nature*, his first important work and his declaration of independence from the religious culture of Unitarianism. He conceived of *Nature,* he modestly wrote to Carlyle, "as an entering wedge, I hope, for something more worthy and significant."[107] Although its reception was tepid, *Nature* represented another important step for Emerson away from the ministry. Print and public lectures helped put him on the road to reaching a far broader audience than the select group of Unitarians who admired his preaching.

The publication of *Nature* and the delivery of several series of public lectures evidenced Emerson's ever-growing interests beyond traditional religion. More than that, publication and popular lecturing offered Emerson the hope of achieving the broader relevance he craved. As Emerson's confidence and energies grew palpably in the mid-1830s, the contrast is unmistakable between his interests and influences within his denomination and those beyond the bounds of religion. Emerson wrote fewer sermons—only five in 1834 and but two more thereafter—and many more lectures. His reading and writing reflected the pull of biography and English literature, to each of which he devoted lecture series, as well as such contemporary issues as education and reform. Emerson began a lifelong and highly rewarding correspondence with Thomas Carlyle. He continued his broad reading. "When shall I be tired of reading?" he asked. "When the moon is tired of waxing & waning, when the sea is tired of ebbing & flowing, when the grass is weary of growing, when the planets are tired of going."[108] In composing *Nature,* he finally succeeded in formulating his own idealized, highly syncretistic religious sentiments. Any additional prodding Emerson needed to speed his transition from the traditional ministry to broader social and intellectual issues his new eccentric acquaintances provided—in spades. New friends with incisive intellects, such as Elizabeth Palmer Peabody, Bronson Alcott, Margaret Fuller, and Henry Thoreau, stormed into Emerson's life between 1835 and 1837, each one bringing to his attention novel ideas, ambitions, and programs only tangentially related, if at all, to traditional religion. Like Emerson himself, they both reflected and engendered the intellectual and social currents on the brink of revolutionizing New England's high culture. Within months of his return to the United States, Emerson's reading, writing, lecturing, correspondence, and conversations took up issues that transcended even the broadest conceptions of a ministerial career. Emerson recorded that he was "on the brink of an ocean of thought into which we do not yet swim."[109]

Trained as a Unitarian minister and boasting a lineage of ministers dating back almost two centuries, Emerson remained reticent about severing his ties to his putative denomination and faith. It would take a few more years of growing disgust with his erstwhile colleagues, and his own steady drift away from Protestant Christianity, to compel a divorce from Unitarianism. In the years between his return from abroad and the Divinity School Address, every Sunday, wherever he was, Emerson attended church, either to deliver a sermon himself or to hear a fellow pastor. More often than not, he came away dissatisfied. "The whole world holds onto formal Christianity," he lamented in a familiar refrain, "& nobody teaches the essential truth, the heart of Christianity."[110] Emerson's frequent complaints, which he diligently copied into his journal and often included in his correspondence, varied from boring ministers and hollow, formulaic sermons to what he considered offensive and arrogant ministerial claims to authority. The best he could write about Newton, Massachusetts, minister James Bates, "a plain, serious Calvinist not winning but not repelling," whose service he attended only ten days after his return from abroad, was that he was

> one of the useful police which God makes out of the ignorance & superstition of the youth of the world. I dare not & wish not speak disrespectfully of these good, abstemious, laborious men. Yet I could not help asking myself how long is the society to be taught in this dramatic or allegorical style? When is religious truth to be distinctly uttered—what it is, not what it resembles? Thus every Sunday ever since they were born this congregation have heard tell of *Salvation*, and of going to the door of heaven & knocking, & being answered from Within, "Depart, I Never Knew You" & of being sent away to eternal ruin.[111]

Bates's Calvinism stood in stark contrast to Emerson's fanciful summation of New England religion in his "Historical Discourse" delivered at Concord. Emerson revised Puritanism into a religion of "sweetness and peace amidst toil and tears," while at the same time praising New England's founders for beholding "God and nature face to face."[112] He hoped in the address at Concord and in *Nature* to convince ministers like Bates to abandon the harsh doctrines of innate human depravity and original sin. Considering Calvinistic dogma so much nonsense, the author of *Nature* embraced an optimistic, even romantic, vision of human nature characteristic of what detractors would soon derisively call New England Transcendentalism. Emerson sought in his sermons, which he continued to compose and deliver, in his public lectures, and in *Nature* to communicate his most hopeful portrait of a nation of right-behaving people. In understanding themselves as the potentially perfect reflection of a perfect God—"A man is a god in ruins," Emerson wrote—Americans would aspire to live up to the divine within them as opposed to descending to the depraved state postulated by Calvinists.[113] "Know then that the world exists for you," he declared. "For you is the phenomenon perfect."[114]

Calvinists like Bates got off easy. Calvinism itself, with its largely misunderstood doctrines concerning human depravity and an omnipotent God, was entirely anathema to Emerson, who repeatedly claimed in *Nature* and his sermons that "God is in every man."[115] Yet, Calvinism and its orthodox advocates retained some praiseworthy characteristics, particularly when contrasted with the Unitarians. At least Calvinism claimed a glorious past when it powerfully stirred the souls of women and men. Calvinists might be "so befooled as to call this sucked eggshell hightoned orthodoxy," but their ancestors did profess a strong, emotional, truly spirited faith.[116] The orthodox had heart. They understood the crucial relationship between vital piety and true faith. The minister's success depended upon his ability to communicate the emotional core of his faith, as Emerson noted after attending a Concord service. "I could not help remarking at church how much humanity was in the preaching of my good Uncle, Mr S. Ripley," he wrote. "The rough farmers had their hands at their eyes repeatedly."[117] Without emotion and heart, preachers offered only the "pale negations" of religion.

The problem with the Calvinists was not their hearts, but their heads, which were stuck in the distant, albeit glorious, past. For all their vital piety, orthodox Calvinists resembled his grandfather Ezra Ripley when they engaged in "the foolishest preaching—which bayed at the moon. Go, hush," Emerson quipped, "whom years have taught no truth."[118] In his essay "Worship" in *Conduct of Life*, Emerson announced that "the stern old faiths have all pulverized" and must be jettisoned. "We live in a transition period, when the old faiths which comforted nations, and not only so but made nations, seem to have spent their force. I do not find the religions of men at this moment very creditable to them, but either childish and insignificant or unmanly and effeminating." Calvinist and Unitarian alike ought to apprehend that among the folk "there is a feeling that religion is gone."[119] "We are born too late for the old," Emerson warned,[120] so the lone solution was to forget the past and to "replace these thread bare rags" of enervated dogma.[121]

Emerson reserved his harshest criticism for the exclusive, educated Unitarian ministers among his brethren. He had been an ordained Unitarian minister and still spent Sundays in its houses of worship. Unitarianism was the faith of his family and his father; it was the creed that he had once fervently pledged to make into the life force of his own congregation. Emerson despaired of Calvinists but derided Unitarians. His colleagues had confined Calvinism to the past, but had failed to substitute a new faith. For the most part, their ministries seemed hollow, devoid of the life-giving force that Emerson understood to be the vital center of any religious experience. Unitarian ministers relied on ritual, adhered to a cold formalism, and tended to sneer at the low and common. Their preaching was almost unbearable. As Emerson traveled throughout New England, his complaints became more strident and his disenchantment with established religion overwhelmed him. By the summer of 1838 and his notorious Divinity School Address, Emerson was bursting with the pent-up frustration accumulated over half a decade of miserable Sundays.

Emerson repeatedly accused his colleagues of foolishly adhering to doctrines and institutions that had no relevance to their lives. Sadly for them and their congregations, "pews, vestries, family prayer, sanctimonious looks & words constitute[d] religion," as opposed to faith and personal devotion. Nowhere was this tendency more apparent than in Unitarians' continued reliance on the external evidence of scripture and miracles when the only true measure of belief was internal conviction, a point Emerson drove home in the Divinity School Address. "There is no miracle to the believing soul," Emerson avowed. "The accepted Christianity of the mob of Churches is now as always a caricature of the real."[122] Even their reading struck him as lacking inspiration. "I looked over the few books in the young clergyman's study yesterday till I shivered with cold," Emerson recorded while supplying a pulpit at Billerica, Massachusetts.[123] Emerson heartily agreed with the Methodist Edward Taylor when he spoke "of poor ministers coming out of divinity schools, &c. as 'poor fellows hobbling out of Jerusalem.' "[124] Interacting with his colleagues confirmed what Emerson had thought while at Harvard Divinity School a decade earlier: that the best men no longer entered the ministry. The Divinity curriculum included courses in biblical exegesis and reformed theology but did nothing to inspire the students. "At the Divinity School this morning I heard what was called the best performance," Emerson recorded in his diary in July of 1835, "but it was founded on nothing & led to nothing & I wondered at the patience of the people."[125]

Emerson particularly decried the preaching he endured every Sunday. Dry, suffused with poor language and stale images, it reflected all the worst traits of the denomination. After attending the services of Concord's new minister, Barzillai Frost, Emerson complained that the "young preacher preached from his ears & his memory, & never a word from his soul. His sermon was loud & hollow."[126] A year later after listening to the same minister, Emerson reached his limit. "At Church all day," he lamented, "but almost tempted to say I would go no more."[127] He found some solace in viewing sermons as a peculiar source of inspiration. "Among provocatives," he wrote, "the next best thing to good preaching is bad preaching. I have even more thoughts during or enduring it than at other times."[128] After yet another bout of Barzillai Frost, Emerson's irony got the better of him as he noted that church was "a good place to study Theism by comparing the things said with your Consciousness."[129] Although he singled out Frost on a number of occasions, Emerson was generous in distributing his opprobrium. He found virtually no Unitarian minister worthy of praise beyond the members of the so-called Hedge Club: Orestes Brownson, James Freeman Clarke, Convers Francis, Frederic Henry Hedge, and George Ripley. Other Unitarian ministers could not possibly deliver truly moving and eloquent sermons because they lacked the "passion, which is the *heat*" to make their oratory come alive.[130] His age was witnessing the sorry eclipse of pulpit eloquence, one of New England's prized institutions. "If there ever was a country where eloquence was a power, it is the United States," Emerson declared in *Letters and Social Aims,* as he lamented the decline of the sermon.[131] "But the minister in these days, how little he says! . . . Go into one of our cool churches, & begin to count the words that might be spared, & in most places, the entire sermon will go."[132]

For a long time Emerson confined his lamentation over the decline of ministerial office to his journals and letters. He continued to preach and attend Unitarian services, though both with less frequency as the decade wore on. Increasingly secure in his still evolving vocation as lecturer and author, Emerson retained his hope that New England pulpits would once again become the source of inspiration and eloquence they had been in the days of his Puritan progenitors. Hardly sanguine about the prospects for such a rebirth, Emerson nevertheless agreed in the spring of 1838 to meet with some Harvard Divinity students to discuss the present state of religion. Emerson met the students on the first of April, a "Cool or cold windy clear day."

> The Divinity School youths wished to talk with me concerning theism. I
> went rather heavy-hearted for I always find that my views chill or shock
> people at the first opening. But the conversation went well & I came away
> cheered. I told them that the preacher should be a poet smit with love of the
> harmonies of moral nature: and yet look at the Unitarian Association & see
> if its aspect is poetic. They all smiled No. A minister nowadays is plainest
> prose, the prose of prose. He is a Warming-pan, a Night-chair at sick beds &
> rheumatic souls; and the fire of the minstrel's eye & the vivacity of his word
> is exchanged for intense grumbling enunciation of the Cambridge sort, &
> for scripture phraseology. [133]

Their apparent satisfaction with this meeting impelled the students to ask
Emerson to present the address at their forthcoming commencement. After
some hesitation, Emerson ultimately acquiesced, believing that he had a
responsibility to the students, if not to the denomination as a whole, to voice
publicly his reservations. Whether Emerson perceived that the address would
signal his formal disunion from the Unitarian powers-that-be remains unclear.

The opportunity to address the gathering at the Harvard Divinity School
in the summer of 1838 came at a propitious moment. Nowhere in his journals
are there more references to the inadequacies of the Unitarian ministry and
the failings of the denomination than in the months leading up to the address.
Emerson had grown increasingly critical of his colleagues the more he listened
to Frost's vacuous sermons, and it seems likely that he had the Concord pastor
in mind when he observed in the address that all too often Unitarian ministers
were "merely spectral." [134] They had not lived, so they could not possibly
preach. Commenting upon his poem "The Problem," a verse commentary on
his own decision to quit the ministry altogether, Emerson jocularly confessed
that he had composed several lines "one Sunday lately at church," which
Henry Thoreau confirmed in his own note: "at least partially written in
church." [135] Thoreau concurred with Emerson that Frost and his brethren were
"as diseased, and as much possessed with a devil as the reformers." [136]

Emerson felt obliged to address publicly the diseased state of the ministry because he had for so long harbored such high hopes for it, for what had
constituted his chosen vocation. "I dislike to be a clergyman & refuse to be
one," Emerson finally resolved after the controversy of the Divinity School
Address. [137] "Yet how rich a music would be to me a holy clergyman in my
town. It seems to me he cannot be a man, quite & whole. Yet how plain is the
need of one, & how high, yes highest, is the function." [138] The ministry, the
sermon, pulpit eloquence—all of which Emerson found so utterly deficient—were institutions with great history and awesome potential. The true

minister who broke away from formalism and sought to express himself and his soul's searching for true religious experience might restore them to glory. "The young preacher is discouraged by learning the motives that brought his great congregation to church. Scarcely ten came to hear his sermon," Emerson wrote in his journal in preparation for his upcoming Harvard talk.

> Never mind how they came my friend; never mind who or what brought them any more than you do who or what set you down in Boston in 1835. Here they are real men & women, fools I grant but potentially divine every one of them convertible. Every ear is yours to gain. Every heart will be glad & proud & thankful for a master. There where you are, serve them & they must serve you. They care nothing for you but be to them a Plato be to them a Christ & they shall all be Platos & all be Christs.[139]

Emerson remained hopeful even as he grew discouraged. Without his characteristic optimism—perhaps one of these six commencing students would become a great preacher, he surmised—Emerson would not have offered his address.[140] Intensely critical to be sure, the Divinity School Address also served as a challenge and a prayer.

Emerson believed himself to be brutally honest and self-critical. His journals and letters are replete with acknowledgements of failures, from his poor showing in college to his decision to abandon his ministry in Boston. His farewell sermon to his Second Church congregation, "The Genuine Man," was a public explanation of his particular shortcomings as well as an eloquent explication for his decision. "It is the essence of truth of character that a man should follow his own thought," he explained. "He therefore speaks what he thinks. He acts his thought. He acts simply and up to the highest motives he knows of."[141] Feeling that he had failed as a supply preacher and poised to forsake altogether the Unitarian church in 1838, Emerson felt constrained as a genuine man to make good on an earlier promise. There was "no better subject for effective writing than the Clergy," Emerson grumbled to himself in his Concord pew on a winter Sunday in 1838. "I ought to sit & think & then write a discourse to the American clergy showing them the ugliness & unprofitableness of theology & churches at this day & the glory & sweetness of the Moral Nature out of whose pale they are almost wholly shut."[142] Emerson fulfilled his promise on a warm summer evening the following July.

Emerson's intent in the Divinity School Address seems clear. Whether the content of the address was singular and revolutionary or more conventional and evolutionary might remain in dispute, but the author's twofold purpose was unambiguous.[143] Emerson sought to suggest to the students in attendance how they might repair the vocation upon which they were about to embark and simultaneously explain why he had resolved to seek a new vocation for himself. That his list of frustrations and disappointments would engender such a harsh response from the Unitarian authorities in the assemblage seems as inevitable now as it was surprising then to the speaker himself. Referring to the aftermath as a "storm in our washbowl," Emerson chose—at the insistence of Lidian—to steer clear of the public debate that ensued, refraining from publishing a single word about the controversy.

To be sure, Emerson chose a most awkward location to offer his critique. The Harvard Divinity School was the seat of American Unitarianism, and the occasion ensured that the likes of Andrews Norton, John Gorham Palfrey, and Henry Ware Jr. would be in attendance. Yet, for Emerson the talk embodied nothing more than the ruminations and observations he had been accumulating over the past several years. Many passages come almost verbatim from his journals, particularly those most critical of the "two errors" of ritualism and formalism that had caused "the famine in our churches."[144] For Emerson, the import of the address had little to do with doctrine. Like the controversy over the Lord's Supper in his dispute with Second Church earlier in the decade, the specific doctrinal and theological issues in the address served only as examples, or symbols, of a larger problem. "It is time," he declared,

> that this ill-suppressed murmur of all thoughtful men against the famine of our churches; this moaning of the heart because it is bereaved of the consolation, the hope, the grandeur that come alone out of the culture of the moral nature; should be heard through the sleep of indolence, and over the din of routine. This great and perpetual office of the preacher is not discharged. Preaching is the expression of the moral sentiment in application to the duties of life. In how many churches, by how many prophets, tell me, is man made sensible that he is an infinite Soul;. . . But now the priest's Sabbath has lost the splendor of nature; it is unlovely; we are glad when it is done; we can make, we do make, even sitting in our pews, a far better, holier, sweeter, [Sabbath] for ourselves.[145]

Emerson admonished the Unitarians that it was high time to acknowledge the obvious. Whatever the doctrinal issues, the denomination was in trouble and "the worshipper defrauded and disconsolate."[146] Dull and lifeless ministers, trained at Harvard for the most part, were wringing the true faith from the church and in no time would relegate it to irrelevance in New England and the nation at large. "I think no man can go with his thoughts about him, into one of our churches, without feeling that what hold the public worship had on men, is gone or going."[147] The growing irrelevance of the church was the heart of Emerson's message. As distasteful as the news was, it was equally obvious.

Not only was Emerson basically accurate in his prognostication, but his warnings proved entirely consistent with his personal and professional misgivings that spanned the previous decade. He had joined the ministry, perhaps as the students at the divinity school that day had, not meekly to follow his father and his father before him, but to do great things. Hugely ambitious, Emerson had chosen the ministry in order to be the "great Teacher" who could "preach God who is, not God who was."[148] Disappointed with the training at Harvard, he had quickly moved on to preaching. More deeply disappointed by the failure of his own ministry, he had resigned it after less than three years. Finally, disgusted with the utter ossification of the profession as a whole, Emerson was prepared to quit preaching—at least from the pulpit—once and for all. As a young man, Emerson had listened to Aunt Mary and had sought glory in the church. By 1838 that quest was over. "Genius leaves the temple to haunt the senate or the market," he concluded.[149] A published author and a successful lecturer, Emerson resolved to follow genius out of the church. He resolved to "go alone," to pursue "the office of a true teacher." If going alone entailed the creation of an entirely novel vocation, that of the minister-poet-pedagogue, then so be it. He was up to the challenge.

Whatever his irenic intentions, Emerson's Divinity School Address caused a crisis in the Unitarian ranks. On the heels of the address, many Unitarians, those in the audience particularly, chose to view it as an outright attack upon their faith. "Unitarian pope" Andrews Norton labeled the speech a "form of infidelity," while Henry Ware attempted to refute the theological claims of his friend and erstwhile colleague. The bitterness and personal animus engendered by the Divinity School Address poisoned Emerson's relationship with his former denomination for years to come. The import of the Unitarian community's harsh reaction for Emerson remains difficult to gauge precisely because the address itself marked a self-conscious and considered turning point. Emerson had already decided that his consuming desire for relevance in America obliged him to move beyond the effete Unitarianism of eastern Massachusetts. By that refulgent July evening in Cambridge, Emerson had already made his separation from Unitarianism, the ministry, and the parochial confines of Brahmin Boston. The rest of the nation and the rest of his life beckoned.

NOTES

1. *JMN* 4:306.
2. *JMN* 4:46.

3. Charles Chauncy Emerson to William Emerson, May 1834, as cited in *Letters* 1:414n.

4. *JMN* 4:27; *JMN* 7:391.

5. *JMN* 4:27.

6. *JMN* 4:27.

7. *JMN* 4:52; "Divinity School Address," *Collected Works* 1:90.

8. The great intellects of Europe whom he visited "have no idea of that species of moral truth which I call first philosophy." *JMN* 4:79.

9. Robert Richardson points to Emerson's quasi-religious inspiration at the Jardin des Plantes in Paris as the critical turning point. See his *Emerson: The Mind on Fire* (Berkeley, Calif., 1995).

10. The entire United States included southerners, free blacks, and slaves, all of whom Emerson firmly believed would eventually become Yankees.

11. Charles Chauncy Emerson to William Emerson, 11/27/32, *Letters* 1:357n.

12. Emerson to Mary Moody Emerson, 4/18/33, *Letters* 1:375.

13. *JMN* 4:103, 105–6.

14. "Conversation," in *Young Emerson Speaks, 60.*

15. *JMN* 4:110.

16. *JMN* 4:115.

17. *JMN* 4:103.

18. Emerson to William Emerson, 6/29/33, *Letters* 1:388.

19. *JMN* 5:141.

20. *JMN* 5:38.

21. Emerson's 1848 trip to Europe became the basis for his 1850 *English Traits.*

22. Emerson to Charles Chauncy Emerson, 6/25/33, *Letters* 1:386.

23. *JMN* 4:75.

24. Emerson to George A. Sampson, 6/25/33, *Letters* 1:371.

25. *JMN* 4:126.

26. *JMN* 4:126.

27. *JMN* 4:74.

28. *JMN* 4:59.

29. *JMN* 4:117.

30. Emerson's aesthetic comments throughout his European journals, his coolness to the great works of the Italian Renaissance in particular, so clearly anticipate the views of Dewey and the pragmatists.

31. *JMN* 4:152.

32. *JMN* 4:153.

33. *JMN* 4:153.

34. *JMN* 4:153.

35. *JMN* 4:75.

36. *JMN* 4:80.

37. *JMN* 4:77.

38. *JMN* 4:203.

39. *JMN* 4:203.

40. *JMN* 7:338–39.

41. Alexander Ireland, *Ralph Waldo Emerson* (London, 1882), 140–42.

42. *JMN* 4:78.

43. *JMN* 4:79.

44. *JMN* 4:219.

45. *JMN* 4:219.

46. *JMN* 4:80.

47. *JMN* 4:80.

48. *JMN* 4:81.

49. *JMN* 4:83. When Samuel Taylor Coleridge had similarly criticized the Unitarians only days earlier, the American had felt compelled to interject that he was a Unitarian, lest he appear mendacious. Not surprisingly, this information did nothing to check Coleridge's disdain. Feeling himself among friends in Dunscore, Emerson took a different tack in his discussion with Carlyle.

50. *JMN* 4:81.

51. *JMN* 4:80.

52. *JMN* 4:81.

53. *JMN* 4:83.

54. *JMN* 4:84.

55. *JMN* 4:306.

56. *JMN* 4:157.

57. *JMN* 4:78.

58. *JMN* 4:78.

59. *JMN* 4:278.

60. A fitting contrast is with Emerson's jotting of the sentiments of Wordsworth concerning the pointlessness of most education of the peasantry. See *JMN* 4:222.

61. Emerson's reading of Plato here is highly selective. Emerson replaces Socrates' ambition of educating the aristocratic few with the Christian conviction that all are educable.

62. "Politics," *Early Lectures* 2:70.

63. *JMN* 4:50–51.

64. *JMN* 4:236.

65. *JMN* 4:240–42.

66. *JMN* 4:81.

67. Edward W. Emerson, *Emerson in Concord* (Cambridge, 1889), 46.

68. Emerson to William Emerson, 10/11/33, *Letters* 1:397.

69. For a review of some of the legal haggling, see Henry F. Pommer, *Emerson's First Marriage* (Carbondale, Ill., 1967), 62–65.

70. Cited in Pommer, *First Marriage,* 67.

71. *JMN* 4:46.

72. *JMN* 4:35.

73. *JMN* 4:253.

74. *JMN* 4:250–51.

75. See introductory remarks by editors of *JMN* 4:249.

76. *JMN* 4:253.

77. *JMN* 4:253.

78. *JMN* 4:252.

79. *Young Emerson Speaks*, 192.

80. *Young Emerson Speaks*, 196.

81. *JMN* 7:312.

82. He delivered it only twice subsequently.

83. All cites in this paragraph are from *Young Emerson Speaks*, 196–97.

84. See Mary Turpie, "A Quaker Source for Emerson's Sermon on the Lord's Supper," *New England Quarterly* 17 (1944), 95–101, and Frederick B. Tolles, "Emerson and Quakerism," *American Literature* 10 (1938), 142–66.

85. *JMN* 4:263.

86. Richardson, *Mind on Fire*, 161.

87. *JMN* 4:263–64; see Plutarch's *Morals* for a discussion of Socrates' decision to follow—correctly as it turned out—the admonition of his "daemon" to avoid the most direct route in favor of a circuitous one to his destination.

88. *JMN* 4:33.

89. Emerson to Edward Bliss Emerson, 5/31/34, *Letters* 1:412–13.

90. David Haskins, *Ralph Waldo Emerson: His Maternal Ancestors* (Boston, 1887), 114.

91. *JMN* 3:236n.

92. Haskins, *Maternal Ancestors*, 118.

93. "George Fox," *Early Lectures* 1:166–67.

94. *JMN* 5:283.

95. "Historical Discourse at Concord," *Works* 11:65.

96. "Historical Discourse," *Works* 11:53.

97. "Historical Discourse," *Works* 11:50.

98. "Historical Discourse," *Works* 11:50–51.

99. "Historical Discourse," *Works* 11:52.

100. *JMN* 9:446.

101. "Historical Discourse," *Works* 11:53.

102. "Historical Discourse," *Works* 11:52.

103. *JMN* 4:357.

104. Some contemporary philosophers praise Emerson specifically for his refusal to come up with a philosophical defense of democracy. In a similar vein, Stanley Cavell argues that Emerson and Ludwig Wittgenstein were both philosophers of the everyday. I find this claim highly dubious. Wittgenstein was a profound thinker, a philosopher of the ordinary who used everyday objects and notions to demonstrate complex philosophical issues. Emerson's language contains some similarities to that of Wittgenstein, but hardly for the same deep purposes. By his own admission, Emerson

was not capable of systematic thinking even remotely approaching the rigor of a Wittgenstein. See Stanley Cavell, *Conditions Handsome and Unhandsome: The Constitution of Emersonian Perfectionism* (LaSalle, Ill., 1990).

105. Emerson chose to call his wife Lidian, as noted earlier.

106. See Philip F. Gura, *The Wisdom of Words: Language, Theology, and Literature in the New England Renaissance* (Middletown, Conn., 1981).

107. *CEC* 1:99.

108. *JMN* 5:72.

109. *JMN* 4:274.

110. *JMN* 4:45.

111. *JMN* 4:91.

112. "Historical Discourse," *Works* 11:44; *Nature, Collected Works* 1:7.

113. *JMN* 5:181.

114. *Nature, Collected Works* 1:44.

115. *JMN* 4:309.

116. *JMN* 4:309.

117. *JMN* 5:445.

118. *JMN* 7:22.

119. "Worship," *Works* 6:195, 199, 201.

120. "The Preacher," *Works* 10:210.

121. *JMN* 4:309.

122. *JMN* 5:478.

123. *JMN* 5:398.

124. *JMN* 5:287.

125. *JMN* 5:58.

126. *JMN* 5:380.

127. *JMN* 5:463.

128. *JMN* 5:334.

129. *JMN* 5:464.

130. "Eloquence," *Works* 8:115.

131. "Eloquence," *Works* 8:128.

132. *JMN* 5:91.

133. *JMN* 5:471.

134. The line in the Divinity School Address from *Collected Works* 1:85 was copied from Emerson's specific comments about Frost in *JMN* 5:463–64; see also Conrad Wright, "Emerson, Barzillai Frost, and the Divinity School Address," *Harvard Theological Review* 49 (1956), 19–43.

135. Emerson to Margaret Fuller, 12/12/39, *Letters* 2:242; Thoreau cited in Kenneth W. Cameron, "Emerson, Thoreau, Parson Frost, and 'The Problem,' " *ESQ* 6 (1957), 16.

136. The full citation from March 15, 1841, is as follows: "The religion I love is very laic. The clergy are as diseased, and as much possessed with a devil as the reformers." See Henry D. Thoreau, *Journal,* ed. John C. Broderick et al. (Princeton, 1981), 1:289.

137. Quitting the ministry freed Emerson to preach to a larger church, the national audience.

138. *JMN* 7:60.

139. *JMN* 5:37.

140. Theodore Parker, of course, did—and he vociferously noted the profound impact of Emerson's address.

141. "The Genuine Man," *Young Emerson Speaks*, 185.

142. *JMN* 5:464.

143. Wright, Stephen Railton, and David Robinson have come to different conclusions about the revolutionary nature of the Divinity School Address; see Railton, *Authorship and Audience: Literary Performance in the American Renaissance* (Princeton, 1991) and Robinson, "Poetry, Personality, and the Divinity School Address," *Harvard Theological Review* 82:2 (1989), 185–99. More recently Lisa Gortis and Tim Jensen have taken up this issue in *The Journal of Unitarian Universalist History* 24 (1997). See Lisa Gortis, "Consecrating a Rebellion: Emerson's Divinity School Address, David Friedrich Strauss, and the Historical Jesus," 1–16, and Tim Jensen, " 'Their own thought in motley. . .': Emerson's Divinity School Address and Henry Ware Jr.'s *Hints on Extemporaneous Preaching*," 17–28.

144. "Divinity School Address," *Collected Works* 1:81, 85.

145. "Divinity School Address," *Collected Works* 1:85.

146. "Divinity School Address," *Collected Works* 1:85.

147. "Divinity School Address," *Collected Works* 1:88.

148. *JMN* 5:75, 5:126.

149. "Divinity School Address," *Collected Works* 1:89.

5

THE TRANSFORMATION
OF GENIUS INTO
PRACTICAL POWER

In April of 1842, four years after he had delivered his momentous Divinity School Address and only weeks after the death of his son Waldo, Emerson characterized his life as a paradox. "I am *Defeated* all the time; yet to Victory I am born."[1] Approaching his fortieth year and at the pinnacle of his intellectual powers, Emerson reflected on a life of seeming defeats. A mediocre career at Harvard punctuated by unhappy stints of teaching school had brought him little more than hugely unfulfilled ambitions. Family tradition and a paucity of alternatives led to divinity school and a promising career in the Unitarian churches. Yet, as the minister of the prestigious Second Congregational Church in Boston at the age of twenty-five, Emerson had endured far more disappointment than satisfaction. Distraught by the tragic death of his young wife and disenchanted by his professional isolation and irrelevance, he had resigned from his pastorship at Second Church after three mostly miserable years. In 1836, he had published *Nature*, which, despite effusive praise from Thomas Carlyle and others, had failed to achieve any great change in New England culture. Effectively severing his ties to the Unitarian establishment with his 1838 address at the Harvard Divinity School, Emerson had once and for all grasped that he would never fulfill his ambitions, such as they were, in any church or within any denomination. Reviewing the singularly undistinguished record that comprised his career until the spring of 1842, he confessed that his vocational tribulations were "a sign of our impotence & that we are not yet ourselves."[2] Stubbornly optimistic even in the face of his son's death and his own professional "failures," Emerson remained hopeful that he would yet achieve greatness. "As long as I am weak, I shall talk of Fate," he confessed; but "whenever the God fills me with his fulness, I shall see the disappearance of Fate."[3]

Ever optimistic in the face of an underlying nagging disenchantment, and driven by grand ambitions, Emerson struggled to break free of his vocational purgatory. After several decades of nay-saying—no to Harvard, no to the ministry, and no to Brahmin Boston—Emerson found himself sufficiently mature and self-reliant to force fate to take the hindmost and to carve out the entirely novel, distinctly American vocation of public orator.[4] "After groaning thro' years of poverty & hard labor," Emerson concluded, "the mind perceives that really it has come the shortest road to a valuable position."[5] With no existing intellectual career to suit him, he assigned himself the task of creating what he called "a new theatre, a new art" by which he could fulfill his awesome aspirations.[6] Like Socrates, whose dialogues he read and reread throughout the 1840s, Emerson discovered that the greatest teachers never discover their pupils within traditional institutions. "Where do we find ourselves?" Emerson asked himself in the spring of 1842. "We wake & find ourselves on a stair; there are stairs below us up which we seem to have come; there are stairs above us many a one, they go up to heaven."[7]

Emerson's grand ascent to becoming a public intellectual came by means of an institution with which he had been familiar for a decade. Almost ten years earlier, on the evening of November 5, 1833, Emerson had delivered his first public lecture at the Masonic Temple in Boston. Conducted under the auspices of the Society of Natural History, it probably netted the lecturer the grand sum of ten dollars.[8] He liked the work and quickly arranged to give seven lectures the following year. Hardly imagining at that point that he would fashion public lecturing into a vocation, within a decade Emerson professed to be a lecturer. "I count this distinct vocation," he wrote in 1843, "which never leaves me in doubt what to do but in all times, places, & fortunes, gives me an open future, to be the great felicity of my lot."[9] In a most fortuitous stroke of fate, the lecture platform, this crucial vehicle of his success, came into its own at the very moment when Emerson had become disenchanted with being a minister, as the 1830s and 1840s witnessed the wholesale proliferation of lyceums, mercantile associations, and other such educational organizations throughout New England and the Northern United States. Similarly, technological innovations in printing, publishing, and distribution drove down the cost of the printed word and in time provided the means to satisfy affordably the public's burgeoning thirst for knowledge. By midcentury, the first hint of the means to create mass culture came into existence, resulting in what sociologist Alvin Gouldner styled "the dialectic of ideology and technology."[10] The rise of a culture industry enabled Emerson's emergence as "an American Prophet,"[11] or as peddler-turned-schoolteacher Amos Bronson Alcott grandiloquently declared: "there was no public lecture till Emerson made it," that Emerson called into being "a public to listen to the master and his disciples.

. . . That were a victory worth a life, since the lecture is the American invention, serving the country with impulse and thought of an ideal cast and conquering virtue. The lyceums are properly *Emersonia*, and we must substitute the founder's name for the thing he has invented."[12] Emerson both created and was created by the public lecture. The transformation of Emerson's genius into practical power illustrated the conjunction of the means and the man.

In the years after the Divinity School Address, Emerson's problem of vocation largely resolved itself. Behind the lectern, he located precisely those elements lacking in the library, classroom, and pulpit. The lecture circuit provided the genuine calling for which Emerson had searched in vain during the first third of his life. It featured a welcome if moderate income and deadlines that compelled the completion of work, as well as an outlet for accumulated knowledge, thus making his prodigious learning serve an eminently public end.[13] James Russell Lowell described him aptly in his 1871 *My Study Windows* when he called Emerson "The Lecturer." From the 1840s until the last decade of his life, a span of almost forty years, Emerson regularly delivered lectures, often as many as seventy or eighty in a year. He consistently ranked at the very pinnacle of his adopted profession. "It is a singular fact, that Mr. Emerson is the most steadily attractive lecturer in America," Lowell concluded. "Mr. Emerson always draws."[14]

Lecturing educated Emerson. Away from home and among the people with whom he shared long trips, cramped quarters, and smoke-filled hotel lobbies, Emerson exchanged his contemporaries' elemental alienation with a growing sense of utility and affinity. The lecture circuit saved the man who at times appeared stilted and uncomfortable in the company of others from the characteristic fate of so many members of the American thinking class. Lecturing and the concomitant weeks and months of annual treks that eventually included twenty-two states and Canada brought Emerson into vital contact with his compatriots. It proved to be the critical means for the Concord sage to observe at close hand the life not only of the self-selective audiences of his lectures but of the average American-in-motion whom he so earnestly sought to incorporate into his work. The road satisfied his determination to be one of those individuals who, he wrote in *Conduct of Life*, "is made of the same stuff of which events are made; is in sympathy with the course of things; can predict it. Whatever befalls, befalls him first; so that he is equal to whatever shall happen. A man who knows men, can talk well on politics, trade, law, war, religion."[15] Lecturing, traveling, and all the hardships they entailed proved the forge in which Emerson tested his mettle. His lecturing practices not only reflected his democratic philosophy, they helped to shape it. Both his linguistic game-playing and his avowed preference for lecturing over traditional philosophical discourse in the academy foreshadow American pragmatism and William James's and John Dewey's predilection for a philosophy embraced by the general public.[16] On the lecture circuit, Emerson achieved the relevance he craved.

Everything in Emerson's character and worldview, even his abiding idealism, steered him toward the lyceum and lecture hall. As early as 1832, two years before his first public lecture at the Natural History Society, Emerson had intimated that his peculiar talents necessitated a novel arena. In a sermon he delivered seven times, entitled "Find Your Calling," Emerson argued that God reveals to all "what his own peculiar talent is," and that with "constant effort" one could "bend his circumstances to his character."[17] Prognosticating his future, the preacher announced:

> We occasionally see an individual forsake all the usual paths of life and show men a new one better fitted than any other to his own powers. And as any man discovers a taste of any new kind, any new combination of powers, he tends toward such places and duties as will give occasion for their exercise. And this because great powers will not sleep in a man's breast. Everything was made for use. Great powers demand to be put in action, the greater they are with the more urgency.[18]

Only when he recognized his "assigned province of action" to be at the lectern, a fact that was "hidden from him for years," did he once and for all acknowledge that his "temporary" career in the church had only served to prepare him for a novel undertaking.[19]

That Emerson came to embrace the public lecture as a type of secular sermon over those in a church by no means meant that he no longer considered himself a preacher. He always did. Only the venue had changed. In "The Preacher," an essay published in the 1860s, Emerson suggested that his generation had come of age at a temporary nadir of religious faith. It was "the misfortune of this period that the cultivated mind has not the happiness and dignity of the religious sentiment. We are born too late for the old and too early for the new faith."[20] Preachers who remained within the church and struggled within the confines of the sermonic form had lost touch with the people and their needs.[21] "And if I had to counsel a young preacher," he continued, "I should say: When there is any difference felt between the foot-board of the pulpit and the floor of the parlor, you have not yet said that which you should say."[22] By the time Emerson perceived that he and even his most well-intentioned colleagues were barred from preaching "the noble Ethics of Nature, as contrast to the poverty stricken pulpit," it became obligatory to deliver the sermon out of doors.[23] He proceeded to preach his pantheistic vision of God-in-the-world where it belonged—in the street.

> We are all very sensible,—it is forced on us every day,—of the feeling that churches are outgrown; that the creeds are outgrown; that a technical theology no longer suits us. It is not the ill-will of people—no, indeed, but the incapacity for confining themselves there. The church is not large enough for the man; it cannot inspire the enthusiasm which is the parent of everything good in history, which makes the romance of history. For that enthusiasm you must have something greater than yourselves, and not less.[24]

Like Luther, Emerson sought to revitalize the intimate connection between religion and everyday life.[25] He abandoned the ministry precisely because it had failed to repair the rift between church and community, clergy and congregation, and metaphysics and physics. "The best study of metaphysics is physics," he declared in one lecture, clearly suggesting that theology and divinity school proved to be the wrong means to access the divine. While he greatly lamented the "unhappy divorce of Religion and Philosophy," he hardly sought to supplant the former with the latter.[26] Whatever was right about religious culture and practiced on Sunday could not help but be the tocsin for culture as a whole and preached every day of the week from all possible platforms. "Is not the meeting-house dedicated because men are not?" he asked. "Is not the Church opened & filled on Sunday because the commandments are not kept by the worshippers on Monday?"[27] In this sense, George Santayana aptly styled Emerson, who as a young man had quit the ministry and severed his ties to the church, "the Psyche of Puritanism."[28]

Emerson made his preference for the lecture platform and the lyceum over the pulpit and the church evident in his journals throughout the 1830s. Contrasting the relative merits of sermon and lecture as media for his personal aspirations and as they related to the broader sweep of American culture, Emerson repeatedly reflected upon the freedom and open-ended nature of the secular lecture. The very best parts of the sermon, he felt sure, could be incorporated into his lectures; and so much that tradition and propriety, so-called, precluded from the sermon occupied a rightful and prominent place in the public lecture. One was traditional and limited, the other, novel and open-ended. For Emerson, who held as his deepest conviction that "God is in every man" and everything, the lecture hall promised to serve as that great step, as well as a bridge, from the artificial and exclusive isolation of the pulpit and church toward a congregation of each and all.[29] "If I were called upon to charge a young minister, I would say Beware of Tradition: Tradition which

embarrasses life & falsifies all teaching. The sermons that I hear are all dead
of that ail[ment]."[30] Emerson believed that it was his calling "to show men
the nullity of churchgoing compared with a real exaltation of their being."[31]
In these transitional years, Emerson devoted far more time and energy to composing lectures than sermons. In fact, of his more than 160 original sermons,
he composed all but two before he delivered his first lecture. Although he continued to preach sermons more frequently than to deliver lectures and earned
more income from supply preaching than from lecture fees, Emerson directed
most of his mental energies into composing and perfecting his carefully
wrought essays in the sermonic tradition almost from the day he returned from
abroad. Virtually everything in Emerson's character drew him to a medium
that promised all the advantages of supply preaching without the estimable
disadvantages. Provided he drew an audience, he could profess whatever he
liked. He could expand his imagery and allusions to include a far more representative survey of his reading. He could deliver his "sermons" more than one
day per week. And at the lyceum there was no tradition compelling the speaker
to offer standard sermons and rote prayers or comparing him to the multitude
of conventional preachers who preceded and surrounded him. "Here is all the
true orator will ask," he noted in an 1839 journal entry titled "Lyceum";

> for here is a convertible audience & here are no stiff conventions that pre-
> scribe a method, a style, a limited quotation of books, & an exact respect
> to certain books, persons, or opinions. No, here everything is admissible,
> philosophy, ethics, divinity, criticism, poetry, humor, fun, mimicry, anec-
> dotes, jokes, ventriloquism. All the breadth & versatility of the most liberal
> conversation highest lowest personal local topics, all are permitted, and all
> may be combined in one speech; it is a panharmonicon.[32]

Emerson cherished this freedom every bit as much as he despised the con-
straints and false notes of the traditional sermon. Emerson drove home his
contrast of the lyceum and the church by concluding that the lecture-platform
was "a pulpit that makes other pulpits tame & ineffectual."[33] Small wonder,
then, that he assured his brother William in the spring of 1838 that he "shall
not preach more except from the Lyceum."[34]

The greatest difference between the lecture and the sermon was the
venue. The lyceum and lecture hall attracted a more diverse, inquisitive, energetic, and eager cross-section of the U.S. population than the Unitarian or any
other church. In contrast to the university classroom and the denominational
church, the lecture hall seemed to be a remarkably egalitarian medium that
one historian suggested "appeared to make knowledge readily accessible to

the common man."[35] Superior to a sermon presented to an exclusive congregation of half-hearted auditors or a book written, alas, to be read by only a few, the lecture, delivered day after day in cities and towns throughout the nation, afforded the prospect of achieving the eminence that resulted only from mass appeal. "A lecture is a new literature, which leaves aside all tradition, time, place, circumstance, & addresses an assembly as mere human beings," Emerson declared in the summer of 1839. "It is an organ of sublime power."[36]

Between Emerson's first public address in 1833 and his last in 1881, Emerson read one or another of his resplendent lectures an astonishing fifteen hundred times. From "Immortality" to "Water" to "New England Reformers" and from Portland, Maine, to St Paul, Minnesota, to San Francisco, California, Emerson carefully crafted his adopted vocation of public speaker. His oratorical career proved to be, as William Charvat astutely noted almost a half-century ago, "one of the most extraordinary phenomena in the history of American culture."[37] In time, effort, and remuneration, it was the central focus of his professional life. By the late 1830s, the time when his lecturing eclipsed his preaching, Emerson's career as a public speaker was poised to explode. It also became his chief source of earned income. In 1838, for example, he delivered thirty-five discourses, all but two in Massachusetts. Although his total earnings are difficult to determine, it is clear that he earned far more from the lecture platform than he could from the pulpit. "The pecuniary advantage of the Course," delivered on consecutive Wednesdays in Boston, "has been considerable."[38]

> Season tickets sold 319 for $620; Single tickets sold 373 for 186; [total] 806; deduct expenses 225; $568 net profit. The attendance on this course adding to the above list 85 tickets distributed by me to friends, will be about 439 persons on the average of an evening—& as it was much larger at the close than at the beginning I think 500 persons at the closing lectures. . . . A very gratifying interest on the part of the audience was evinced in the views offered—which were drawn chiefly out of the materials already collected in this Journal. The ten lectures were read on ten pleasant winter evenings on consecutive Wednesdays.[39]

Emerson's success in Boston translated to the surrounding towns, and, within a few years, to the whole of New England. He could not garnish such handsome fees outside of Boston, but he could expect a regular stipend of between ten and twenty dollars over and above his expenses.

The income Emerson generated from his lecture engagements proved critical to his entire family's financial security. The settlement of the Tucker estate in the mid-1830s relieved the economic distress that had forced the Emersons to move from place to place, caused Ruth to take in boarders, and otherwise compelled Ralph to scramble to secure sufficient resources. Emerson's purchase of Coolidge Castle, the family home in Concord, with the second installment of the Tucker legacy marked the turning point in his family's security. Nevertheless, until the death of his mother in 1853, Ralph assumed much of the financial responsibility for the family. After the tragic deaths of Edward and Charles, he still provided for his younger brother Bulkeley and materially assisted William, whose law practice and investments remained shaky for years. Emerson was not about to secure easy circumstances from his lecture fees, particularly before the 1860s and the height of his fame. The money generated from the circuit, nonetheless, made a huge difference in the family's finances. Emerson well understood that his income from investments and book sales, such as it was, did not meet their expenses. With an elderly mother, a wife, and young children to look after, Emerson's career as a lecturer provided income that he could procure nowhere else.

In the almost four decades of his lecturing, Emerson acquired between one-third and one-half of his income and almost all of his earnings on the road. At times, he lamented the fact that economics played such a large role in his professional machinations. "Whenever I get into debt," he facetiously intoned in 1843, "which usually happens once a year, I must make the plunge into this great odious river of travellers, into these cold eddies of hotels, and boarding houses—farther into these dangerous precincts of charlatanism, namely lectures."[40] The size of his audiences and the resulting receipts figure prominently in his letters home, often in humorous ways. "The first evening I thought the audience very small, perhaps 200 but they told me it was made of some of their best people," he wrote Lidian. "This night the audience was considerably increased, possibly there were 300. . . . I doubt I am not in the way of paying my debts pecuniary, which I dimly call to mind, was one of my wife's reasons for sending me forth into this remote field."[41] At other times, Emerson saw lecturing as the best means then available to make money doing that work for which he considered himself peculiarly suited. A successful evening always elicited a happy note in his letters. "And they listen intelligently enough," he wrote of a Philadelphia audience, "nay declare that they are delighted."[42] As much as he might have liked to ignore the financial issues involved, Emerson indubitably discerned his dependence on the continued success of his lecturing.

Emerson's lecture tours represented a financial venture replete with risks and up-front expenses, such as those for advertising and transportation. Despite the fact that lecturing was "always attended with a degree of uncertainty," Emerson understood that it could also be lucrative.[43] As the editor of his early lectures noted, "If, as he once wrote, his journals were his savings bank, his lecture series were his capital investment, and one that paid on the whole excellent returns."[44] Even as early as 1835, Emerson counseled Carlyle that a lecture tour of New England could pay handsomely for a speaker of his stature, or "names' sake."[45] He informed his English friend that individuals such as he "have undertaken courses of lectures, and have been well paid. Dr. Spurzheim received probably three thousand dollars in the few months that he lived here. Mr. Silliman, a Professor of Yale College, has lately received something more than that for a course of fifteen or sixteen lectures on Geology."[46] Under the heading "Income and Expenses" in the same letter, Emerson elaborated further on the pecuniary aspects of the trade.

> All our lectures are usually delivered in the same hall, built for the purpose. It will hold 1,200 persons; 900 are thought a large assembly. The expenses of rent, lights, doorkeeper, &c. for this hall, would be $12 each lecture. The price of $3 is the least that might be demanded for a single ticket of admission to the course,—perhaps $4; $5 for a ticket admitting a gentleman and lady. So let us suppose we have 900 persons paying $3 each, or $2,700. . . . If the lectures succeed in Boston, their success is insured at Salem, a town thirteen miles off, with a population of 15,000. They might, perhaps, be repeated at Cambridge, three miles from Boston, and probably at Philadelphia, thirty-six hours distant. At New York anything literary has hitherto had no favor. The lectures might be fifteen or sixteen in number, of about an hour each. They might be delivered, one or two in each week. And if they met with sudden success, it would be easy to carry on the course simultaneously at Salem, and Cambridge, and in the city.[47]

It is clear, then, that even as early as 1835 and in only his second year of lecturing, Emerson not only understood the relatively large sums involved in the lecture business, but also already understood both the benefits and shortcomings of the lyceum system. At least in Boston, financial considerations prompted him to offer his own series of lectures whenever possible.

It is difficult to calculate Emerson's exact year-to-year income from lecturing. At the beginning of his career in the 1830s, Emerson's pay averaged fifteen dollars per lecture. By the 1860s and the height of his popularity, Emerson commanded five times that amount. In 1865, for example, for the sixty-five of seventy-five lectures for which there is a record of payment (Emerson regularly read a Sunday lecture *gratis*) the total receipts came to $3,077. From another perspective, in Massachusetts alone, where his expenses were minimal, he delivered at least nine hundred lectures between 1833 and 1881, or slightly over half of his total. Subtracting the hundred or so talks for which Emerson received no compensation, even at the modest stipend of twenty-five dollars per lecture, Emerson earned not less than twenty thousand dollars in his home state alone. Of course, not everyone fared as well as the Concord sage. Stipends depended upon both the lecturer and the location, as Emerson explained to his Scottish friend and Unitarian minister, Alexander Ireland.

> In regard to the remuneration of Lectures here, we have all rates as we have all merits. I have formerly read courses of Lectures on my own account to classes collected by advertisement in the newspapers: and for a course of ten lectures I once received, after the payment of all expenses, 576 dollars; or, 57 dollars for each lecture. That is the highest payment I ever received. From the Boston Lyceum, last winter, I received 50 dollars for each lecture of a course of seven; by a previous agreement. And the Lyceum was no loser, as I was told. These are city prices. I often read lectures to our country Lyceums, which usually pay their Lecturer $10.00, & his travelling expenses.[48]

By the late 1840s, Emerson regularly delivered at least fifty public lectures annually and grossed in excess of two thousand dollars. This sum represented many times the profits generated by his publications. In fact, Emerson fully grasped that sales of his books often depended upon his success on the lecture circuit. After a series of well-attended lectures in Philadelphia in January of 1843, Emerson wrote his publisher, James Munroe & Company, that there were "several persons in Philadelphia who desire me to see that my little books should be put into the shops here for sale. Mr. John Pennington, Bookseller, is very willing & desirous to receive them, *on sale*. I wish you would send to him 50 copies of the 'Essays,' and, say, Ten or Twenty copies of 'Nature,' & as many copies of the 'Orations,' at Dartmouth, & at Waterville, & at Cambridge."[49] As his books sold inconsistently, Emerson could not live without the lecture fees, as he wrote his brother in 1843. "I am poor enough to need to lecture."[50]

That a significant percentage of his annual earnings derived from lecturing was not lost on Emerson. His voluminous correspondence devoted to arrangements, schedules, and fees testified to the close attention he paid to the financial angle of the vocation. Despite his 1833 lamentation, "O what a wailing tragedy is this world considered in reference to money-matters," his letters are full of observations and calculations related to income.[51] With the lyceum and lecture business in its infancy in the 1830s and 1840s, Emerson was obliged to blaze his own path through the maze of self-promotion, advance bookings, travel logistics, and the like. Generally, Emerson engaged in two distinct types of arrangements: guest speaking and private subscription. The guest lectures, which were done by invitation, proved far easier on a number of levels, though they often did not pay so well as the private ones. For the invited public lectures, Emerson simply agreed to give one or more performances under the auspices of a lyceum, mercantile association, or some similar organization, which generally paid a flat fee in addition to expenses. In the 1840s and 1850s the honorarium averaged approximately twenty-five dollars. By 1865, it had doubled. More than 80 percent of Emerson's lectures were by invitation. Although fewer in number, the private subscriptions could be highly remunerative; for example, he earned over $1,000 in a series of six lectures delivered in Philadelphia in January of 1854.[52] Of course, these entailed more risk, as it was always possible that inclement weather or other unanticipated circumstances might greatly diminish attendance. "I beg you to know," he wrote Lidian of one unfortunate series of lectures, "that as far as money results go, my lecturing in N.Y. has had no success. The price of tickets is one half the price of last year & the expenses of the hall &c are the same as last year . . . , so that my payment for my work is as I counted something less than $9.00 per lecture the modest compensation I ever received except once in Billerica."[53] Probably more importantly, the privately organized lectures necessitated a great deal of effort relating to booking the hall, promotion, and other incidental arrangements. Emerson particularly disliked attending to these details, so that with the exception of Boston, Emerson preferred lecturing through the agency of the lyceum or some other organization. Making travel arrangements proved sufficiently daunting by itself.

Emerson seems to have been highly successful in distinguishing between commodity and commercialism in his work. He sold his lectures and depended upon their marketability, to be sure. Lecturing was big business for the scholar. Nevertheless, he never reified his intellectual product over which he worked so passionately. To be successful, he had to be popular, but he was not in the same business as P. T. Barnum, nor even Wendell Phillips, who delivered his "The Lost Arts" oration more than one thousand times.[54] No absent-minded professor, Emerson exhibited a keen awareness of the tenuous relationship between the scholar and the nascent capitalist system. He understood that no agency of the government or of society was about to confer upon him the sort of honorific benefice that, for example, Periclean Athens bestowed upon its Olympic victors. Like it or not, Emerson and other intellectuals who had voluntarily departed the circumscribed boundaries of the church or college were obliged to earn their own livelihood. Rather than railing against the materialistic spirit of the times, at least as it related to the production of culture, Emerson simply demanded that his contemporaries (and posterity) understand the nature and necessity of his foray into the marketplace.

> Society quarrels with the clerisy or learned class if they sell their wisdom for money. But Society compels them to this course. The Church is not now the resort of all or almost all this class. They are gone out hence, & the ecclesiastics are not drawn to the church by their nature but by convenience. Of course the church has lost the veneration of the people & they do not like to pay for its support. Meantime the Scholars out of the church have the same needs as before. . . . Shall they then, since the state is no state, gives them no place, desert also their function in the commonwealth, untimely deny themselves & those whom they ought to serve the first means of education? . . . Or shall they forsake their duties since they are so straitened by your penury, & go dig in the fields & buy & sell in the markets to the detriment of all learning & civility in the Commonwealth, in order that they may have that share of external power which their insight has made a higher need to them? If not, then leave open to them the resource of selling the works which are the only vendible product of so many laborious days & watching nights, & whose price ought to be esteemed sacred & not vile.[55]

After resigning his pastorate, Emerson consigned himself to the vicissitudes of the emerging literary marketplace and a mercurial public. He understood that the necessity of hawking intellectual commodities contained a silver lining, serving as an impediment to the snobbish elitism of his erstwhile Brahmin colleagues. Often animated by the prospect of putting his work "on the block," Emerson disdained the sour grapes of those who felt their intellects slighted by "the era of Trade," in which "every thing is made subservient to that agency."[56] Producers and disseminators of culture had to make their learned discourses compelling and relevant. As with all illustrious figures in history, they were responsible for creating the means to be ingenuously representative; as Emerson put it, "the greatest men have been most thoughtful for the humblest."[57]

For Emerson, as with all individuals whose success depended upon a degree of public appeal, there existed a substantial and unmistakable distinction between popularity and pandering. He held equally in contempt those effete scholars who stumbled feebly among the common folk and the strumpetting entertainers whose sole end was the fleeting glory of a momentary notoriety. With his characteristic optimism, Emerson fervently believed that the representative nature of his ideas ensured him an audience; at once, he could remain true to his inner convictions and have a broad appeal. "It is a secret which every intellectual man quickly learns," he wrote in *Essays: Sec-*

ond Series, "that, beyond the energy of his possessed and conscious intellect, he is capable of a new energy by abandonment to the nature of things; that beside his privacy of power as an individual man, there is a great public power, on which he can draw." That the citizenry could recognize and pay obeisance to a genuine teacher constituted the very marrow of Emerson's political thinking. His enduring repute justified his faith in his fellow Americans.[58]

Contemporaries had difficulty accounting for Emerson's growing renown, particularly insofar as he did not possess charisma in any traditional sense. Detractors and admirers alike called attention to his peculiar demeanor on the lecture platform as well as to his manner of delivery, which all agreed was uniquely and deceptively engaging. In contrast to many others who met with great success on the lyceum circuit, Emerson eschewed the usual physical gestures and gyrations that were part of the evolving practice of delivering a lecture. Disdaining wild hand gestures, foot stomping, or similarly staged antics, Emerson and his unimpressive voice more resembled Jonathan Edwards than P. T. Barnum. "We call it a singular fact" that Emerson is popular, noted James Russell Lowell, "because we Yankees are thought to be fond of the spread-eagle style, and nothing can be more remote from that than his."[59] Anyone attending an Emerson lecture was likely to be a bit disappointed by the appearance of this "slender and bony" person who "in his plain suit of ill-fitting black, looked not unlike a New England country schoolmaster."[60] One admirer in 1870 wrote that "the lectures themselves are poetry and music," while William Cullen Bryant, a rather unsympathetic observer, noted that the lecturer "possesses great powers of language, great felicity of illustrations which he manages with a certain poetical grace."[61] One listener rhapsodized that "his voice was unmatchable by any I ever heard; it had a potency and effect of eloquence with not a single one of the traditional characteristics of it."[62]

Even as Emerson consistently drew audiences, critical assessments varied considerably, with negative reviews outnumbering positive ones by a wide margin. Some faulted Emerson for his utter lack of showmanship, and others, like a writer in the Hartford, Connecticut, *Courant*, thought him "fully saturated" with what he called "Boston Conceit,"[63] which explained his apparent contempt for histrionics. Even Margaret Fuller, who believed, as Emerson put it, that "the best of me" was in his public performances, noted that her friend "always seemed to be on stilts" when lecturing.[64] Partisan critics often offered the harshest assessments, like the writer to the Milwaukee *Sentinel* in 1854 who considered Emerson to be spreading "a scurrilous Tom-Paine-ism" that was a distinct danger to the morals of that frontier community. "In all the lecture, there was not one recognition of Christianity as the foundation of culture any more than if it had been a Pagan speaker and a Pagan audience."[65] Similarly, in Kenosha, Wisconsin, in 1860, the editor of the *Democrat* accused Emerson of a trinity of sins: "He is an infidel—an abolitionist—a monarchist—all these, though he talks as musically as any dying swan."[66] Lumped together with Theodore Parker, Wendell Phillips, and William Lloyd Garrison, Emerson "formed a moral and political cabal which is a curse to the country."[67] As for content, reviewers seemed to be in a singular quandary. When it came to their obligatory terse summary of the substance of the lecture, they found themselves utterly at a loss, as encapsulating an Emerson oration proved an exercise in futility. A writer for the Providence, Rhode Island, *Manufacturers' and Farmers' Journal* confessed that "there was much that he said that I could not possibly understand. . . . Some persons here in Providence have not yet acquired a taste for Germano-Sartor-Resartorism."[68] Emerson himself confided to Lidian that a typical evaluation called him "very fine & poetical but a little puzzling."[69]

On the whole, Emerson dismissed reviewers and their criticisms, so long as they seemed to have no measurable impact upon his ability to draw an audience.[70] Always prepared to be misquoted, mistaken, and misunderstood, he easily reconciled himself to the critics, reasoning that misunderstanding was both inevitable and the perpetual plight of all great intellects. "Speak what you think now in hard words, and to-morrow speak what to-morrow thinks in hard words again, though it contradict every thing you said to-day," he declared in "Self-Reliance." "—'Ah, so you shall be sure to be misunderstood.'—Is it so bad then to be misunderstood? Pythagoras was misunderstood, and Socrates, and Jesus, and Luther, and Copernicus, and Galileo, and Newton, and every pure and wise spirit that ever took flesh. To be great is to be misunderstood."[71] Emerson consistently acknowledged that he was directly responsible for many of the difficulties audiences had with his lectures, particularly those pertaining to grasping his overall argument. "I need hardly say to any one acquainted with my thoughts that I have no System," he confessed in a journal entry in 1839.[72] As frustrating as it was for reviewers and listeners alike, there was no way to synopsize Emerson.

Throughout his public career Emerson remained acutely conscious of his connection to the people who came to hear him at lyceums, library societies, mercantile associations, and similar venues. Few topics elicited more ink in his journals and letters than the process and problems of communication in lecture hall. He readily conceded the inevitability of misunderstandings between himself and his audiences, especially since he proffered no facile answers. Anyone looking for a quick fix or a lecture on "philosophy made simple" was bound to be disappointed. "People came, it seems, to my lectures with expectation that I was to realize the Republic I described, & ceased to come when they found this reality no nearer. They mistook me."[73] Very much like Socrates' message to Glaucon in the *Republic*, Emerson's teaching of self-reliance explicitly precluded the possibility of directly communicating the ultimate lessons. The teacher can show the way, can provide encouraging glimpses along the journey, but cannot undertake it for anyone else. "It is the essence of truth of character that a man should follow his own thought; that he should not be accustomed to adopt his motives or modes of action from any other but should follow the leading of his own mind like a little child," Emerson frequently repeated. "The genuine man is always consistent for he has but one leader."[74] Self-culture necessitated a solitary voyage.

Emerson did not shy away from the implications of his doctrine of self-reliance and its ramifications for his chosen vocation. His disdain for communicating easy, spurious answers to audiences hungry for them entailed risk. "I fear the popular notion of success stands in direct opposition in all points to the real and wholesome success. One adores public opinion, the other private opinion; one fame, the other desert; one feats, the other humility; one lucre, the other love; one monopoly, the other hospitality of mind."[75] Echoing a theme from his Divinity School Address, what he termed "real and wholesome success," he believed, emanated directly from his provocation of his audience to seek their own solutions. Learning through even the most felicitous medium was a challenge, so anyone who attended his discourses intent on gaining easy answers was apt to be disappointed. Emerson made it clear that he had no patience for laziness. "I hate this shallow Americanism," he quipped in his famous lecture on success, "which hopes to get rich by credit, to get knowledge by raps on midnight tables, to learn the economy of the mind by phrenology, or skill without study, or mastery without apprenticeship, or the sale of goods through pretending that they sell, or power through making believe that you are powerful, or through a packed jury or caucus, bribery and 'repeating' votes, or wealth by fraud."[76] Emerson was equally contemptuous of lyceum lecturers who professed to have all the answers. Of Horace Greeley, he ironically observed: "He preceded me, by a few days, and people had flocked together, coming thirty and forty miles to hear him speak; as was right, for he does all their thinking and theory for them, for two dollars a year."[77] Emerson offered no shortcuts.

For a nation of people in a hurry to make a quick buck, who seemed to partake in the "popular notion of success," articulating such an uncompromising, even caustic, directive might well have proven unpopular.[78] At times, Emerson could be harsh indeed. In "Books," an oration he delivered on numerous occasions, Emerson upbraided the lazy and ignorant.

> If you know that—for instance in geometry, if you have read Euclid and Laplace,—your opinion has some value; if you do not know these, you are not entitled to give any opinion on the subject. Whenever any skeptic or bigot claims to be heard on the questions of intellect and morals, we ask if he is familiar with the books of Plato, where all his pert objections have once for all been disposed of. If not, he has no right to our time. Let him go and find himself the answer there.[79]

Nevertheless, Emerson remained popular, drawing large and mostly enthusiastic audiences, for several complementary reasons. First, his exemplary personal demeanor and consistency of character disclosed themselves wherever he ventured. According to contemporary observers, everything about him suggested that here was a man who lived precisely as he lectured. Typical are the words of Lowell who observed that "the whole life of the man is distilled in the clear drop of every sentence, and behind each word we divine the force of a noble character."[80] His utter lack of hypocrisy, or even the semblance of it, Emerson well understood, was critical to his success on the lecture platform. "The same reality pervades all teaching," he noted; "The man may teach by doing, and not otherwise. If he can communicate himself he can teach, but not by words."[81] In Emerson's characteristic fashion, he turned what might be considered his special genius or talent into a universal quality. His success merely reflected his "connection" with a theme so widespread that everyone perceived its truth. Emerson hoped that, like the true poet, he was "representative," that he stood "among partial men for the complete man, and apprises us not of his wealth, but of the commonwealth."[82] Assiduously avoiding self-congratulation, Emerson regularly reflected upon the genius necessary for and the great barriers to effective instruction, especially for the hugely diverse audiences he regularly addressed as he toured the nation. A passage in "The American Scholar," his Phi Beta Kappa oration of 1837, focused on the critical element of self-revelation in the art of teaching.

> The orator distrusts at first the fitness of his frank confessions,—his want of knowledge of the persons he addresses,—until he finds that he is the complement of his hearers;—that they drink his words because he fulfils for them their own nature; the deeper he dives into his privatest secretest presentiment,—to his wonder he finds, this is the most acceptable, most public, and universally true. The people delight in it; the better part of every man feels, This is my music; this is myself.[83]

One way or another, those who found themselves enchanted by Emerson felt wholeheartedly that the full man was contained in his lecture. Audiences came away with the conviction that the word and the man were one. To them, Emerson was neither showman nor charlatan.

In addition to the lecturer's unmatched sincerity, Emerson's public achievement rested on his ability to convey his sanguine, resolute conviction that his audience—each and every listener in fact—had the wherewithal to undertake the kind of intellectual journey he proposed in his orations. Determined "to make the acquaintance with the spiritual dominion of every human mind," Emerson sought to impart in his lectures the fundamental tenet that everyone possessed strong, capable intellects characterized by largely untapped reasoning faculties, which as citizens and free individuals they were obliged to develop to the fullest. In so many words, Emerson congratulated his audiences for attending the lyceum, for here was a first step and irrefutable sign of their desire for knowledge. It could not be gainsaid that they were in attendance to improve their intellects. "I shall assume that the aim of each young man in this association," he declared before the Mechanics' Apprentices' Library Association on January 25, 1841, "is the very highest that belongs to a rational mind."[84] Emerson relied on his unique ability to communicate these two intangibles in his auditors: both the desirability and possibility of developing their spiritual and intellectual selves. Inside each person resided the requisite materials for fulfillment. "If I could persuade men to listen to their interior convictions, if I could express, embody their interior convictions, that were indeed life," he confided in his journals. "It were to cease being a figure & to act the action of a man."[85]

Acutely attuned to the intimate relationship of style and substance in his public orations, Emerson believed that a heartfelt teaching, whether positive or negative, admonitory or hopeful, of necessity had to permeate both components of any discourse. The mode Emerson strove to develop to complement his message was at once simple, powerful, and indigenous. Eloquence entailed trying to speak in an unstilted, simple style that acknowledged rhetorically what he proclaimed to be the essence of the lectures. The nation's aggressive, expansive, democratic institutions, as reflected in the marketplace, the courthouse, and on the hustings, produced a language with an eloquence all its own. Admiration of these commercial and political institutions required not just their praise but the adoption of their uniquely American expressiveness. "Every one has felt how superior in force is the language of the street to that of the academy," Emerson unflinchingly declared. "The street must be one of his schools. Ought not the scholar to be able to convey his meaning in terms as short and strong as the porter or truckman uses to convey his?"[86] Even as he fell far short of a rough streetwise eloquence, his respect for a common style represented the very heart of Emerson's intuitive democratic sense.

Nowhere else did he proclaim so unambiguously his faith in the American workingman's latent talents than in his conscious attempt to grasp the rhetorical power of everyday language.

To Emerson the simple style was uniquely American. Contemptuous of what he considered the stilted, foreign demeanor of his father's generation that so many of his Brahmin contemporaries lamely copied, Emerson sought to leapfrog "that early ignorant & transitional *Month-of-March* in our New England culture" in order to revive the plain style of his Puritan precursors. Emerson disdained the orator who was detached from the vital wellspring of the everyday, from life and death. "It is true undoubtedly that every preacher should strive to pay his debt to his fellowmen by making his communication intelligible to the common capacity," he noted to himself. " 'John Evangelist,' says Luther, 'was simple & spake also simply but every word in John weigheth two tons.' " The Puritans had understood that whatever the congregation— and it should be that of all people—eloquence required a style that engendered forceful communication. All else was deception. As much as he dismissed the theology of Calvin and his New England descendants, Emerson respected its earthy, emotive style, which he frequently praised over that of his erstwhile Unitarian colleagues. With virtually the sole exception of William Ellery Channing, Emerson scoffed at the dullness of Unitarian preaching. The vitality of the democracy demanded a forceful technique like that of the Methodist Edward Taylor, who "by seeing the man within the sailor" incorporated a robust earthiness into his sermons. "How he conciliates, how he humanizes! how he exhilarates & ennobles! Beautiful philanthropist! godly poet! the Shakspeare of the sailor & the poor." Taylor had tapped into that vigorous American tradition of oratory that the Puritans had richly prized.[87]

Emerson's style also reflected his deep conviction concerning the splendor of everyday language. "Beauty must come back to the useful arts, and the distinction between the fine and the useful arts be forgotten," he wrote in *Essays: First Series*. "In nature, all is useful, all is beautiful."[88] With Walt Whitman, whom he inspired, Emerson discovered what he required in the everyday, which he celebrated with the relish of a poet. Emerson's poetry never rose to the level of greatness to be sure, but his prose occasionally soared in large measure because of his intuitive sense of the comeliness of everyday speech and imagery. Like his friend the sculptor Horatio Greenough, Emerson believed that the "beautiful rests on the foundation of the necessary." A plain, simple style, "as the carpenter's stretched cord, if you hold your ear close enough, is musical in the breeze."[89] For Emerson, listening was the critical analog of lecturing, just as he understood that "the teacher should be the complement of the pupil."[90] Lecturers, no matter how great, did not create beauty, but collected, refined, and returned to their audiences what was their creation all along. Beauty and truth, which for all Platonists are inseparable, the great poet might more readily recognize, but their essence was nonetheless as universal as humanity itself. "I ask not for the great, the remote, the romantic; what is doing in Italy or Arabia; what is Greek art, or Provencal Minstrelsy," Emerson asserted in his 1837 "American Scholar" address. "I embrace the common, I explore and sit at the feet of the familiar, the low."[91] A Harvard graduate, a truly prodigious reader, and a traveler thrice to Europe and once to Africa, Emerson nonetheless felt inspired by what he called "the ballad in the street."[92]

The beauty of everyday language translated into force. The simple style of plain prose worked because it was the best and only means to communicate with the diverse audiences on the lecture circuit. Lecturers or intellectuals had to seize upon the rudimentary toughness of the language of the street and use it to advantage or all their efforts would come to naught. "And I confess to some pleasure from the stinging rhetoric of a rattling oath in the mouth of truckmen & teamsters. How laconic & brisk it is by the side of a page of the North American Review. Cut these words & they would bleed; they are vascular & alive; they walk & run." Perhaps eloquence could be taught in a college class, but as Emerson wrote in *Society and Solitude*, it could only be tested outside the academy. The real measure of the intellectual came when he or she sought to communicate with the people at large. Thinking of his own evolution, Emerson opined: "The best university that can be recommended to a man of ideas is the gauntlet of the mobs."[93]

Emerson criticized his friends of the Transcendentalist circle for an eccentricity that needlessly inhibited vital communication. As much as he admired his companion and neighbor Bronson Alcott, Emerson lamented his inability to reach the common man. "Alcott & [Charles] Lane want feet," he wrote in his journal; "they are always feeling of their shoulders to find if their wings are sprouting; but next best to wings are cowhide boots, which society is always advising them to put on."[94] Even Thoreau at times failed Emerson's democratic test. "Talking one day, of a public discourse, Henry remarked, that whatever succeeded with the audience was bad. I said, 'Who would not like to write something which all can read, like Robinson Crusoe? and who does not see with regret that his page is not solid with a right materialistic treatment, which delights everybody?' "[95] Far less contemptuous of his audiences than his young friend, Emerson concurred with Thoreau that one must never pander to the public or seek popular acclaim as its own end. He routinely whispered to himself, "when you come to write Lyceum lectures, remember that you are not to say, What must be said in a Lyceum? but what discoveries or stimulating thoughts have I to impart to a thousand persons? not what they will expect to hear but what is fit for me to say."[96] There could be no other proper audience than the people, and their critical judgment he believed to be more often right than wrong. It was a matter of faith that the people could discern the great from the pretenders. This faith, which developed largely through his observations of his fellow countrymen, fueled Emerson's devotion to the public lecture.

Despite the countenance of a country pastor and the awkward demeanor of a scholar, Emerson steadfastly pursued his lecturing career, always thrilled by the possibilities therein. The combination of a profound desire for relevance and his unwavering conviction that all knowledge had to be put to some great purpose proved a potent impetus driving him from Concord and his cozy familial surroundings. Emerson never lost sight of the potential power he wielded each time he mounted the stage. "When I address a large assembly, as last Wednesday, I am always apprised what an opportunity is there," he observed in the winter of 1844, "for painting in fire my thought, & being agitated to agitate."[97] By his late thirties, Emerson fully comprehended that, far more than merely a means to a livelihood, his lecturing had come to constitute the cornerstone of his professional life. His special gift, as inapt as it seemed to his talents, manifested itself most forcefully before a live audience. Calling himself an "incorrigible spouting Yankee," he exclaimed to Carlyle, "how natural it is to me to run to these places! Besides, I am always lured on by the hope of saying something which shall stick by the good boys."[98]

Also critical to Emerson's success was his unfeigned admiration for the achievements and progress he saw all around him. As he traveled from place to place, Emerson bore witness to the energy and ingenuity of the people who came to hear him. He utilized with brilliant effectiveness a keen awareness of his immediate environment, or what one Cincinnati commentator called his "plain *common sense.*" By urging Americans to address their cultural development with the same vigor and urgency with which they pursued fortunes, Emerson endeavored to link the material and intellectual, the commonplace and the ethereal. Unlike itinerant preachers who so vigorously contrasted spirit and matter, Emerson delighted in the natural and material. As early as the publication of *Nature*, Emerson had praised prosperity as a "mercenary benefit" that "has respect to a farther good. A man is fed, not that he may be fed, but that he may work." He possessed a gift, perhaps unique among his contemporaries, for calling upon his audiences to engage in intellectual pursuits foreign to their lives without disparaging their hard-won material victories in establishing their communities, pursuing their livelihoods, and providing for their families. Convinced that the mental and the material were hardly antithetical, Emerson declared in "The Young American" that he sought "to speak of the signs of that which is the sequel of trade" rather than its antithesis. He envisioned his message of self-culture as the intellectual complement to Americans' headlong pursuit of material prosperity. As a national idealist prophet, Emerson believed himself to be the harbinger of the nation's next giant step toward greatness.[99]

In the course of decades on the lecture circuit, Emerson had ample opportunity to hone what he believed was his truly American vocation. Emerson ultimately viewed the lecturer as a uniquely American figure, connected with the great New England Congregational ministers of the past and their tradition of skilled oratory and pulpit eloquence. Emerson identified himself with the Puritan ministers of the past, who "were the victims of the same faith with which they whipped & persecuted other men, and their sermons are strong, imaginative, fervid, & every word a cube of stone."[100] Like them, he forcefully combined the material and spiritual, the mundane and the transcendent, in a manner that he hoped infused his message with a divine quality. In the new era, where God was immanent and notions of human depravity had been discarded, Emerson sought to imbue his lectures, even those on such worldly topics as success and books and clubs, with a type of eloquence once manifested in the meetinghouse. The lecture functioned as the bridge to a new spiritualism that in time would supplant the dead worship of forms so characteristic of contemporary religious institutions. "Cursed is preaching,— the better it is, the worse. A preacher is a bully," he sniped in his journal.[101] "But presently there will arise a race of preachers who will take such hold of the omnipotence of truth that they will blow the old falsehoods to shreds with the breath of their mouth."[102] When he wrote to Carlyle in 1837, that he "religiously read lectures every winter," the particular adverb had been painstakingly chosen.[103] What he had sought but failed to find as an ordained Unitarian minister, he resolutely pursued in the lyceum and from the lecture platform. Emerson never doubted the rectitude of his move from the ministry to the lecture hall, which ironically he undertook to conserve the revolutionary aspects of pulpit eloquence. "The common experience is, that the man fits himself as well as he can to the customary details of that work or trade he falls into, and tends it as a dog turns a spit," he declared in "Self-Reliance." "Then is he a part of the machine he moves; the man is lost. Until he can manage to communicate himself to others in his full stature and proportion, he does not yet find his vocation. He must find in that an outlet for his character, so that he may justify his work to their eyes."[104] The lecture platform provided Emerson with that crucial medium by which he could express himself. Emerson's communicative endowment proved to be the irreducible key to his eloquence, which in turn undergirded his extraordinary popularity. It was the sum and substance of his genius.

Eloquence was a subject to which Emerson returned time and again during his long public career. What it was, how it worked, and whether he in fact possessed it were frequent topics in his journals, letters, and essays. Even at the age of twenty-five, Emerson was already preoccupied by the subject, as he recounted to his brother Charles his disappointment with an oration delivered by Edward Everett. "In short during this very pleasing performance," he noted with an ironic twist,

> I was many times reminded of Mr Everett's remark upon the ancients that they made the greatest advances in arts & commerce & politics & yet in each, thro' some strange mischance fell short of the last advance. So Mr E. with noble elements for eloquence, was all but eloquent. I felt that the voice should have thrilled me as a trumpet. I only heard it with pleasure. I felt that he should have made me laugh & cry at his will. He never touched me.[105]

As he turned to the lecture platform, Emerson sought the very emotional connection with his audience that Everett had failed to achieve. With nothing like the forensic skills of his old teacher, Emerson nevertheless possessed that singular filament that had eluded Everett. True eloquence, the ability to connect with an audience on an emotional level, required a combination of humility and engagement that could neither be learned nor pretended. "Eloquence is the appropriate organ of the highest personal energy," he explained in his essay on the topic.[106]

> No gifts, no graces, no power of wit or learning or illustration will make any amends for want of this. All audiences are just to this point. Fame of voice or of rhetoric will carry people a few times to hear a speaker; but they soon begin to ask, "What is he driving at?" and if this man does not stand for anything, he will be deserted. A good upholder of anything which they believe, a fact-speaker of any kind, they will long follow; but a pause in the speaker's own character is very properly a loss of attraction. The preacher enumerates his classes of men and I do not find my place therein; I suspect then that no man does. Everything is my cousin; and whilst he speaks things, I feel that he is touching some of my relations, and I am uneasy; but whilst he deals in words we are released from attention. If you would lift me you must be on higher ground. If you would liberate me you must be free. If you would correct my false view of facts,—hold up to me the same facts in the true order of thought, and I cannot go back from the new conviction.[107]

The expressiveness largely denied him in the confines of the pulpit, he readily discovered while preaching to multitudes in lyceums and lecture halls across the nation. "But eloquence must be attractive, or it is none. The virtue of books is to be readable, and of orators to be interesting."[108] Emerson's eloquence was proof of his efficacy.

The middling sorts of people on the make who attended the lyceum fueled Emerson's creative energies. He fed off the folk and relished his interaction with the people he addressed. By making his lectures sparkle with an eloquence his audiences naturally intuited and to which they responded so warmly, Emerson found the fulfillment that he had written about in his youthful journals and sermons. Nearly all his auditors were struck by how the force of his convictions came through in his lectures. "I have observed that in all public speaking," he remarked in one essay, "the rule of the orator begins, not in the array of his facts, but when his deep conviction, and the right and necessity he feels to convey that conviction to his audience,—when these shine and burn in his address; when the thought which he stands for gives its own authority to him, adds to him a grander personality, gives him valor, breadth, and new intellectual power, so that not he, but mankind, seems to speak through his lips."[109] Emerson located the substance of his discourses, then, in that vital region he wonderfully staked out between pomposity and pandering, avoiding the hollow display of a detached genius on the one hand and the "mere prostitution of the intellect," as Aunt Mary Moody Emerson once styled it, on the other.[110] Neither did Emerson use artifice or rhetorical ruses in order to win the easy approval of the public he deeply respected, nor did he haughtily throw metaphysical dust in their eyes. That was his special and unique talent, for which he was repaid by an enduring popularity.

Emerson had high hopes for his audiences. As limited as he believed his abilities—"our perception far outruns our talent"—he doggedly set forth on the lecture circuit with the assurance that even with his mediocre talents, he could help his audiences discover in themselves their own awesome capacity for intellectual and moral development.[111] He steadfastly retained the belief, succinctly articulated in his essay "Circles," that a "new degree of culture would instantly revolutionize the entire system of human pursuits."[112] Not that he or any other teacher could deliver an education in culture—not in fifty minutes, nor in fifty years. The culture that Emerson had in mind resembled the German word *Bildung*, which might be translated as acculturation. His job in his brief lectures entailed convincing, cajoling, and otherwise enticing the people to pursue culture for themselves. "The whole secret of a teacher's force lies in the conviction that men are convertible," he declared. "And they are. They want awakening."[113] Like Socrates, Emerson understood that he could only teach by example. In every lecture and public performance, he revealed his love for learning and for self-reliance, and otherwise sought to inspire his auditors. He hoped they would detect the fundamental resemblance between speaker and listener, teacher and pupil. Accomplishment of such a tall order necessitated a ruthless honesty, because from the Merrimac to the Miami to the Mississippi, Emerson sanguinely believed, people detected even the slightest hint of hypocrisy in the earnest lecturer.[114] Emerson's power as a public speaker rested in his unsurpassed ability to convey his profound openness to all classes of people, who delighted in hearing this awkward and brilliant Harvard graduate and former Unitarian minister proclaim the potential of the average American. Throughout his career, Emerson resolutely held fast to the conviction that with his inspiration his audiences could, and perhaps would, achieve greatness. "He seems to feel that his best and deepest sayings," observed William Cullen Bryant, "are the spontaneous utterances of *one soul*, which dwells in *all men*, and that thus whenever they are authentic, they must, of necessity, be recognized and received."[115] Neither showman nor supreme egotist, Emerson viewed himself—as he wrote so eloquently in the introduction to *Representative Men*—as nothing more than a simple teacher who had learned "to speak according to the power of understanding of ordinary people."[116] His design was always didactic.

Emerson remained convinced throughout his life that teaching, learning, lecturing, and listening were of a piece. They were inseparable companions to the human search for enlightenment. As much as he naturally took to his study and preferred solitude to society, he forced himself to take to the road virtually every year for four decades. It was more than the money that impelled him. He fully comprehended that the most vital filaments of his learning came from his experiences beyond Concord and home. "Shall I tell you the secret of the true scholar?" he asked in one of his lectures. "It is this: Every man I meet is my master in some point, and in that I learn of him."[117] The road for Emerson, with all its difficulties, discomforts, and downright miseries, provided him with an unparalleled education. He composed his lectures and essays on America on the basis of firsthand observations culled from traveling thousands of miles throughout the nation.[118] So long as Emerson appreciated that "no man believes any more than he has experienced," the people he met and the places he visited constituted the essence of his work.[119]

Emerson's annual treks, especially to the west, contributed vitally to his basic consanguinity. On the shores of the Ohio, the Wabash, the Mississippi, and hundreds of other rivers and tributaries, Emerson found confirmation of his optimistic belief in the energy, ingenuity, and basic good sense of the American people. For Emerson, there was far more to admire than censure in the westward expansion to which his generation bore witness, as his voluminous journal entries and letters home attest. The awesome hunger for land, material security, and personal success was a benign force that for the most part summoned the creative energies of the people. "I am greatly pleased with the merchants," he noted in 1843. "In railcar & hotel it is common to meet only the successful class, & so we have favorable specimens," and even taking the selective sampling into account, the men Emerson met abroad in the land impressed him.[120] "We rail at trade, but the historian of the world will see that it was the principle of liberty, that it settled America, & destroyed feudalism, and made peace & keeps peace, that it will abolish slavery."[121] Although after 1850 he realized that slavery could only be eradicated by means of a cataclysmic struggle, Emerson consistently celebrated the potential of commerce to produce good. The merchants and westward migrants gained Emerson's steady admiration. He found their company highly satisfactory. In his travels Emerson shied away from staying in private residences, preferring hotels or whatever passed for one in the towns he visited. Still, he regularly devoted his evenings to informal social gatherings. In fact, much to the delight and gratitude of his hosts in town after town, he spent far more hours in conversation in parlors and social gatherings than he did behind the lecture podium. The sincere dialectical engagements he had despaired of having while at Harvard he enjoyed time and again in hamlets and villages across the nation. "I am certified of a common nature," he declared in "The Over-Soul"; he readily favored the company of regular folks that "stir in me the new emotions we call passion; of love, hatred, fear, admiration, pity; thence come conversation, competition, persuasion, cities, and war."[122] Exaggerating a bit, he insisted he "much prefer[ed] the company of plough-boys and tin-pedlers, to the silken and perfumed amity which celebrates its days of encounter by a frivolous display, by rides in a curricle and dinners at the best taverns."[123]

Lecturing outside of his native New England brought another reward, as the western reaches of the nation inspired Emerson. "And what a future it opens," he declared. "I feel a new heart beating with the love of the new beauty. I am ready to die out of nature, and be born again into this new yet unapproachable America I have found in the West."[124] The western United States with its spirited settlement of the frontier and its rousing natural beauty promised to serve as the inspiration for generations of indigenous poets and artists who would find in the West the images and ideals necessary to jettison their wearisome dependence on a European past tied to the east, as it were.[125] In one of his most beautiful essays, "The Poet," Emerson lamented how no writer or artist had yet captured the sublime character of the nation that so abundantly manifested itself in his western travels:

We have yet had no genius in America, with tyrannous eye, which knew the value of our incomparable materials, and saw, in the barbarism and materialism of the times, another carnival of the same gods whose picture he so much admires in Homer. . . . Banks and tariffs, the newspaper and caucus, methodism and unitarianism, are flat and dull to dull people, but rest on the same foundations of wonder as the town of Troy, and the temple of Delphi, and are as swiftly passing away. Our logrolling, our stumps and their politics, our fisheries, our Negroes and Indians, our boasts and our repudiations, the wrath of rogues and the pusillanimity of honest men, the northern trade, the southern planting, the western clearing, Oregon and Texas, are yet unsung. Yet America is a poem in our eyes; its ample geography dazzles the imagination, and it will not wait long for metres.[126]

Always tending toward the Romantic, Emerson thrilled to the sheer immensity and apparent boundlessness of the West that he believed would play a pivotal part in the nation's historical mission. "The land is the appointed remedy for whatever is false and fantastic in our culture," he declared in "The Young American" in 1844. "The land, with its tranquilizing, sanative influences, is to repair the errors of a scholastic and traditional education, and bring us into just relations with men and things."[127] From the Mammoth Cave in Kentucky to the Yosemite Valley in California, Emerson visited natural wonders with the conviction that in some way they were as intimately connected with the destiny of the nation as were the town meeting and the Constitution.

Emerson equated the rapidity of westward expansion and the relative ease of travel with the general improvement of American culture. Journal entries and letters home contained commentary about frightful travel and logistical nightmares, but the very fact that he could go about his business at all elicited the most notice. The peripatetic Emerson made extensive use of the expanding transportation network, especially the railroads, in his travels. A recent biographer notes that during a swing through upstate New York in the winter of 1855, Emerson delivered twelve speeches in one two-week period. That the lectures were scheduled for ten different cities, each one many miles apart, necessitated a train trip every single day.[128] Considering himself on the cutting edge, he was especially proud that such an undertaking could be accomplished at all. The Concord sage's approving commentary about roads, rails, and river travel anticipated the observations of fellow New Englander Henry Adams. Both men invoked transportation as a measure of and metaphor for cultural improvement.[129] For the young Adams, who mordantly observed that "Bad roads meant bad morals," the horrid conditions of Virginia's rutted cart paths served as indisputable proof of the backwardness of a people plagued by chattel slavery.[130] Analogously, Emerson championed the extension of the railroad and the universal improvement of the transportation system north of the Ohio

River as key indices of the cultural progress of the "Universal Yankee nation" residing there.[131]

In contrast to his friend Henry Thoreau, Emerson found little to worry about in the "market revolution" to which they bore witness. In essays such as "The Progress of Culture" and "Young America," Emerson strongly attended to the benefits of freedom, both material and intellectual, which he believed greatly exceeded the dangers. Even the Boston railroad that Thoreau so famously complained "rides on us," Emerson viewed with pride and hope.[132] "I hear the whistle of the locomotive in the woods," he wrote with gusto.

> Wherever that music comes it has a sequel. It is the voice of the civility of the Nineteenth Century saying "Here I am." It is interrogative: it is prophetic: and this Cassandra is believed: Whew! Whew! Whew! How is real estate here in the swamp & wilderness? Swamp & Wilderness, ho for Boston! Whew! Whew! Down with that forest on the side of the hill. I want ten thousand chestnut sleepers. I want cedar posts and hundreds of thousands of feet of boards. Up my masters, of oak & pine! You have waited long enough—a good part of a century in the wind & stupid sky. Ho for axes & saws, and away with me to Boston! Whew! Whew! I will plant a dozen houses on this pasture next moon and a village anon; and I will sprinkle yonder square mile with white houses like the broken snow-banks that strow it in March.[133]

An inveterate ambler, a lover of nature, and even a sometimes naturalist who found a kindred spirit in John Muir, Emerson perceived no inherent conflict between love of the outdoors and the inevitable encroachment of progress.[134] National growth did not necessarily entail the wanton destruction of nature any more than material progress came at the expense of ethics and spiritual values. Nor was there an intrinsic contradiction between his unceasing attempt to spread the gospel of self-culture and his admiration of American material advancement. Although by no means an end in itself, the pursuit of property and prosperity goaded people into productivity and hard work.

Emerson was neither dedicated to free markets nor in any measure a materialist. At times, he felt pangs of contrition for the insubstantial property he did possess. He soberly considered joining his friends at Brook Farm, George and Sophia Ripley's socialist experiment in West Roxbury, and underwrote a small portion of Alcott's own communal venture, Fruitland's. Aware that the quest for wealth too often devolved into a destructive fetish, Emerson remained convinced that the fault did not lie with property per se, or markets, or the free enterprise system, but with Americans themselves. Proclaiming the "infinitude of the private man," he believed that the only way to change the

world was to change oneself, all else being futile.[135] "Progress is not for society," Emerson declared in one of his earliest lectures. "Progress belongs to
the individual."[136] He sympathized with the ideals of Brook Farm and the
other socialist experiments of the day, but in the end concluded that they were
not for him.

> The two parties in life are the believers & unbelievers, variously named.
> The believer is poet, saint, democrat, theocrat, free-trade, no church, no
> capital punishment, idealist. The unbeliever supports the church, education,
> the fine arts, &c as *amusements* . . . But the unbelief is very profound: who
> can escape it? I am nominally a believer: yet I hold on to property: I eat my
> bread with unbelief. I approve every wild action of the experimenters. I say
> what they say concerning celibacy or money or community of goods and
> my only apology for not doing their work is preoccupation of mind. I have
> a work of my own which I know I can do with some success. It would leave
> that undone if I should undertake with them and I do not see in myself any
> vigour equal to such an enterprise. My Genius loudly calls me to stay where
> I am, even with the degradation of owning bankstock and seeing poor men
> suffer whilst the Universal Genius apprises me of this disgrace & beckons
> me to the martyr's & redeemer's office.[137]

As much as he classed himself with the "believers," as he styled it, Emerson
could not in good faith adopt, and ultimately fight for, a system that he did
not fully understand. He confessed plainly that such a radical undertaking, as
promising as it might be, he had no choice but to leave to others. Honesty
compelled him to live in the world such as it was with his property and his
conscience.

One of the qualities that Emerson most admired in Ripley, Thoreau, Margaret Fuller, and other associates was that they were in some form or other
active souls who sought to change the world. Like him, they sought to transform their genius into practical power. In his journals and lectures Emerson
frequently contrasted energetic doers with the effete scholars he had left
behind in the Unitarian churches. The states through which he traveled on his
lecture tours bore witness to an American future largely devoid of bookish
professors and preachers. The road was populated by people on the make and
by headstrong merchants, who for all their faults and material aspirations were
possessed of an energy and vitality that Emerson effortlessly respected. The
homesteader, tradesman, and merchant "discover more manly power of all
kinds than scholars," Emerson remarked in a journal entry scribbled while
riding between Philadelphia and Baltimore; they "behave a great deal better,
converse better, and have independent & sufficient manners."[138] Emerson

returned time and again to the shortcomings of the usual scholarly types who lived and wrote in fear of the masses. "He is no master," Emerson sharply concluded, "who cannot vary his form and carry his own end triumphantly through the most difficult conditions."[139]

Emerson persistently called for the advent of a new generation of intellectuals. In contrast to the previous scholars and clerical intellectuals of Brahmin Boston, new, democratic intellectuals would fully comprehend that the value of their knowledge and years of study would be measured by a single yardstick. Erudition had to be immediately useful. As implausible as this claim might seem for the nineteenth century's most famous idealist, there can be no gainsaying that Emerson repeatedly and earnestly gave obeisance to precisely that type of measure, both for himself and his class. Emerson detested the fact that "our geniuses cannot do anything useful," as he ruefully noted in his lecture "Nominalist and Realist." Scholars have considered "The American Scholar" to be Emerson's revolutionary call for the new national genius without grasping the more urgent appeal of his lectures and letters for the practical genius. Breaking away from European influence was necessary for the creation of a national poetry and literature to be sure, but it paled in comparison to the need to break down the artificial barriers between the intellectual and the people.[140] Compared to his call for a democratic culture, the worries over foreign influence featured in his Phi Beta Kappa oration were nothing more than an *obiter dictum* to the Harvard College Class of 1837.

Despite his distrust of most academic intellectuals, Emerson did not play upon, much less partake in, what historian Richard Hofstadter once lucklessly styled the "anti-intellectual tradition" in America.[141] Emerson devoted the bulk of his mature life to calling people from their material pursuits. Prosperity was nothing more than a means to spiritual and cultural ends. In all of his lectures and essays, Emerson never departed from the theme of self-culture and the singular value of education. He did not disparage the great learning of Harvard- and Yale-educated young men and self-educated women any more than he refrained from further study himself. If anything, Emerson continued his prodigious reading in philosophy, history, literature, and the natural sciences that he had begun as a boy. The issue was never the acquisition of knowledge, even from the most obscure and unlikely sources; Emerson loved cogitation and those few folks, such as Theodore Parker, who excelled him in their erudition. Emerson focused his criticism on the ends of learning, which he insisted must be practical or they proved merely fetishistic. Perry Miller incisively noted that Emerson detected an unmistakable ennui among his Brahmin associates—"overcome with lassitude," wrote Miller—which was generated largely from their lack of utility and relevance.[142] "It does seem as if history gave no intimation of any society in which despondency came so readily to heart as we see it & feel it in ours. Young men, young women at thirty & even earlier seem to have lost all spring & vivacity," Emerson wrote in 1838.[143] This spiritual languor drove Emerson from his inherited Brahmin institutions and on to the road. In the appropriately titled essay "Considerations By the Way" from his 1860 *Conduct of Life*, Emerson issued his prescription for the ailment of the intellectual class.

> Genial manners are good, and power of accommodation to any circumstance; but the high prize of life, the crowning fortune of man, is to be born with a bias to some pursuit which finds him in employment and happiness,—whether it be to make baskets, or broadswords, or canals, or statutes, or songs. I doubt not this was the meaning of Socrates, when he pronounced artists the only true wise, as being actually, not apparently so.[144]

Emerson sought to communicate what he had learned from two decades of "rough riding," of taking "the last & worst bed in the tavern."[145] Satisfaction entailed "the wish to serve, to add somewhat to the well-being of men."[146]

Emerson's annual treks across America redeemed him from ennui and spiritual desolation. "On the highway," where John Dewey insisted "all Truth lies," Emerson rescued himself by ferreting out a metier—no matter how unsuited to his talents and natural inclinations—that enabled him to achieve the relevance he craved and had failed to find "in the dead pond which our church is."[147] The public lecture yielded him those crucial elements that empowered his genius: money to make ends meet, an ideal means to observe the salubrious development of the nation, as well as an unmatched opportunity to commune with his fellow citizens. Most importantly, lecturing guaranteed that his knowledge had—as William James would shortly describe it—a practical "cash-value." The lyceum and lecture hall provided Emerson with a vocation that enabled him to become the democratic intellectual he called for in his "American Scholar" address in 1837 and in the ensuing decades. As a lecturer Emerson solved his vocational dilemma by transforming himself into one of the nation's greatest public intellectuals.

NOTES

1. *JMN* 8:228; Emerson also used the phrase in "New England Reformers."
2. *JMN* 8:228.
3. *JMN* 8:228.
4. On Emerson as aloof critic, see, for example, Taylor Stoehr, *Nay-Saying in Concord: Emerson, Alcott, and Thoreau* (Hamden, Conn., 1979).

5. *JMN* 4:302.

6. *JMN* 7:338–39.

7. *JMN* 8:238; for a slightly different version of the same, see "Experience," *Collected Works* 3:27.

8. For observations on the lecture, which went off very well according to Charles, see 11/6/33, *Letters* 1:397n.

9. *JMN* 9:49.

10. Alvin Gouldner, *The Dialectic of Ideology and Technology: The Origins, Grammar, and Future of Ideology* (New York, 1979).

11. See Mary Kupiec Cayton, "The Making of an American Prophet: Emerson, His Audiences, and the Rise of the Culture Industry in Nineteenth-Century America," *American Historical Review* 92 (1987), 597–620.

12. Odell Shepard, ed., *Journals of Bronson Alcott* (Boston, 1938), 279.

13. As for deadlines, Emerson asked himself in 1834 just before his lecture career commenced whether it was "possible that in the solitude I seek I shall have the resolution the force to work as I ought to work—as I project in highest most farsighted hours?" See *JMN* 4:272.

14. James Russell Lowell, *My Study Windows* (Boston, 1884), 375. Just who attended Emerson's lectures remains open to debate. That few free blacks, recent immigrants, or working poor heard him seems clear; yet it is equally apparent that the lyceum and lecture hall boasted a diverse clientele that included women and men, merchants, journeymen, and apprentices, as well as other intellectually curious persons. In Emerson's day there existed little distinction in antebellum America between highbrow and lowbrow, and a performance of Shakespeare or Emerson's reading of his essay "Shakespeare" from *Representative Men* drew a remarkably diverse crowd whose class composition would be difficult to characterize. The lyceum, for example, where Emerson frequently spoke, was "a working-class institution," Robert Richardson had recently reminded us, "founded, supported, and directed by local boards made up originally of working people intent on bettering themselves through practical education." Robert D. Richardson, *Emerson: The Mind on Fire* (Berkeley, Calif., 1995), 419.

15. "Power," *Works* 6:58.

16. The similarities do not stop there. Like Emerson, James delivered most of his works as public lectures, most notably *Pragmatism*.

17. *Young Emerson Speaks*, 164–65.

18. *Young Emerson Speaks*, 166.

19. *Young Emerson Speaks*, 167.

20. "The Preacher," *Works* 10:210.

21. See Philip Gura, *The Wisdom of Words: Language, Theology, and Literature in the New England Renaissance* (Middletown, Conn., 1981).

22. *Works* 10:224.

23. *JMN* 5:464.

24. "Address Before the Free Religious Association," *Works* 11:382.

25. See Emerson's lecture, "Martin Luther," in *Early Lectures* 1:118–43.

26. *JMN* 4:335.

27. *JMN* 4:313.

28. See George Santayana, *Interpretations of Poetry and Religion* (1900; rep., New York, 1922), 231; and, of course, *The Last Puritan: A Memoir in the Form of a Novel* (1935, rep. New York, 1994), 198, where one of his characters blusters that Emerson was "simply a distinguished-looking old cleric with a sweet smile and a white tie."

29. *JMN* 4:309.

30. *JMN* 4:380.

31. *JMN* 4:382; the quote continues: "I think [it] might even promote parish objects & draw them to church."

32. *JMN* 7:265.

33. *JMN* 7:265.

34. Emerson to Ruth Haskins Emerson and William Emerson, 3/14/38, *Letters* 2:120.

35. Donald M. Scott, "The Public Lecture and the Creation of a Public in Mid-Nineteenth-Century America," *Journal of American History* 66 (1980), 791.

36. *JMN* 7:224; Emerson referred to Socrates' preference for the spoken word over the written in his journals.

37. William Charvat, "A Chronological List of Emerson's American Lecture Engagements," *New York Public Library Bulletin* 64 (1960), 492.

38. *JMN* 5:451.

39. *JMN* 5:451.

40. Cited in Charvat, "Chronological List," 492.

41. Emerson to Lidian Jackson Emerson, 1/25/43, *Letters* 3:133.

42. Emerson to Lidian Jackson Emerson, 1/25/43, *Letters* 3:133.

43. Emerson to Thomas Carlyle, 4/30/35, *CEC* 123.

44. *Early Lectures* 2:xi–xii.

45. *CEC* 123.

46. *CEC* 122–23. On Johann Gaspar Spurzheim's tour of 1832, see Charles Colbert, *A Measure of Perfection: Phrenology and the Fine Arts in America* (Chapel Hill, N.C., 1997).

47. *CEC* 123–24.

48. Emerson to Alexander Ireland, 2/28/47, *Letters* 3:380.

49. Emerson to James Munroe & Company, 2/2/43, *Letters* 3:140–41.

50. Emerson to William Emerson, 10/16/43, *Letters* 3:214.

51. *JMN* 4:344.

52. See Charvat, "Chronological List," 557.

53. Emerson to Lidian Jackson Emerson, 2/26/43, *Letters* 3:150.

54. See Carl Bode, *The American Lyceum: Town Meeting of the Mind* (Carbondale, Ill., 1968), 206. Phillips offered his antislavery lectures for free, but if the audience wanted something else he charged a fee.

55. *JMN* 7:312.

56. *JMN* 5:237.

57. *JMN* 4:315. Both Lawrence Levine and David S. Reynolds offer interesting discussions of the distinction of highbrow and lowbrow culture in their recent works. See, for example, Levine's *Highbrow/Lowbrow: The Emergence of Cultural Hierarchy in America* (Cambridge, 1988) and Reynolds's " 'A Chaos-Deep Soil': Emerson, Thoreau, and Popular Literature," in *Transient and Permanent: The Transcendentalist Movement and Its Contexts*, ed. Charles Capper and Conrad Edick Wright (Boston, 1999), 282–309.

58. "The Poet," *Collected Works* 3:15–16. Willard Thorp astutely observed that "no one can maintain that Emerson flattered his audiences. In fact, he frequently shocked and alarmed them with the fervent desire of disturbing the conventional patterns of their lives." See "Emerson on Tour," *Quarterly Journal of Speech* 16 (1930), 23.

59. Lowell, *My Study Windows*, 375.

60. Cited in Thorp, "Emerson on Tour," 25.

61. Annie Adams Fields, "Mr Emerson in the Lecture Room," in *Ralph Waldo Emerson: A Profile,* ed. Carl Bode (New York, 1968), 85.

62. Cited in Thorp, "Emerson on Tour," 24–25.

63. Thorp, "Emerson on Tour," 26.

64. *JMN* 7:301. It is not entirely clear from the entry whether Fuller or Emerson's Concord neighbor, Samuel Staples, made the comment about Emerson being on stilts.

65. (Milwaukee) *Sentinel*, February 20, 1854.

66. (Kenosha) *Democrat*, February 17, 1860.

67. (Kenosha) *Democrat,* February 17, 1860.

68. (Providence) *Manufacturers' and Farmers' Journal*, June 10, 1837.

69. *JMN* 8:203.

70. The one exception was the reviewers who stole his best lines, as it were. A sharp letter to Elizur Wright, editor of the *Commonwealth*, is a good example. "I am exceedingly vexed by finding in your paper, this morning, precisely such a report of one of my lectures, as I wrote to you a fortnight since to entreat you to defend me from. My lectures are written to be read as lectures in different places, & then to be reported by myself. Tomorrow, I was to have read this very lecture in Salem, & your reporter does all he can to kill the thing to every hearer, by putting him in possession beforehand of the words of each statement that struck him, as nearly as he could copy them. Abuse me, & welcome, but do not transcribe me" (1/7/52, *Letters* 4:272–73).

71. "Self-Reliance," *Collected Works* 2:33–34.

72. *JMN* 7:302.

73. *JMN* 9:49.

74. "The Genuine Man," in *Young Emerson Speaks*, 184–85.

75. "Success," *Works* 7:290.

76. "Success," *Works* 7:273–74.

77. *CEC* 499. The ambiguity stems from Emerson's belief that the editor of the *Tribune* was engaged in a great service in spreading culture at the clip of one hundred thousand copies a day.

78. "Success," *Works* 7:290.

79. "Books," *Works* 7:183.

80. Cited in Charles I. Glicksberg, "Bryant on Emerson the Lecturer," *New England Quarterly* 12 (1939), 530–34; James Russell Lowell, "Emerson the Lecturer," in *The Recognition of Ralph Waldo Emerson: Selected Criticism since 1837,* ed. Milton R. Konritz (Ann Arbor, Mich., 1972), 45.

81. "Spiritual Laws," *Collected Works* 2:88.

82. "The Poet," *Collected Works* 3:4.

83. "The American Scholar," *Collected Works* 1:63.

84. "Man the Reformer," *Collected Works* 1:145.

85. *JMN* 4:346.

86. "Eloquence," *Works* 8:121. How successful Emerson ultimately was in this endeavor remains open to debate.

87. Emerson to William Emerson, 2/10/50, *Letters* 4:179. *JMN* 4:348–49. *JMN* 5:255. *JMN* 5:287. In time, however, Emerson decided that Taylor was more show than substance.

88. "Art," *Collected Works* 2:218.

89. "The Poet," *Collected Works* 3:8–9. With its democratic imagery "The Poet" also contains a searing critique of the mediocre.

90. *JMN* 9:449.

91. "The American Scholar," *Collected Works* 1:67.

92. This citation was written after Emerson's first trip to Europe in 1833–34.

93. *JMN* 7:374. "Eloquence," *Works* 7:95.

94. *JMN* 9:54.

95. "Thoreau," *Works* 10:426.

96. *JMN* 4:372.

97. *JMN* 9:70.

98. *JMN* 9:70 and similarly *Works* 7:338–39. *CEC* 343.

99. *Cincinnati Gazette*, May 24, 1850. *Nature*, in *Collected Works* 1:12. "The Young American," *Collected Works* 1:234.

100. *JMN* 8:231.

101. *JMN* 8:367.

102. *JMN* 4:313.

103. *CEC* 168.

104. "Self-Reliance," *Collected Works* 2:83.

105. Emerson to Charles Chauncy Emerson, 7/15/28, *Letters* 1:239.

106. "Eloquence," *Works* 7:81.

107. "Eloquence," *Works* 7:70.

108. "Eloquence," *Works* 7:69.

109. "Greatness," *Works* 8:292.

110. Mary Moody Emerson to Charles Chauncy Emerson, 1822, Emerson Family Papers, Houghton Library, Harvard University Archives.

111. "Success," *Works* 7:283.

112. "Circles," *Collected Works* 2:184.

113. *JMN* 4:278.

114. Entertainers such as P. T. Barnum were a different issue entirely.

115. Glicksberg, "Bryant," 534.

116. Baruch Spinoza, "A Portrait of the Philosopher as a Young Man," in *A Spinoza Reader: The* Ethics *and Other Works,* ed. Edwin Curley (Princeton, 1994), 6.

117. "Greatness," *Works* 8:296.

118. More precisely, Emerson traveled throughout the North and West, as his only foray into the South was one trip to Kentucky and another, well after the Civil War, to Virginia.

119. *JMN* 8:373.

120. *JMN* 8:335.

121. *JMN* 9:61–62.

122. "The Over-Soul," *Collected Works* 2:164.

123. "Self-Reliance," *Collected Works* 2:121.

124. "Experience," *Collected Works* 3:41.

125. For an extended discussion of nature as "God's second book," see Sacvan Bercovitch, *The Puritan Origins of the American Self* (New Haven, 1975), 136–63.

126. "The Poet," *Collected Works* 3:21–22.

127. "The Young American," *Collected Works* 1:226.

128. Richardson, *Mind on Fire*, 419.

129. Lewis Perry writes that for Emerson "the conditions of travel became a test of the quality of civilization" in *Boats Against the Current: American Culture Between Revolution and Modernity, 1820–1860* (New York, 1993), 8.

130. Henry Adams, *The Education of Henry Adams* (Boston, 1918; rep., 1989), 47.

131. *JMN* 5:196.

132. Henry David Thoreau, *Walden or Life In the Woods* (1854; rep. New York, 1939), 98.

133. Cited in *Emerson in His Journals*, ed. Joel Porte (Cambridge, 1982), 297.

134. For Emerson and his trip to Yosemite, see James B. Thayer, *A Western Journey with Mr. Emerson* (Boston, 1884).

135. John Flanagan in 1937 arrived at much the same conclusion. See his "Emerson and Communism," *New England Quarterly* 10 (1937), 243–61.

136. *Early Lectures* 2:173–76.

137. *JMN* 9:62.

138. *JMN* 8:335.

139. Cited in James Elliot Cabot, *Memoir of Ralph Waldo Emerson* (Cambridge, 1887), 564.

140. See Harold Bloom, *The Anxiety of Influence: A Theory of Poetry* (New York, 1973).

141. "With delight he scourged the academic retinue," writes Paul Conkin, "who could not even state the great questions, let alone answer them." See Conkin, *Puritans and Pragmatists: Eight Eminent American Thinkers* (Bloomington, Ind., 1968; rep.,

1976), 197. See also, Richard Hofstadter, *Anti-Intellectualism in American Life* (New York, 1964).

142. Perry Miller, "Emersonian Genius and the American Democracy," *New England Quarterly* 26 (1953), 27–44; cite is on 28.

143. *JMN* 7:73.

144. "Considerations by the Way," *Works* 6:253. Most translators use "artisans" in place of Emerson's "artists," which makes a great deal of difference.

145. Emerson to Lidian Jackson Emerson, 1/2/56, *Letters* 5:4.

146. "Considerations by the Way," *Works* 6:263.

147. *JMN* 5:491.

6

ABOLITIONISM AND THE STRANGE CAREER OF EMERSON AND RACE

By 1850 and his mid-forties Emerson was in the midst of carving out for himself the vocation of democratic intellectual. An increasingly eminent lecturer, thinker, and writer, he had largely fulfilled his driving ambition to devote himself to delivering didactic secular sermons to a national audience. In the portentous year of the Compromise of 1850 and the passage of what he called the dreaded Fugitive Slave Law, Emerson was frenetically engaged in his lecturing activities. He traveled thousands of miles, which incorporated his first trip to Ohio, in order to deliver something over sixty lectures in eight states on topics ranging from "Politics" and "Eloquence" to the "Humanity of Science." As an individual who had recorded his revulsion to the institution of slavery as early as his first college journals, Emerson was greatly dismayed by the turn of events of the preceding several years. He was especially distraught by the apostasy of Massachusetts Senator Daniel Webster, whom he had previously admired as the embodiment of the energetic and effective American politician-statesman. As a public figure who had dedicated himself to a type of secular preaching, Emerson felt obliged to cease his avoidance of the fight over slavery and to confront the issue head-on. Convinced that the stirring, malevolent power maintaining the peculiar institution was driving out the forces of right, Emerson reasoned that he had no choice but to join the ranks of those fighting to abolish it. From 1850 Emerson was an abolitionist.

Abolitionism represented Emerson's single great foray into active politics. It forced him as perhaps no other issue could to come to grips with the role of the intellectual in a republic. Here was the chance to work mightily for a just political cause to which the public intellectual might wholly devote himself. For the next fifteen years, which represented the bulk of his remaining years of great intellectual vitality, Emerson engaged himself, as did the nation in which he lived, with the crucial issues of slavery, race, and civil war. Slav-

ery and the fate of the "African race" came to play a crucial role in his understanding of the United States and the promise of self-reliant individuality.

Despite his great flurry of activity after 1850, assessing Emerson's relation to the antebellum abolitionist movement has long been problematic.
Friends, family members, and acquaintances offered hugely conflicting
accounts of his activities and beliefs concerning slavery and antislavery.[1]
Scholars, too, have found situating Emerson within abolitionist democracy
particularly elusive. For those who would like to make him into an abolitionist, Emerson's nagging racism, his disdain for activism and agitation, as well
as his avowed disgust for many abolitionists and reformers must be somehow
overcome or explained away.[2] Scholars who would like to portray Emerson as
an armchair idealist, indifferent to the plight of African Americans, are in a
similar quandary. It requires some sleight-of-hand to reconcile their image of
Emerson as a recluse with the man who delivered stirring speeches in support
of West Indian emancipation, John Brown, and the Emancipation Proclamation, as well as those decrying the Fugitive Slave Law and the proslavery
atrocities in Kansas.[3] At times, Emerson condemned the abolitionists and pitied the planter class; at others, he immoderately praised William Lloyd Garrison and Wendell Phillips while calling slavery "wholly iniquitous" and the
slaveholder a criminal.[4] Simultaneously intimate with the abolitionist Senator
Charles Sumner and the English reactionary and the author of "The Nigger
Question," Thomas Carlyle, Emerson took great pride in these divergent associations.[5] Always unsystematic, often aphoristic, and occasionally contradictory, Emerson evades easy categorization.

As much as Emerson considered himself an outsider in Brahmin Boston
and as much as he found himself dissatisfied with elite Boston's attitudes
toward education, religion, and vocation, Emerson was not radical when it
came to antislavery. As atypical as he was in so many respects, when it came
to slavery, early in his life Emerson professed some fairly representative attitudes of the children of Boston Federalists.[6] Antislavery virtually from birth,
he nonetheless believed in the superior "genius of the Saxon race" and otherwise gave little thought to slavery issues until about 1840.[7] He never especially
warmed to the great wave of Romantic reformers and their social palliatives
and for the most part dismissed utopian idealists with whom Emerson, and so
many Brahmins, associated the abolitionists. Believing himself unsuited to the
antislavery movement, and convinced that the relevance he craved would not
come from abolitionism, which for many years he thought to be a waste of
time, Emerson participated in antislavery activities only marginally until
1850. On the whole, Emerson had little regard for the abolitionist, whom he
derisively styled "the fool of virtue." Nothing could have been more anathema

to his eclecticism than the monomania of a Garrison or a Phillips. Although claimed by them, Emerson held himself aloof from the abolitionists during their critical first decades of labor.[8]

Emerson's assumptions concerning race, as was the case with so many of his contemporaries, thoroughly circumscribed his thinking about slavery as well as his relation to the abolitionist movement.[9] The stark fact of black inferiority, of which Emerson for years had no doubt, muted his condemnation of slavery as well as his criticism of slaveholders. Even his famous "faith in the great Optimism" failed to inspire Emerson to imagine a society in which African Americans might equal or excel their Saxon and Caucasian counterparts.[10] They would surely follow the American Indian into extinction as the superior Saxon race established its rightful hegemony. Nonetheless, as with so much of his thought, Emerson's notions about race were flexible and open to revision.[11] As events unfolded, Emerson modified his views. When proslavery apologists and their allies used to advantage many of the same arguments for Negro inferiority that he had scribbled in his journal, Emerson seems to have resolved neither to write nor speak of them again. Emerson slowly extricated himself and his core ideas about progress from the confines of his racial assumptions, a process that culminated in his 1844 address marking the tenth anniversary of emancipation in the British West Indies. Like those of Abraham Lincoln and unlike those of Thomas Jefferson, who refused to change his views in the face of contradictory evidence, Emerson's ideas evolved.[12] By the Civil War, Emerson believed that African Americans demanded, deserved, and would make the most of full equality before the law.[13]

The evolution of Emerson's views on slavery can be separated roughly into three periods. His youth and early career were characterized by a basic indifference that lasted until 1837 when he presented his first lecture on slavery. In the ensuing decade, Emerson remained largely mute on slavery, only gradually becoming more engaged in antislavery issues as he rethought many of his earlier assumptions about the intractable inferiority of Africans in America and elsewhere. In this second stage of his evolution, his views showed the most dramatic change, as highlighted by his 1844 public celebration of emancipation in the West Indies and his sharp reaction to southern machinations surrounding the annexation of Texas and the Mexican War. The final stage of Emerson's evolution dates from the Compromise of 1850, after which Emerson often joined the ranks of antislavery activists, at least in his own measured, prosaic way, as he came to embrace the necessity of espousing and working toward the political equality of blacks and whites. By the conclusion of the Civil War, such radicals as Phillips and Sumner could without exaggeration claim Emerson as one of their own. In his 1867 address dedicating the Soldiers' Monument in his hometown of Concord, Massachusetts, Emerson alluded to the gradual but steady evolution of his antislavery thought. "The war made the Divine Providence credible to many who did not believe the good Heaven quite honest," he admitted. The nation's commitment to the war had taken him by surprise. "Every man was an abolitionist by conviction, but did not believe that his neighbor was. The opinions of masses of men, which the tactics of primary caucuses and the proverbial timidity of trade had concealed, the war discovered; and it was found, contrary to all popular belief, that the country was at heart abolitionist, and for the Union was ready to die."[14] By 1867, New England had come a long way from the gross indifference of earlier decades. Emerson had as well.

In his youth and into his thirties Emerson seemed almost indifferent to the plight of blacks in America. Slavery was not a critical issue. His few encounters with chattel slavery and race include a few early entries in journals, several allusions in his sermons, his 1827 trip to South Carolina and Florida, his decision four years later to welcome abolitionist Samuel J. May to his pulpit, and his "rescue," with brother Charles, of Harriet Martineau from a hostile Boston crowd in 1835.[15] Yet, these few episodes offer important clues to his conception of chattel slavery, particularly in the context of his evolving views of history, human nature, and the uniqueness of American society.

Emerson's first recorded examination of the institution dates from a journal entry in 1822. The young Harvard graduate, nineteen years old, had never been outside his native New England and likely had never exchanged even a few words with a slave. To be sure he had encountered slaveholders, including Robert Woodward Barnwell, the brilliant and smug South Carolinian with whom Emerson had attended Harvard. Unlike Barnwell, who graduated as valedictorian of their class, Emerson fervently believed slavery to be barbaric. He used his journal, dedicated to the "Genius of America," to reconcile his conviction that the institution was evil with his equally strong and sanguine assurance of divine providence. Slavery had existed for centuries and seemed entrenched in the American South, so the benevolent Unitarian deity whom Emerson worshipped must have incorporated it into His grand scheme. Seeking to "aid our faith by freer speculation," Emerson marshaled whatever facts he could in a theoretical defense of slavery. "I believe that nobody now regards the maxim 'that all men are born equal,' as any thing more than a convenient hypothesis or an extravagant declamation," he rationalized in 1822.

> For the reverse is true,—that all men are.born unequal in personal powers and in those essential circumstances, of time, parentage, country, fortune.

> The least knowledge of the natural history of man adds another important particular to these; namely, what class of men he belongs to—European, Moor, Tartar, African? Because Nature has plainly assigned different degrees of intellect to these different races, and the barriers between are insurmountable. This inequality is an indication of the design of Providence that some should lead, and some should serve. For when an effect invariably takes place from causes which Heaven established, we surely say with safety, that Providence designed that result.[16]

Speculating about an institution that seemed to have no direct bearing upon him, Emerson offered the similar rationale that masters had endlessly paraded as unimpeachable evidence for enslaving others.[17] Slavery only appeared iniquitous and malevolent, but in fact was part of a larger benign celestial design. God dictated through nature that "some should lead, and some should serve"; the ubiquitous "relation of king & subject, master & servant" proved as much.[18] Perhaps slavery was justifiable, Emerson mused, so long as "the same pleasure and confidence which the dog and horse feel when they rely upon the superior intelligence of man is felt by the lower parts of our own species with reference to the higher."[19]

Following Aristotle and Locke, Emerson then defended bondage by analogizing slaves with beasts of burden. He proposed three basic criteria by which humans were justified in domesticating animals: "their want of reason; their adaptation to our wants; and their own advantage (when domesticated)."[20] The question turned on whether "those three circumstances which are the foundations of our dominion over the beasts, very much may be said to apply them to the African species." Choosing not to address the debatable point of the slave's adaptability to bondage, he proceeded to compare favorably life in servitude in the South with freedom in Africa. Feeling obliged to "pursue a revolting subject to its greatest lengths," Emerson concluded "that many a slave under the warm roof of a humane master with easy labours and regular subsistence enjoys more happiness than his naked brethren parched with thirst on a burning sand or endangered in the crying wilderness of their native land."[21] The exercise may have been academic, but the verdict seemed unimpeachable. Emerson suggested that black servitude must somehow have been sanctioned by God and might well be benign.

The more formidable issue hinged on whether "Man and Beast" were distinguishable by the former's capacity to "reason." Emerson was not sanguine in his assessment of Africans:

> It can hardly be true I think that the difference lies in the attribute of Reason; I saw ten, twenty, a hundred large lipped, lowbrowed black men in the

streets who, except in the mere matter of language, did not exceed the sagacity of the elephant. Now is it true that these were created superior to this wise animal, and designed to controul it? And in comparison with the highest orders of men, the Africans will stand so low as to make the difference which subsists between themselves & the sagacious beasts inconsiderable.[22]

With the argument framed in this way, Emerson felt compelled to speculate: "are not they an upper order of inferior animals?" Robert Barnwell, Emerson's plantation-born classmate, could not have offered a balder assertion of African inferiority.[23]

As much as Emerson believed that slavery itself was a gross injustice, he had trouble refuting his own defense of it, as it seems clear that his statement that the intelligence of black men "did not exceed the sagacity of the elephant" was hardly academic. Unable to refute the proslavery arguments systematically, Emerson turned instead to sentiment and intuition. No matter what the arguments in its favor—even the inferiority of the African race—the enslavement of humans by humans was anathema.[24] "To establish by whatever specious argumentation the perfect expediency of the worst institution on earth is *prima facie* an assault upon Reason and Common sense. No ingenious sophistry can ever reconcile the unperverted mind to the pardon of *Slavery*; nothing but tremendous familiarity, and the bias of private *interest*."[25]

Emerson's resolute conviction that slavery was unjustifiable did not lead him to conjecture that equality was the natural condition of all humankind.[26] He offered no argument against African inferiority in 1822, nor would he for many years to come. His best guess was that the demise of slavery would spell the extinction of American blacks altogether. "The negro must be very old," he wrote as late as 1840, "& belongs, one would say, to the fossil formations. What right has he to be intruding into the late & civil daylight of this dynasty of the Caucasians & Saxons? It is plain that so inferior a race must perish shortly like the poor Indians."[27] "Divine Providence" had decreed that inferior races would disappear in a "genocide by natural causes," as the historian George Fredrickson once characterized it.[28] The entire history of slavery in the Americas was nothing short of a tragedy, which, he quoted Edward Gibbon, "accuses the guilt of Europe and the Weakness of Africa." Barely twenty years old, Emerson reasoned that he could do nothing to alter the course of history and the triumph of the Saxon race.[29]

The result of study and contemplation, as his 1822 notebook ruminations demonstrated, Emerson's thinking on race was largely "scientific" and ideological. As with the vast majority of intellectuals of the early nineteenth century, novel developments and discoveries in biology, zoology, geography, and archaeology seemed to validate a racialized account of history. With the proliferation of the ideas of Lord Kames, whose *Sketches of the History of Man* was arguably the catalyst for modern racial conceptions, and of Immanuel Kant, who wrote that "the negro . . . occupies the lowest of the remaining grades we have called racial differences," race-based theories came to dominate the nineteenth-century historical imagination.[30] Intellectuals from Thomas Carlyle and Samuel Taylor Coleridge to Victor Cousin and Johann Gottfried Herder justified European expansion, English domination of the Irish, the origins of popular government in the North Atlantic nations, and much more on the basis of race. Under the heading "Fate," Emerson approvingly cited the correspondent for the New York *Tribune*, Karl Marx, as writing that "races too weak to master the new conditions of life must give way."[31] The successive displacement of one race (or class) by another was the progressive engine of human history.

Emerson's racist assumptions proved equally critical to his understanding of the United States and its history, as well as what he believed to be its crucial role in human progress. Virtually from birth, Emerson inherited a set of racial assumptions about Saxon genius that played perfectly into his evolving nationalism. Like many of his contemporaries, his friend Louis Agassiz most prominently, Emerson adopted a type of biological "life-cycle theory" that sought to explain Continental, English, and American history as the successive development and unfolding of a divine scheme. The "wild liberty" of the Druid and Berserker manifested itself in the American "Hoosier, Sucker, Wolverine, Badger, or whatever hard head" that felled the trees, trapped the beaver, and tamed the wilderness.[32] The fortune of the Republic, Emerson argued, depended upon these Saxon "rough riders" who understood "the necessity of balancing and keeping at bay the snarling majorities of German, Irish, and native millions."[33] The nation's vitality as manifested in its explosive expansion, its commercial might, its democratic institutions, and its auspicious destiny, rested upon the elemental virtues of a young and vital race. Insofar as Emerson's faith in popular government was rooted in his conviction that "The instinct of the people is right," his definition of "the people" necessarily remained highly circumscribed.[34] Only some races had attained a sufficiently advanced culture to be able to compete and survive.

Emerson considered racial distinctions to be one of the primary determinative elements in human history, even as it contradicted his ahistorical notions of individual self-reliance.[35] In his 1856 *English Traits* he sought to elucidate the unique qualities of the Saxons, whose world domination and pantheon of great men he unabashedly celebrated. Emerson set himself the task of explicating the historical causes of the undeniable greatness of the Saxon. "It is race, is it not?" he asked rhetorically.[36] Yet, as often as he used the word, race became for Emerson less a matter of blood and biology than a convenient metaphor for a constellation of determinative traits that more closely corresponds to the contemporary term *ethnicity.* Not blood alone, but historical contingency, culture, environment, and geography played critical roles in the elaboration of national character. Philip Nicoloff sympathetically characterized Emerson's discussion of the term in *English Traits* as "one of the more liberal and perceptive statements on the question of race to be written by a layman in the middle of the nineteenth century."[37] Nicoloff's generous representation highlights how Emerson's mature explication of race, then, reveals a distinct progression in his thinking. At the same time that he wrote that "Race is a controlling influence in the Jew" and "Race in the negro is of appalling importance," he refused to preclude the possibility of racial intermixture at some future moment.[38] What Emerson called "mongrelism," his sense of the benign mixing of racial stocks, was deliberately intended to counter theorists such as Robert Knox who argued that "races are imperishable."[39] Emerson disputed Knox's polygenicism as well as his fallacious belief that rigid racial distinctions forbade miscegenation.[40] Accordingly, a multiracial nation like the United States at some distant juncture might even converge into a single amalgamated people, whose hybridization promised to be the very source of its vigor.

The racial propositions of *English Traits* and elsewhere represent one element in a basically sanguine outlook. Emerson's underlying, elemental optimism stands in marked contrast to the pessimistic mood that pervades the work of Spengler, for example, who wrote at a time of societal decline and crisis. Where Spengler viewed his work as grave portents of imminent disaster, Emerson believed himself to be writing for a nation characterized by great promise and poised to be the rightful heir of Athens, Rome, Florence, Geneva, and London. Rejoicing "in the birthright of a country where freedom of opinion & action is so perfect that every man enjoys exactly that consideration to which he is entitled," Emerson did not invest his vision with the brutal urgency of a call for racial purity.[41] He had no such end in mind. Africans might not play a part in the American nation's "forward step in the path of her greatness," but they were not the scourge of its destiny either.[42] At his most ebullient, Emerson envisioned "in this Continent—asylum of all nations, the energy of Irish, Germans, Swedes, Poles, & Cossacks, & all the European tribes—of the Africans, & of the Polynesians, will construct a new race, a new religion, a new State, a new literature, which will be as vigorous as the new Europe which came out of the smelting pot of the Dark Ages, or that which earlier emerged from the Pelasgic & Etruscan barbarism."[43] This optimism, for which Emerson was famous, ultimately proved critical to the evolution of his egalitarian thought.

In the context of contemporary American society, Emerson's early axiomatic assumption of African racial inferiority had significant ramifications, including his sympathy toward southern slaveholders and antipathy toward the abolitionists. With Jefferson, he believed that planters were to be pitied, as they held tightly to a "wolf by the ears," neither able to let it go nor animated by the prospect of the perpetual maintenance of so dangerous an institution. Southerners deserved sympathy, as slavery in some measure injured the master, even as he seemed to profit from it. In 1833 Emerson noted with approval a citation forwarded from his brother Edward quoting "from [James-Henry Bernardin de] St Pierre the saying that 'when the chain is put upon a slave the other end is rivetted around the neck of the master' & sanctions warmly the observation."[44] Although the brothers expressly had in mind the ethical implications of one race holding another in bondage, Emerson extended this image to suggest that the yoke around the slaveholder's neck presaged economic catastrophe as well. Like many northerners, Emerson held that slavery had grossly inhibited the economic development of the southern states, a judgment partly confirmed by his 1827 excursion to South Carolina and Florida. "St Augustine is the most idle of towns," he wrote Concord minister Ezra Ripley. "It is indeed the Castle of Indolence."[45] The very fact of the South's retarded progress contributed to Emerson's downplaying the efficacy of abolitionism. In time, the North and its economic juggernaut would overwhelm the South, thus precluding the need for an organized movement to abolish slavery. The South's peculiar institution was destined to die a natural death. Although the progression of events after 1845 changed his mind, until 1837 and his first public lecture on slavery, Emerson consistently struck an irenic note on behalf of the distressed slaveholder. "Far be it from me to reproach the planter," he wrote. "I think His misfortune is greater than his sin."[46]

As central to much of his thinking as his racial assumptions were, Emerson never questioned the savagery of the slave trade or the iniquity of chattel slavery itself. Deeply troubled by the very notion of one person holding another in bondage in what he believed to be a benevolent universe, Emerson was still a long way from resolving the fundamental question of slavery. If all persons possessed souls, then slavery must be a sin. "Canst thou ponder the vision," he asked, "and shew why Providence suffers the land of the richest productions to be thus defiled? Do human bodies lodge immortal souls,—and is this tortured life of bondage and tears a fit education for the bright ages of heaven and the commerce of angels?"[47] Closer to earth, he railed against the abhorrent international trade in human flesh. "To stop the slave traffic the nations should league themselves in indissoluble bands [and] should link the thunderbolts of national power to demolish this debtor to all Justice human & divine."[48] The slave trade was an institutionalized form of "kidnapping," for which there could be no justification except for a dreadfully corrupted "private interest."[49]

His racial prejudice notwithstanding, Emerson did express his antipathy to the institution in other ways. On May 29, 1831, the year Garrison began publication of the *Liberator*, Emerson welcomed Samuel J. May, abolitionist minister from Brooklyn, Connecticut, to his pulpit at Boston's Second Congregational Church. At a time when Brahmin Boston wanted nothing to do with Garrison and his holy war against slavery, and abolitionists like May were unwelcome in Unitarian pulpits, Emerson's invitation constituted a bold act at least in defense of the propriety of airing the issue in public. The following year Emerson again signaled his support for antislavery by once more opening Second Church's pulpit to the abolitionist cause, this time to Arnold Buffum, the Quaker cofounder of the New England Anti-Slavery Society.[50] The fact that Emerson was not only the ordained minister of Second Church but also held the esteemed public office of chaplain of the Massachusetts Legislature (the same office his father had once retained) lent an added measure of significance to this antislavery gesture. One can only speculate about his motives, as Emerson never explained them.

A few years later, in 1835, Emerson peripherally participated in another public act against slavery when he found himself embroiled in a scene that would be repeated in Boston many times in the years to come. A group of self-appointed keepers of the peace had gathered to silence an abolitionist speaker, in this case, Harriet Martineau, the English abolitionist and author of *Illustrations of Political Economy*. The all-but-deaf Ms. Martineau was "nearly mobbed" until the Emersons rescued her.[51] "At the time of the hubbub against me in Boston," she recalled, "Charles Emerson stood alone in a large company in defence of the right of free thought and speech, and declared that he had rather see Boston in ashes than that I, or anybody, should be debarred in any way from perfectly free speech. His brother Waldo invited me to be his guest, in the midst of my unpopularity. . . ."[52] In this instance and throughout virtually his entire antislavery career, such as it was, Emerson followed the lead of other family members. Charles was first to offer a public condemnation of slavery, while his elder brother held back, his 1837 slavery lecture following that of his younger brother by more than two years. Similarly, Lidian Jackson Emerson, Emerson's wife, was consistently the more active partner in Concord's antislavery circles. Emerson delivered the famous speeches, often at Lidian's prompting, but she proved the tireless worker for emancipation.[53] "She joined the Anti-Slavery Society," recalled their daughter, "and remained a zealous member until Slavery was abolished."[54] It was Lidian who "grieves aloud about the wretched negro in the horrors of the middle passage."[55] Mary Moody Emerson felt "the terrors of the retribution" for American slaveholding more than her famous nephew; she repeatedly prodded him to make the antislavery cause his own.[56] "Let him . . . lecture on this subject with zeal," she explained to Lidian in 1835, "& I will rejoice like Simeon of old."[57] Emerson needed to look no further than his family to commune with those who heeded the antislavery call more strongly than he.[58]

As in the Martineau imbroglio, it is clear that while slavery might have been the proximate cause of the trouble, the more immediate issue for the Emersons was the right of free speech. This subject remained an important, at times central element in Emerson's thinking and activities, frequently at the expense of the antislavery fight itself. For Emerson, the fight for freedom of expression impacted directly upon his own life and vocational struggles with the Congregational clergy. In some sense he resigned his pastorate at Second Church because he felt pressured to make his sermons, public prayers, and other utterances conform to established rituals and rules. It was but a small step to associate his personal struggle to break free of the circumscribed world of Unitarian convention and dogma with the larger crusade for freedom of expression so intimately tied to the antislavery movement. In preparation for his first public antislavery lecture in 1837, Emerson noted without equivocation that it was his "great duty" in regard to the abolition of slavery to enable antislavery crusaders to speak their minds without fear of retribution anywhere in Massachusetts.[59]

The Concord lecture of November 14, 1837, represented the culmination of Emerson's early thinking about chattel slavery. Delivered exactly one week after the murder of Elijah Lovejoy in Alton, Illinois, Emerson resolved to speak out at least in part because of his fellow New Englanders' indifference, particularly considering that the mayor of Boston had just refused Channing's request for the use of Faneuil Hall for a memorial in the slain man's honor.[60] Emerson expressly eulogized the abolitionist "martyr" in his "Heroism" lectures in the first months of 1838. "It is but the other day, that the brave Lovejoy gave his breast to the bullets of a mob for the rights of free speech and opinion," he declared before disapproving audiences, "and died when it was better not to live."[61] Ironically, he delivered his first antislavery lecture in the vestry of the Concord Second Congregational Church, all other accommodations being closed to discussion of so controversial a topic.

Emerson commenced by calling slavery "wholly iniquitous," after which he relegated further discussion of the peculiar institution to the latter part of his talk. In his outline, he listed the topics for consideration in order of importance: "Duty to us/Duty to Negro/Practicability/Slavery." Significantly, duty is repeated in succession, and "us" is distinguished from "Negro" and placed ahead of it. Consistent with his other considerations of the moment—his relation to his Unitarian faith in particular—Emerson began with his usual question concerning personal obligation; what should he and the members of the audience do?[62] Without the lecture manuscript itself, it is impossible to know precisely what the author presented as his duty. In preparation for his lecture, Emerson had noted that when it came to abolitionism it was his "great duty . . . to open our halls to the discussion of this question steadily day after day year after year until no man dare wag his finger at us." This "great duty of freedom," as he called it, was likely what he had in mind.[63] It is evident that Emerson explicitly privileged his obligations to himself over those to the slaves and free blacks. His brief notes make clear that, whatever his responsibilities concerning slavery, he understood them to be distinct and subordinate to other more pressing issues. "Beyond this [single lecture]," he concluded in 1837, "I do not feel a call to act. . . . Nearer duties." True to his word, Emerson refrained from offering another public pronouncement on slavery for nearly seven years.[64]

In the few paragraphs that followed his outline, Emerson carefully subsumed antislavery under the "one important revolution" of the day, which he called "the new value of the private man." Accordingly, Emerson believed that the onus fell upon him as well as his audience to remind their neighbors about the immorality of human bondage and leave them alone to decide the proper course of action. In contrast to the abolitionists, Emerson believed that the calm articulation of the obvious would do the trick; letting the public "know the truth" would bring slavery to its knees.[65] "Our duty in the matter is to Settle the right & wrong so that whenever we are called to vote in the matter, we may not dodge the question; we may not trifle with it. We may not be ignorant but do an act of reason & justice in the vote we cast. A vote of a freeholder is a rising power."[66] Much to the consternation of the abolitionists, Emerson insisted upon focusing on the need, as he put it, for "practicability." Unlike the abolitionists, whose "plan to awaken the conscience" Emerson cheered, the author refused to conceive of antislavery as more than a political movement with praiseworthy goals. As for slavery itself, Emerson again ranked his observations. Slavery was "self destructive [crossed out]/wholly iniquitous/self destructive [and]/a dreadful reagent." That Emerson at least initially considered slavery more self-destructive than "iniquitous" or "a dreadful reagent" is significant and helps to explain his reticence concerning abolitionism. Sounding Panglossian, Emerson reasoned that if the institution was on its way toward inevitable collapse, then abolition was superfluous. The free institutions of the North had engendered an economic dynamo that, when combined with right voting, guaranteed the demise of the plantation South.[67]

Emerson still excoriated slavery itself. Believing his "little plain prose" on the subject to be "somewhat tedious by often repetition," the lecturer nonetheless went on to condemn the institution. It "yet needs to be said again & again until it has perforated the thick deaf ear, that no man can hold property in Man; that Reason is not chattel; cannot be bought & sold; and that every pretended traffic in such stock is invalid & criminal." Emerson's use of the term *dreadful reagent* is more interesting, suggesting that at this point he still pitied the planters for their predicament. Anticipating Harriet Beecher Stowe by proclaiming slavery to be "almost an unmixed evil to the Southerner," Emerson appeared more concerned with its collateral effects on southern society than upon the slaves themselves. Not slaveholders but slavery "is the most striking example in the history of the world of the evil of taking one wrong step." Not present-day plantations but the long ago "introduction of slaves unfortunately distinguishable by color has entailed all these crimes on the states." Emerson insisted that the "trials of the master are innumerable & inappreciable by the northerner," and that he therefore needed help instead of harassment.[68]

Emerson continued by urging his white audience "to befriend" the "amiable" blacks, but not necessarily to consider them as equals.[69] "I think it cannot be maintained by any candid person," he stated, falling back on his historical and empirical understanding of race, "that the African race have ever occupied or do promise ever to occupy any very high place in the human family. Their present condition is the strongest proof that they cannot. . . . Before the energy of the Caucasian race all the other races have quailed and done obeisance."[70]

In sum, then, Emerson's first foray into antislavery agitation proved limited. For the Concord sage, slavery had no place in the unfolding drama of American civilization, nor did Africans. The institution was on the road to ultimate extinction with or without the assistance of abolitionists and public figures like himself. "But when we have settled the right & wrong of this question," he concluded, "I think we have done all we can. A man can only extend his active attention to a certain finite amount of claims. We have much nearer duties than to the poor black slaves of Carolina," he wrote, "and the effect of the present excitement [abolitionism] is to exaggerate that." Small wonder the abolitionists in attendance that November day departed disheartened.[71]

Between 1837 and 1850 Emerson underwent a change of heart concerning many aspects of slavery and race. This transformation, or evolution, however, took place almost exclusively in private. Despite the entreaties of friends and abolitionists, Emerson eschewed speaking in public on slavery during the seven years following his lecture in Concord's church. Not until his speech on the anniversary of emancipation in the West Indies on August 1, 1844, did he again speak out against slavery. Emerson hardly shied away from public controversy in these highly charged years, during which he delivered his infamous address at the Harvard Divinity School. In "these flying days," as he called them, Emerson established himself as one of the nation's leading public figures, its greatest essayist, and one of the central players of the amorphous philosophical movement derisively styled Transcendentalism. In these productive and stimulating times, as his journals and notebooks demonstrate, Emerson thought a great deal about slavery, race, the planter class, abolitionism, and the relation of them all to the nation's manifest destiny.[72]

In these private ruminations, Emerson's thinking developed significantly. By 1844, he still believed that slavery was a retrograde and barbaric institution that would die of its own accord. Similarly, he remained adamant that the laudable efforts of the abolitionists were often misplaced, as was their saccharine moralizing. More importantly, with the diminution of the racist assumptions he had held so strongly in previous years, Emerson came to express his admiration for the African race and his hope that its unfolding faculties entailed its ultimate survival. Inversely proportional to this calculus was Emerson's estimation of the planter class, which through the 1840s was clinging more than ever to its peculiar institution. With the annexation of Texas and the war with Mexico, Emerson increasingly lambasted the slaveholders and their political allies, in the North as well as the South, for their selfish and inexcusable refusal to see slavery for the injustice it was. By 1850 and the national Compromise of that year, Emerson had jettisoned his old optimistic nostrums about slavery ending of its own accord any time in the foreseeable future. He was ready to join the fight to abolish slavery and assume the cause of the slave wherever it led.

In this middle period Emerson most conspicuously altered his attitude toward the abolitionists. At the beginning of the 1840s Emerson remained adamant that abolition was the futile gesture of New Englanders who would be better served by working closer to home. In his journals, he hurled more invective against slavery's opponents than against their southern adversaries, as his animus toward the reformer and the abolitionist waxed despite the fact that he enjoyed warm friendships with several of their number, Wendell Phillips foremost among them. As much as he respected the antislavery cause in theory, he loathed the haughty, self-righteous, patronizing, increasingly rote cant that spewed from the mouths of interchangeable agitators. The author of "Self-Reliance" found the typical abolitionist or reformer anything but. His devotion to individual autonomy proved antithetical to the preachiness of the benevolent Christian evangelizers of the movement. "At dinner, today we wickedly roasted the martyrs," Emerson quipped about the abolitionists. "I say that nothing is so disgusting in our days as nothing is so dog-cheap as martyrdom."[73] Living in Concord "where every third man lectures on Slavery" inevitably exasperated Emerson's patience.[74] Never one to suffer fools or imitators gladly, Emerson perceived these reformers and moral suasionists to be possessed of the same psychological motivations of personal insecurity and displaced guilt that David Donald, Richard Hofstadter, and Stanley Elkins gestured at a generation ago.[75] "We will almost sin to spite them," Emerson observed.[76]

Emerson's at best tepid support of abolitionism was typical of a number of Transcendentalists. Henry Thoreau and Margaret Fuller echoed many of Emerson's reservations.[77] Like him, they found anathema the religious and moralizing mode of myriad reformers. The late 1830s and early 1840s, the efflorescence of romantic reform in New England, marked the point in Emerson's career when he most emphatically rejected organized Christianity in the United States. The author of the Harvard Divinity School Address and apostate from "the dead pond" that was Unitarianism could hardly have been drawn to the Christian overtones and saccharine religious message of moral regeneration bandied about by some abolitionists. In all of Emerson's antislavery addresses from 1844 on, he never gestured at what so many others called the movement's efforts to atone for sin and thereby revitalize a waning Christian piety.[78] Slavery was depraved, but it was a sin no greater than a multitude of evils closer to home. "Society gains nothing," he had declared in his dramatic "New England Reformers" lecture in March of 1844, "whilst a man, not himself renovated, attempts to renovate things around him: he has become tediously good in some particular, but negligent or narrow in the rest."[79]

The author of "New England Reformers" no more condemned the pure soul fighting injustice than he condoned slavery. In 1844, for example, Emerson praised Garrison for being "so masterly an agent of good . . . I cannot speak of that gentleman without respect."[80] Emerson eulogized the slain abolitionist "martyr" Elijah Lovejoy in his "Heroism" lectures of 1838. Emerson also praised Phillips whom he called "such an artist that he ought to be walking all the galleries of Europe, and yet he is fighting these hard questions."[81] But Garrison, Lovejoy, Phillips, and Lucretia Mott were the exceptions. Only in the 1850s did Emerson's estimate of abolitionists in general turn from scorn to admiration.

Despite his personal dislike for many abolitionists and his conviction that they did as much to harm their cause as help it, Emerson made selective stands on behalf of abolitionists and their right to trumpet their cause. From welcoming May and Buffum to his pulpit in the early 1830s to fighting for Phillips's right to speak at the Concord lyceum a decade later, Emerson labored on behalf of their cause, especially when he found himself in the minority. Indeed, he relished a good fight for an unpopular principle. Only such a perverse character would have elaborated on "the attractiveness of war" before Garrison and the annual meeting of the American Peace Society.[82] "We want to be expressed, and yet you take from us War," he proclaimed to an astonished audience, "that great opportunity which allowed the accumulations of electricity to stream off from both poles the positive & the negative."[83] When in January of 1845 the Concord Lyceum took up the question of offering its platform for "a Lecture on Slavery by Wendell Phillips," Emerson "pressed the acceptance." In ringing terms he argued for the need to take up this great issue,

> because I thought in the present state of this country the particular subject of Slavery had a commanding right to be heard in all places in New England in season & sometimes out of season, that as in Europe the partition of Poland was an outrage so flagrant that all European men must be willing once in every month or two to be plagued with hearing over again the horrid story; so this iniquity of Slavery in this country was a ghost that would not down at the bidding of Boston merchants, or the best democratic drill-officers; but the people must consent to be plagued with it from time to time until something was done, & we had appeased the negro blood so.[84]

Emerson colloquially summarized his views by declaring that like "a shoe-shop," a lyceum "must be boundless in its hospitality."[85]

In the aftermath of the decision to welcome Phillips, Emerson and Henry Thoreau, who with his mentor had risen in defense of Phillips and free speech, became curators of the lyceum in Concord, two of their number having resigned in protest.[86] After the great orator appeared before them in March, Emerson lauded Phillips's performance in a letter to his friend Samuel Ward. He declared that he had not heard "a better lesson in many weeks than last night in a couple of hours."[87] Predictably, Phillips was the exception; as a curator and a concerned citizen, Emerson sat through many tedious talks by a variety of abolitionists and reformers with barely disguised dismay, much as he did though dry and dull sermons in the Unitarian churches of eastern Massachusetts. "Rain rain," he lamented. "The good rain like a bad preacher does not know when to leave off."[88] Emerson rationalized that his suffering for the cause, as it were, was a just retribution for his own refusal to speak out. "Plato says that the punishment which the wise suffer who refuse to take part in the government, is to live under the government of worse men," Emerson paraphrased Socrates in the *Republic*. "That is the penalty of abstaining to speak in a public meeting, that you shall sit & hear wretched & currish speakers."[89]

Either in spite or because of his suffering through too many abysmal antislavery speakers, Emerson refrained from joining the fray. The sage of Concord, who in time derived between one-half and one-third of his income from public lecturing, chose not to speak on slavery between his 1837 lecture and his 1844 emancipation address. True to his convictions, Emerson publicly ignored the issue. If the vast majority of abolitionists were wasting their time in public posturing and wasted words, it would be that much more futile, even hypocritical, for him to preach antislavery. Emerson fretted a great deal about the dangers of hypocrisy, as was only natural for a social critic. As preacher and public lecturer, in one way or another Emerson's job entailed instructing others how to live. Always Socratic, Emerson constantly questioned himself in his journals about the relation of public preaching and private action. Like his Athenian hero, he insisted on constant self-examination in order to ensure that he was living up to his exhortations and admonitions. The fine line Emerson drew between appropriate public gestures and inappropriate ones can be glimpsed in the swirl of events surrounding the death of Salem, Massachusetts, minister and freedom fighter Charles T. Torrey. Torrey had died in a Maryland prison where he had been languishing since his conviction for abetting runaway slaves. Emerson chose to attend Torrey's funeral, which he thought moving enough to comment upon several times in his journals.[90] Several months earlier, however, he had refused to sign a petition on Torrey's behalf. He endorsed the martyr's death by his presence at the funeral, but withheld his signature, as he explained to John Greenleaf Whittier, because he was not intimate enough with the specifics of the matter. "I do not get as much of the facts as I want," he elucidated with care, "and too much of another element."[91] What seemed rote and obligatory to others provoked reticence in Emerson.

One of the reasons Emerson refrained from publicly denouncing slavery until his 1844 emancipation address stemmed from the fallout of his single previous foray into public posturing. In 1838 he read an "Appeal for the Cherokees" to a Concord gathering and, more famously, addressed a scathing letter to President Martin Van Buren that was printed in newspapers in New England and in the nation's capital.[92] With New Englanders of all stripes, Emerson bitterly opposed Van Buren's noxious order to begin the last and most grievous stage of the campaign of forced removal of the Cherokee peoples, which resulted in the "trail of tears." For his part, he felt passionately about the undeniable duplicity and repugnance of the removal policy, as had the 492 Concordians who signed a petition of protest, calling it "a dereliction of all faith and virtue, [and] such a denial of justice, and such deafness to screams for mercy."[93] Nevertheless, as much as "this disaster of Cherokees" had come "to blacken my days & nights," Emerson quickly regretted his letter to President Van Buren.[94] "Yesterday went the letter to V[an] B[uren]," he wrote in his journal, "a letter hated of me. A deliverance that does not deliver the soul."[95] The letter and the speech, he was convinced, "look to me degrading & injurious do what I can. It is like dead cats around one's neck." He confessed that he had written the letter "for the sad reason that no other mortal will move & if I do not, why it is left undone."[96] For Emerson, this negative motivation, like all external forces, was insufficient and false. He would think twice before undertaking similar actions in the future.

For as long as abolitionists had made their rounds and delivered their rousing speeches, Emerson had believed that changing certain personal habits would do more for the movement than their "dog-cheap" eloquence. Slavery was as much a New England problem as a southern one, Emerson sustained; things could and should be done closer to home before taking to the lecture platform. "I confess I do not wish to live in a nation where slavery exists," Emerson had remarked in 1835, yet had not exiled himself from his native land.[97] In a similar vein, three years later he accused himself and his New England neighbors of hypocrisy. "In the base hour, we become slaveholders. We use persons as things, & we think of persons as things," he lamented.[98] "We swell the cry of horror at the slaveholder, & we treat our laborer or grocer or farmer as a thing, & so hold slaves ourselves."[99] Conscious of their inconsistency in relation to two domestic hires, the Emersons tried several egalitarian experiments albeit without much success. Emerson's idea that the entire household—help included—should share meals together resulted in much embarrassment and a flat refusal. Equally as ill-fated was the family's attempt to do without domestic help entirely, Lidian's poor health and the great number of houseguests being the deciding factors. Nevertheless, Emerson felt strongly about the relationship between New England luxury and southern slavery. "The antislavery agency like so many of our employments is a suicidal business. Whilst I talk, some poor farmer drudges & slaves for me." For Emerson, "he who does his own work frees a slave."[100] Despite his estimable Concord residence and a steady dividend income—both part of the windfall of his tragic first marriage—Emerson constantly sought to live sensibly and without ostentation. "If my debts, as they threaten, should consume what money I have, I should live just as I do now," he insisted. "I should eat worse food & wear a coarser coat and should wander in a potato patch instead of in the wood—but it is I & not my Twelve Hundred dollars a year, that love God."[101] Far more than an outward gesture, this frugality reflected the underlying praxis of Emerson's commitments as well as the residue of Puritan experimental piety. He did not preach what he could not live.

Phillips and other abolitionists relentlessly pressed Emerson to become more active in the movement, simultaneously reminding him of the iniquity of slavery and his growing fame and influence.[102] The sheer volume of their efforts suggests that even if they feared that Emerson was no abolitionist and that his cosmic optimism threatened to undermine the movement's total commitment to immediatism,[103] they readily grasped the impact his support would carry. Despite the entreaties of abolitionists, Emerson remained unwilling to become an antislavery activist. At the very moment when he was composing his 1844 West Indian emancipation address, the speech that proved to be the high point of his antislavery statements, he recorded his uneasiness with activism. "My Genius loudly calls me to stay where I am," he confided to his journal.[104] "Things are to be done which I have no skill to do, or are to be said which others can say better. . . . All my virtue consists in my consent to be insignificant," he concluded.[105] Emerson's racial assumptions surely played a part in his disinclination to do more toward the abolition of slavery before 1844. Active participation seemed implausible for anyone who believed that the "degradation of the black race . . . is inevitable to the men they are, and nobody can redeem them but themselves."[106] As long as Emerson assented to the pernicious claim of African inferiority, as he decidedly did until 1844, he had no leg to stand on. Emerson could only take up the abolitionist cause after his racial prejudice abated.

The first evidence of any melioration of Emerson's racial beliefs emerged in the summer of 1844. The notes he made while composing his "Emancipation in the British West Indies" address are the earliest indication of a critical turning point, containing the most generous and egalitarian statements on race he ever pronounced. He insisted that "the alleged hopeless inferiority of the colored race" could be and must be refuted.[107] By the summer of 1844 he had come to realize that no matter what the facts of the situation were, there was no way to fight slavery and its planter-apologists without taking on their pivotal assertion of African American inferiority.[108] His visceral sense that the proslavery argument demanded refutation inspired him as nothing else could to challenge the supposition of African inferiority. Emerson showed his determination to unburden himself on this matter by the choice of the anniversary of this particular event to speak out. The First of August anniversary celebrations of British emancipation in the West Indies had a significant biracial context in the North, as "blacks often joined with whites to celebrate" British emancipation, according to Will Gravely.[109] It was a day in which New Englanders might go beyond the evils of southern slavery and glimpse a multiracial American future.

Even in his address, which was delivered in Concord as one of many celebrations that day, Emerson betrayed uneasiness. He began his address with a self-deprecating nod to the fact that there were many reasons why he was not the ideal person for the present task. "I might well hesitate, coming from other studies, and without the smallest claim to be a special laborer in this work of humanity, to undertake to set this matter before you," he confessed.[110] Hardly a champion of abolition, Emerson up to that point had delivered exactly one antislavery address in his estimable oratorical career, and that a rather unremarkable one. Never having been a leader in the fight against slavery and without a claim to any distinctive knowledge of the events surrounding British emancipation, Emerson nevertheless politely asserted: "I shall not apologize for my weakness." The essential justice of the matter was sufficient to make it everyone's concern. He would rely on the fact that the "subject is said to have the property of making dull men eloquent."[111]

Several elements of the 1844 speech suggest his rationale for breaking his long silence. In part, Emerson believed that he might offer the many abolitionists in attendance some unsolicited advice on at least two counts. In their headlong rush to free the slave and vilify the master, abolitionists damaged their own worthy cause. Emerson advised the abolitionists first to see their own work in the context of slavery's inevitable demise. After all, West Indian emancipation had proved the "history of mankind . . . exhibits a steady gain of truth and right" that no human could alter.[112] Providence foretold that emancipation in the American South would shortly follow. Additionally, the speaker urged his audience to "withhold every reproachful, and, if we can, every indignant remark" directed toward the slaveholders. "In this cause, we must renounce our temper, and the risings of pride," because the masters were victims as well as perpetrators in this American ordeal of slavery and freedom.[113] "We sympathize very tenderly here with the poor aggrieved planter, of whom so many unpleasant things are said."[114] Emerson admonished the abolitionists in the audience to moderate their harsh tone. They ought to remind themselves that emancipation promised to be part of the inevitable unfolding of a benign providence. Speaking on the occasion of the anniversary of West Indian emancipation was no accident, as Emerson fully grasped that this particular historical event, at least in his teleological reading of it, bolstered his own peculiar form of quietism.

There had been little time in the months before his address to research the story of West Indian emancipation. Yet his reading about it, about the revolution in Saint Domingue and the heroism of Toussaint L'Ouverture, as well as his initial impression of Frederick Douglass, had forced him to reconsider his blatant racial prejudice.[115] "The First of August," Emerson declared, "marks the entrance of a new element into modern politics, namely, the civilization of the negro. A man is added to the human family. Not the least affecting part of this history of abolition, is, the annihilation of the old nonsense about the nature of the negro."[116] Emerson chose this occasion to admit that events had proven him wrong. He was in public to declare: "It now appears that the negro race is, more than any other, susceptible of rapid civilization."[117]

His reading about emancipation in the West Indies provoked him not to dwell on the "concession of the whites" or the achievements of British abolitionists William Wilberforce and Granville Sharpe, but on the slaves and freedmen, "the earning of the blacks," as he put it, who had demanded and attained emancipation for their people. "They won the pity and respect which they have received, by their powers and native endowments."[118] Emerson found himself coming to understand that there were "many styles of civilization, and not one only."[119] The promising events of the previous decade in the Caribbean, Emerson fervently hoped, pointed toward an unfolding multiracial drama in the West in which "the black man [who] carries in his bosom an indispensable element of a new and coming civilization"[120] would play an important part. In stark contrast to the sad history of the Native Americans, whom Emerson believed had been destined for extinction, the Africans transported over the centuries to the Western Hemisphere were in the midst of freeing themselves from bondage and thereby creating their own destiny. Having undergone what amounted to a revolution in his thinking, Emerson at least on this day became an eloquent spokesman for "this race [which] is to be honored for itself" and which was on the brink of a new era. "I say to you," Emerson announced, deftly mixing his passion for self-reliance with his emerging respect for African Americans,

> you must save yourself, black or white, man or woman; other help is none. I esteem the occasion of this jubilee to be the proud discovery, that the black race can contend with the white; that, in the great anthem which we call history, a piece of many parts and vast compass, after playing a long time a very low and subdued accompaniment, they perceive the time arrived when they can strike in with effect and take a master's part in the music.[121]

Blacks were persons, capable of individual identity and improvement. These were radical sentiments that were consistent with the Emersonian doctrine of self-reliance and gave eloquent public testimony to a new stage in Emerson's thinking about race.

Emerson's searching reexamination of blacks' capabilities did not signal a predisposition to join the ranks of the abolitionists. They would do well, he informed Wendell Phillips on several occasions, not to look for more public declarations from him.[122] In 1844 Emerson held fast to the notion that in a crucial sense the abolitionist movement was a waste of time. Abolitionists' speeches and accusations were sentimental gestures offered in the right spirit, but futile in the face of the "single noble wind" of emancipation. "So now, the arrival in the world of such men as Toussaint, and the Haytian heroes, or of the leaders of their race in Barbadoes and Jamaica," Emerson declared, "outweighs in good omen all the English and American humanity. The anti-slavery of the whole world, is dust in the balance before this,—is a poor squeamishness and nervousness: the might and the right are here: here is the anti-slave; here is man: and if you have man, black and white is an insignificance."[123]

Just below the surface optimism of the address lay a single but important note of caution that portended the political crisis of the 1850s. Pitted against the "laws of nature" and the "moral sense" were the twin perils of narrow self-interest and the ubiquitous desire for luxury. Human weakness for sugar, coffee, tobacco, rum, cotton, and other commodities produced by slave labor all too easily convinced masters with slaves and without that Africans "seemed created by providence to bear the heat and the whipping, and make these fine articles."[124] There remained the looming danger of sordid material interest throwing itself in the way of progress, and using all means available to postpone the inevitable. Even in Massachusetts, conscience had not yet overcome cotton.

On the eve of events about which Emerson could only have guessed—Polk's election, the annexation of Texas, the defeat of the Wilmot Proviso, and war with Mexico—the author worried about the prospects of emancipation in the United States. "Forgive me, fellow citizens, if I own to you, that in the last few days that my attention has been occupied with this history, I have not been able to read a page of it, without the most painful comparisons. Whilst I have read of England, I have thought of New England."[125] Planter intransigence and universal prejudice threatened emancipation in the United States at precisely the moment when the English had adopted an act "signal in the history of civilization."[126] Emerson's cosmic optimism did not blind him to the plain facts of America's peculiar institution and its deep roots in the psychology, property, and politics of the nation. Politics concerned him particularly. Before his Concord audience, Emerson reproached the politicians of Massachusetts for their failure to abolish slavery, for it was in their power to do so. The inherent justness of emancipation had sparked the Englishman to action, so why not them, he demanded. "There is a disastrous want of *men* from New England," Emerson proclaimed, as he blasted the "tameness and silence of the two senators and ten representatives of the State" that enabled them "to sit dumb at their desks, and see their constituents captured and sold." Emerson found his confidence in government and its limited but critical capacities slipping as hoped-for political heroes, Daniel Webster first among them, were "bullied into silence by southern gentlemen."[127] West Indian emancipation had made manifest the propriety and benefit of abolitionism to all humanity. Only time would tell if New Englanders and other Americans would rise to the occasion.

Despite his reproach of the abolitionists and his concern about the dangers of a sordid materialism, Emerson ultimately chose to be upbeat and hopeful in 1844. There is little sense of imminent crisis in his address. "The conscience of the white & the improvement of the black cooperated," he wrote in the days after finishing a draft of his address, "& the Emancipation became inevitable."[128] Surely the same forces were at work in the United States. This characteristic optimism enabled the Concord sage to remain only a fellow traveler of abolitionism for several more years, sanguine that Americans of all stripes would come to see as he had that "the negro has saved himself."[129] Having publicly questioned the validity of the arguments for black inferiority, Emerson asked in his journal, "Does not he do more to abolish slavery who works all day steadily in his garden, than he who goes to the abolition meeting & makes a speech?"[130]

Between 1845 and 1850, events close to home slowly drew Emerson into the antislavery fray, turning the pedagogue toward outright activism. Duty compelled Emerson to attend a January 1845 meeting in support of his Concord neighbor and friend Samuel Hoar, who had been harassed out of South Carolina while serving as an agent of the state of Massachusetts on behalf of its free blacks illegally kidnapped into slavery. Even on this occasion in which his state, community, and friend had been "insulted," as he put it, Emerson counseled caution: "we can do nothing, only let us not do wrong."[131] When the following year Thoreau refused to pay his poll tax, "not approving some uses to which the public expenditure was applied," Emerson found fault with his young friend and protégé.[132] A night in jail at the public's expense smacked of showmanship and impetuousness. Nevertheless, in his journals he conspicuously contrasted Thoreau's activism with that of the abolitionists.[133]

"My friend Mr Thoreau has gone to jail rather than pay his tax," Emerson affirmed. "The abolitionists denounce war & give much time to it, but they pay the tax."[134] As much as he denounced the Mexican War, Emerson attempted to keep to his regular work regime, devoting a great deal of 1846 to researching and writing the essays that would comprise *Representative Men*. In 1848 Emerson fled the war and sectional strife altogether for England and a triumphal lecturing tour during which he attained celebrity status. As late as the spring of 1850 he was writing of his "misfortune that his virtues are all on paper, & when the time comes to use them, he rubs his eyes & tries to remember what is it that he should do."[135]

The Compromise of 1850 and Webster's Seventh of March speech forced Emerson's hand. Only then did he cease to characterize his support of abolition, as he had to Carlyle in 1844, as "an intrusion . . . into another sphere & so much loss of virtue in my own."[136] Webster's apostasy and the land grab that was the national settlement of the Mexican War confirmed his worst fears. Worst of all, the venomous Fugitive Slave Law, the product of weak and selfish men, supplied ample proof that interests had defeated ideals in the nation's capital. Emerson altered his emphasis when writing about abolitionism, converting what had been a dubious single-issue campaign into a moral crusade. With the seeds of equalitarianism having been planted some years earlier in his West Indian emancipation address, Emerson was equipped to take up the antislavery cause with the conviction he was fighting for freedom and the higher law. The political process in shambles and the slave power intransigent, Emerson understood that like it or not he was obliged to devote himself to the immediate abolition of slavery. Still uncomfortable with his newly adopted role, Emerson accepted discomfort as a small price to pay for fighting a holy war. After 1850 duty to himself and duty to the Negro became one and the same, and his 1837 distinction between "us and them" evaporated in the heat of battle.

Emerson, in 1850, would have preferred to avoid meddling in politics. He could not have been more honest when he declared in 1851 that "the last year has forced us all into politics," as he would have liked to devote his energies elsewhere.[137] In this sense, throughout the 1850s and the Civil War, Emerson remained a reluctant abolitionist. His major contribution to the antislavery cause came largely from the lecture platform. He delivered significant addresses—most of which were posthumously published—on the Fugitive Slave Law, American slavery, Bleeding Kansas, the caning of Sumner, John Brown, and the Preliminary Emancipation Proclamation, as well as moving poems on emancipation and the heroism of the black soldiers of the Massachusetts 54th Regiment. He offered countless more informal talks and lectures and participated in numerous other events, as well as attending meetings and the lectures of others. From his home in Concord, Emerson joined his wife and friends in raising money for the New England Emigrant Aid Society and other antislavery causes, hosting prominent abolitionists such as John Brown, and opening their home to other antislavery activists. In 1854, Bush, the Emersons' residence on the Boston Road, became a stop on the Underground Railroad, joining those of the Alcotts, Brooks, and Thoreaus.[138] It is impossible to imagine the Concord sage, who assiduously protected his solitude, becoming so publicly engaged in any other issue.

Congressional passage of the Fugitive Slave Law forcefully intruded into the lives of New Englanders.[139] In breaking the gentlemen's agreement of 1793 and binding every citizen of Massachusetts to assist when summoned in the recapture of runaway slaves, the law compelled everyone to choose sides, effectively reversing decades of exertion to disown slavery in Massachusetts.[140] Emerson heaped opprobrium on Webster and the hated Fugitive Slave Law in a journal entry in 1851.

> In the weakness of the Union the law of 1793 was framed, and much may be said in palliation of it. . . . It was a little gross the taste for boiling babies but as long as this kind of cookery was confined within their own limits, we could agree for other purposes, & wear one flag. The law affirmed a right to hunt their human prey within our territory; and this law availed just this much to affirm their own platform,—to fix the fact, that, though confessedly savage, they were yet at liberty to consort with men;—though they had tails, & their incisors were a little long, yet it is settled that they shall by courtesy be called men; we will all make believe they are Christians; & we promise not to look at their tails or incisors when they come into company. This was all very well. The convenient equality was affirmed, they were admitted to dine & sup, & profound silence on the subject of tails & incisors was kept. No man in all New England spoke of Ghilanes in their presence. But of course on their part all idea of boiling babies in our caboose was dropt; all idea of hunting in our yards fat babies to boil, was dropt; & the law became, as it should, a dead letter.[141]

No one worth their salt could retreat to their study and avert their eyes from an act which "bring[s] down the free & Christian state of Massachusetts to the cannibal level." The act legalized "the crime of kidnapping," which as Emerson expressed, "is on a footing with the crimes of murder & of incest."[142]

Worse still, so many Boston Brahmins, following Webster and Edward Everett, acceded to the act without so much as a whimper of protest. While southerners cheered the fact that men such as Thomas Sims and Anthony Burns were returned to slavery in shackles, Bostonians did nothing.[143] "The lesson of these days is the vulgarity of wealth," Emerson curtly observed. "We know that wealth will vote for the same thing which the worst & meanest of the people vote for. Wealth will vote for rum, will vote for tyranny, will vote for slavery, will vote against the ballot. . . . Plainly Boston does not wish liberty, & can only be pushed & tricked into a rescue of the slave. Its attitude as loving liberty is affected & theatrical."[144] The fact that Webster, Everett, Chief Justice Lemuel Shaw, who "declined to affirm the unconstitutionality of the Fugitive Slave Law," and virtually the entire enclave of Boston elite had sacrificed principle for pecuniary interest even ostensibly in the name of union drove Emerson from his study as nothing else could.[145] "If the motto on all palace-gates is 'Hush,' the honorable ensign of our town-halls should be 'Proclaim.' "[146] For a decade Emerson upbraided the inhabitants of the Bay State for the "degradation & personal dishonour" that their acquiescence to the slave catchers lowered "on every house in Massachusetts."[147] More in disgust than approbation, the *Boston Daily Advertiser* noted that the capture and "repatriation" of Burns had made "a decided abolitionist" of Emerson.[148]

Even as Emerson wrote that he "had quite other slaves to free than those negroes,"[149] for at least a decade he became a tireless agent of antislavery, making countless public appearances and engaging in many activities in support of abolition. In one thirteen-month span in 1854–55, Emerson delivered no fewer than nine antislavery lectures throughout the Northeast, including four readings of his "American Slavery" address.[150] As James Cabot aptly noted, in the years after 1850 "the politics of the day occupy an unusual space in Emerson's journals, and intrude themselves upon all his speculations."[151] Like his friend Charles Sumner, whom South Carolina Congressman Preston Brooks would shortly cane in the Senate chamber for his inflammatory "Crime Against Kansas" speech, Emerson seemed to have had his worst fears confirmed by the passage of the Fugitive Slave Law. Only days after Sumner's vicious caning at the hands of Brooks, Emerson composed a ringing defense of his friend and sufferer in the abolitionist cause, in which he declared "we must get rid of slavery, or we must get rid of freedom."[152] Sumner may have been silenced (temporarily), but not so Emerson. In the months during which Sumner slowly recuperated, Emerson ratcheted up his abolitionist message.

In the 1850s Emerson enjoyed good relations with most abolitionists, who for their part welcomed him to the cause. Having become acquainted with Sumner in 1837 when the young Harvard graduate had obtained from Emerson a letter of introduction to Thomas Carlyle, by the 1850s the two men were fast friends, Sumner having displaced Webster in Emerson's estimation as the most able American political figure. In addition to Sumner, the Concord sage found himself surrounded by a set of devoted abolitionists whose activities and beliefs he respected implicitly. There was Thoreau, of course, who had prodded his neighbors with his abolitionist sentiments and speeches since he had graduated from Harvard, and Bronson Alcott, the visionary and teacher, who risked his life by single-handedly attempting to run a Boston gauntlet in order to rescue Anthony Burns from slave catchers.[153] And there was the Reverend Theodore Parker, who himself was indicted for his part in the failed effort to liberate Burns. When Parker lived in nearby West Roxbury, he had been a frequent visitor to Concord and the Emerson household. The two ministers had become intimate since Parker had been enraptured by Emerson's notorious Divinity School Address in 1838, which he walked several miles to attend in Cambridge. Although Emerson demurred from the social activism that characterized Parker's career, the two Unitarians made common cause against slavery after 1850.

Parker often came to town to meet with Franklin Sanborn, the Concord schoolteacher, who like Parker was one of the "Secret Six" that funneled money to John Brown. After graduating from Harvard, Sanborn had come to Concord at Emerson's prompting.[154] He frequently solicited his mentor's help, particularly on matters relating to the local chapter of the New England Emigrant Aid Society, which raised funds to procure supplies and guns for Free-Soil settlers in Kansas. At either Parker's or Sanborn's request, Emerson consented to be the featured speaker at a September 1856 rally for "Kansas Relief" in Cambridge. When John Brown spoke about Kansas at Concord's Town Hall the following year, Emerson donated twenty-five dollars to the cause and cordially invited the Hero of Osawatomie to be his houseguest. Emerson found much to admire in this rough "freedom fighter," whose activities since President Franklin Pierce had signed the Kansas-Nebraska Act had done more to end slavery than all the abolitionists' speeches combined. A man of few words, Brown nevertheless "gave a good account of himself" at the Concord Town Hall.[155] Listening to the iron-willed abolitionist on this day and at another appearance, on Brown's fifty-ninth birthday, when he was soliciting funds for his ill-fated raid on Harpers Ferry, Emerson found himself strangely drawn to Brown, although it seems unlikely he fathomed precisely what the old man was about to undertake. Nevertheless, Emerson implicitly understood Brown's dictum: enough words; it was time for action.

In the fall of 1859, while Brown awaited execution in Virginia after his abortive raid, Emerson "privately" wrote to Governor Alexander Wise imploring him to show Brown clemency. John Brown, he declared, was "the rarest of heroes a pure idealist, with no by-ends of his own. He is therefore precisely what lawyers call crazy, being governed by ideas, & not by external circumstance. He has afforded them the first trait marked in the books as betraying insanity, namely, disproportion between means & ends."[156] After Brown's execution, Emerson joined mourners in Boston in an effort to raise money for his family. "John Brown was an idealist," Emerson declared, who "believed in his ideas to that extent, that he existed to put them all into action. He did not believe in moral suasion;—he believed in putting the thing through."[157] Emerson greatly respected Brown for his ability to put his ideas into action. For Emerson, who is too often accused of aloofness, ideas had to find validation in daily existence. The idealist was always the man of the world.

Emerson's antislavery activism in the 1850s and its consequence for the abolitionist movement should not be underestimated. The passage of the Fugitive Slave Law and the forceful return of fugitive slaves in Massachusetts galvanized Emerson as no other events could. Firmly in the abolitionist camp, Emerson powerfully utilized his talent for public speaking and his estimable fame to speed the downfall of the Slave Power.[158] His actions made abundantly clear what he had claimed for years. Just as soon as he sensed the vital need for an abolitionist movement and the efficacy of his participation in the movement, he immediately joined the fray. Slavery had always been the nation's most despicable institution. Only after 1850 did he realize that only an advance guard of abolitionists could effect the means to eradicate it.

At the outbreak of the Civil War, Emerson was approaching his fifty-eighth birthday. For several decades he had been preaching an encomium to the Union in his characteristic optative mood.[159] "Our political constitution is the hope of the world," he declared as late as 1860.[160] In the uncertain times after the firing on Fort Sumter, Emerson remained optimistic about the destiny of the nation. "If the abundance of heaven only sends us a fair share of light & conscience," he penned to a friend, "we shall redeem America for all its sinful years since the century began."[161] Although he had neither predicted nor desired war, and like most New Englanders when it came thought it would be brief, he understood with the now deceased John Brown the necessity "to purge this land with blood." Emerson fervently believed, as he had written in his "Speech on Affairs in Kansas," that when it came to chattel slavery, "extirpation is the only cure."[162] A decade before the outbreak of hostilities, he had declared the utter impossibility of "peace whilst this devilish seed of war is in our soil. Root it out. Burn it up."[163] Even as he dissuaded his son Edward from enlisting, Emerson wrote that the conflagration was preferable to peace with slaveholders. "The war,—though from such despicable beginnings, has assumed such huge proportions that it threatens to engulf us all—no preoccupation can exclude it, & no hermitage can hide us," he admitted. "And yet, gulf as it is, the war with its defeats & uncertainties is immensely better than what we lately called the integrity of the Republic, as amputation is better than cancer."[164] The great war promised an end to the greatest of American evils.

Like other abolitionists, Emerson vociferously urged the enlistment of black troops into the Union Army. Consistent with his 1844 emancipation address, in which he applauded the actions of "Toussaint and the Haytian heroes," Emerson believed that free blacks and slaves had to prove to themselves and to a white America steeped in racial prejudice the depth of their character as well as their ample moral fortitude. The philosopher of self-reliance was nothing if not consistent on this score; the "infinitude of the private man" demanded that blacks had to free themselves from their bonds, and not only the tangible ones of chattel slavery.[165] Enlistment into the Union Army constituted precisely such a self-reliant act, after which, as Frederick Douglass proclaimed, "no power on earth" could deny "the right of citizenship in the United States."[166] In his 1863 poem "Voluntaries," commemorating the Massachusetts 54th Regiment's heroic assault on Fort Wagner, and in his wartime journals Emerson advanced the same powerful sentiments about black agency that he had expressed for decades. Whites might take credit for "freeing slaves," but the only genuine freedom was self-made. "The negro has saved himself," he noted, "and the white man very patronisingly says, I have saved you," Emerson scoffed.[167] Always as much a critic of the North as the South, he hoped that African American heroism would compel "men of Northern brain" to reconsider their prejudicial reservations concerning blacks' bravery and courage.[168] "For freedom he will strike and strive," Emerson wrote, "And drain his heart till he be dead."[169]

Like most antislavery advocates, Emerson rapidly lost patience with Abraham Lincoln. As long as the president frankly proclaimed that his task was to preserve the Union even if that entailed freeing no slaves, Emerson was disheartened. "And for the Union with Slavery," he had written at the time of Webster's apostasy, "no manly person will suffer a day to go by without discrediting disintegrating & finally exploding it. The 'union' they talk of, is dead & rotten."[170] A union with slavery could no longer exist. In the midst of the somber days of January 1862, Emerson went to Washington to deliver his "American Civilization" lecture at the Smithsonian Institution. Whether Lincoln attended the address is unclear, but Emerson met the president the next day at the White House. Introduced by Sumner, Emerson came away from the meeting encouraged by what he heard and saw. "The President impressed me more favorably than I had hoped. A frank, sincere, well-meaning man . . . with a sort of boyish cheerfulness," Emerson wrote in his journal. "All this showed a great fidelity & conscientiousness very honorable to him."[171]

Emerson was especially energized by Lincoln's Preliminary Emancipation Proclamation issued after the Battle of Antietam. At last, Emerson felt certain that the nation was headed in the right direction, even if at an all-too-deliberate pace. Emerson chose the occasion of Lincoln's proclamation of September 22 to deliver his last major antislavery address.[172] It is largely the work of a person who felt both vindicated and sobered by the storm of recent events. Without hostility and with high praise for Lincoln, who with the proclamation "has been permitted to do more for America than any other American man," Emerson articulated what he knew to be the awesome importance of the act.[173] In Lincoln's capable hands, emancipation would remove the great impediment to genuine union of North and South. It would profit the nation in all ways, gain the respect and admiration of the high-minded both at home and abroad, enable citizens to reclaim their honor; and most importantly, the Proclamation would be irreversible. "We shall cease to be hypocrites and pretenders, but what we have styled our free institutions will be such."[174]

Significantly, at this uniquely auspicious moment, Emerson declined to reflect on the impact of the proclamation upon American blacks or offer any hopeful vision of the freedman's future. The lecturer seemed more concerned for his white neighbors and how "life in America had lost much of its attraction in the later years" than for blacks.[175] The best Emerson could muster was a vague nod toward "a new audience [which] is found in the heart of the assembly," and a coda calling on Americans through their national government to protect "that ill-fated, much-injured race."[176] As "a race naturally benevolent, joyous, docile, industrious, and whose very miseries sprung from their great talent for usefulness," African Americans would have "to find their way" under "the protection of American Law."[177] His "Emancipation in the British West Indies" address, delivered almost twenty years earlier, went infinitely farther toward imagining equality. Emerson's 1862 speech, like his addresses of the 1850s and his other wartime lectures, unfortunately highlighted by omission the stirring sentiments of his 1844 pronouncement whose soaring rhetoric he never matched again. In the midst of a horrific war and on the verge of a second American revolution, Emerson's imagination largely failed him.

In the ensuing years, during Reconstruction, Emerson steadfastly supported the radicals. Like his Concord neighbor Henry Thoreau, Emerson before the Civil War had betrayed only marginal faith in the ability of governments to do good. And like his reclusive friend, he refused to reify the state or blame it for the nation's ills; government was not good or bad but people made it so. Indeed, he defined his public vocation around the need to educate the enfranchised citizenry of the nation about the importance of following the dictates of individual conscience and a higher law. In this sense, Emerson had always concurred with the abolitionists and a long line of American antinomian thinkers. Unlike Thoreau, Emerson's belief in a higher law never precluded a certain faith in the political process, which for the most part enabled the free, self-reliant citizens of the nation to follow the dictates of their consciences as they dispersed across the continent.[178] According to Emerson, the United States government had played several useful functions in society and certainly would need to enact positive law in the ensuing decades. This pragmatic view of the state, in contrast with that of some reformers and abolitionists, proved particularly useful in the Reconstruction. Emerson readily grasped the new activist role of the national government necessitated by the exigencies of war and, like Sumner, championed the need for governmental action to protect the freedom critical to individual expression. In the decades prior to the Civil War, a minimal central authority governed well enough, allowing Emerson and others like him to pursue their destiny without much political interference or assistance. Civil War, emancipation, and the intransigence of the defeated South necessarily transformed his vision. With Sumner, Thaddeus Stevens, and many other Republicans, Emerson endorsed the Freedman's Bureau, the Fourteenth Amendment, and the expanded function of the central power entailed in protecting the rights of all citizens of the nation.[179] "We have seen slavery disappear like a painted scene in a theatre," he declared in "Resources," a lecture he gave frequently in the 1860s; "we have seen the most healthful revolution in the politics of the nation,—the Constitution not only amended, but construed in a new spirit."[180]

Toward the end of his life, Emerson adroitly understood the politics of the possible, as he unwaveringly stood by Sumner, Stevens, and the Radicals in their defense of the basic rights of African Americans and the national government's role in protecting them. Indeed, it is in his balanced, sensible, and progressive articulation of an equitable political settlement in Reconstruction that the grand irony of Emerson's intimate relation to race and abolitionism most clearly manifests itself. For much of his life, he had avoided direct participation in the fight against slavery exactly because by his own admission he was a scholar and teacher merely. Hardly shirking his duty, Emerson had reserved for himself what he defined as the infinitely subtler task of envisioning and expressing the greater glory of a self-cultured and ethical nation of free citizens. As politically progressive as he was, Emerson balked at undertaking the elaboration of the basic equality of all peoples. If the marrow of Emerson's political philosophy was a "behavioral nonconformity [that] loosens the hold of narrow or conventional methods of seeing and feeling (as well as preparing a person to take a principled stand in favor of those denied their rights)," as political philosopher George Kateb has written, then the lack of a more grandiloquent statement on race is conspicuous by its absence.[181] With his incomparable gifts and the affection of a nation of self-making men and women, he never became that great American intellectual who elaborated a genuinely multiracial vision of the United States. Consistent with his earlier inhibitions, Emerson turned silent on race after emancipation. No sooner had the Union been restored and slavery abolished than Emerson, who once had seemed poised to slough off his racial assumptions, felt free to disown the issue of race in America.

For Americans who would look to Emerson and the Transcendentalists for a stirring example of a radical indigenous intellectual movement, the strange career of Emerson and race is hardly encouraging. Even as the Concord sage remained a singularly deep and challenging thinker, who with Henry Thoreau, Margaret Fuller, Theodore Parker, and others offered a profoundly important critique of American society, when it came to race Emerson proved representative of his times. To be sure, his ideas evolved in important ways. He did speak out against slavery, his 1844 emancipation address representing a major imaginative triumph. And he did join the abolitionist movement. Like all too many of his fellow intellectuals, however, throughout his life and works Emerson remained convinced that the characteristics that made the United States, for all its flaws, the great nation of the world were largely the product of its Saxon heritage and history. Proclaiming publicly as late as 1851 that "Asia and Africa are [Europe's] ox and its ass," Emerson, it seems, always doubted that the promise of American freedom was anything but white.[182]

That Emerson was largely silent on race after emancipation is consistent with his earlier activities and public professions. Abolitionism was Emerson's one great political commitment to which he dedicated an awesome amount of energy for over a decade in the prime of his life. Slavery had been the nation's great, inexcusable sin, to be sure, and Emerson rejoiced in its demise. Yet no sooner had the Union destroyed it than Emerson felt free to return to his larger project—the problem of democracy and the role of the intellectual in it.

NOTES

1. Among his contemporaries, Oliver Wendell Holmes and Moncure Conway represent the two extremes concerning Emerson's antislavery activities. Declaring that

"Emerson had never been identified with the abolitionists," the conservative Holmes utterly rejected the notion that the sage of Concord was of any radical disposition whatsoever (234). Ironically, Nathaniel Bowditch, a former associate of William Lloyd Garrison, agreed with Holmes, concluding that making Emerson into an abolitionist did a great injustice to those like his mentor who were the real article. On the other hand, Conway, a slaveholder-turned-abolitionist, dedicated an entire chapter of his 1883 biography to Emerson's antislavery activities, erroneously calling his friend "the first American scholar to cast a dart at Slavery"(242). Other defenders of Emerson's abolitionist credentials included Elizabeth Palmer Peabody, Alexander Ireland, Thomas Wentworth Higginson, Franklin Sanborn, his literary executor and biographer James Elliot Cabot, and Harriet Martineau, who wrote that Emerson "is now, and has long been, completely identified with the abolitionists in conviction and sentiment." See, for example, Oliver Wendell Holmes, *Ralph Waldo Emerson and John Lothrop Motley* (Boston, 1884); Nathaniel Bowditch, "Did Mr. Emerson Sympathize with the Abolitionists?" in the *Index* (November 1885); Moncure Conway, *Emerson at Home and Abroad* (New York, 1882); *Harriet Martineau's Autobiography*, ed. Maria Weston Chapman (Boston, 1877), 1:375.

2. Rollo G. Silver, "Emerson: Abolitionist," *New England Quarterly* VI (March 1933), 151–57; Marjory M. Moody, "The Evolution of Emerson as an Abolitionist," *American Literature* 17 (1945–46), 1–21; Gay Wilson Allen, *Waldo Emerson: A Biography* (New York, 1981); Maurice Gonnaud, *An Uneasy Solitude: Individual and Society in the Work of Ralph Waldo Emerson* (Princeton, 1987); Len Gougeon, *Virtue's Hero: Emerson, Antislavery, and Reform* (Athens, Ga., 1990); Len Gougeon, "Historical Background," in *Emerson's Antislavery Writings*, ed. Len Gougeon and Joel Myerson (New Haven, 1995), xi–lvi. The latest biography of Emerson, Robert Richardson, *Emerson: The Mind on Fire* (Berkeley, Calif., 1995), a nuanced, subtle intellectual study, largely dodges Emerson's racism.

3. Stephen E. Whicher, *Freedom and Fate: An Inner Life of Ralph Waldo Emerson* (Philadelphia, 1953); Stanley M. Elkins, "Intellectuals without Responsibility," Slavery: A Problem in American Institutional and Intellectual Life (Chicago, 1959); George Fredrickson, *The Inner Civil War: Northern Intellectuals and the Crisis of the Union* (New York, 1965); Taylor Stoehr, *Nay-Saying in Concord: Emerson, Alcott, and Thoreau* (Hamden, Conn., 1979); John McAleer, *Ralph Waldo Emerson: Days of Encounter* (Boston, 1984).

4. *JMN* 12:151.

5. Not surprisingly, Carlyle's essay proved popular in the American South.

6. For an interesting, if dated, take on the children of Federalists and abolitionism, see David Donald's 1955 essay, "Toward a Reconsideration of Abolitionists," in *Lincoln Reconsidered: Essays on the Civil War Era*, ed. David Donald (New York, 1956), 19–36.

7. "Address on the Emancipation of the British West Indies," *Works* 11:175.

8. Many abolitionists underwent something of a moment of insight or conversion. Emerson's boyhood friend Henry Furness is an example. Resistant to abolitionism, he

suddenly embraced radicalism with a fervor that suggested he was atoning for previous silence. Emerson was far more consistent. His thinking evolved; he never converted to abolitionism.

9. See Christopher Newfield, *The Emerson Effect: Individualism and Submission in America* (Chicago, 1996), 195–96, for an insightful if brief discussion of Emerson's racial assumptions.

10. *JMN* 8:10.

11. Phillip Nicoloff, *Emerson on Race and History: An Examination of English Traits* (New York, 1961); and Cornel West, *The American Evasion of Philosophy: A Genealogy of Pragmatism* (Madison, Wis., 1989).

12. I have in mind here Benjamin Rush's presentation to Jefferson of the work of Benjamin Banneker.

13. Racism is a serious allegation that most students of Emerson and antislavery fail to take seriously; it is also a loaded one. It would be futile, as well as anachronistic, to search for some twenty-first-century ideal of color blindness in antebellum America. Scholars would do well to keep in mind the words of W. E. B. Du Bois when he intoned that John Brown was the sole "European American" before the Civil War whom he could with confidence claim to be immune from the sorry taint of racism. As for Emerson, even if he was only a "typical nineteenth-century North Atlantic 'mild racist,' " as Cornel West has suggested, his prejudices nevertheless limited his thinking in important ways. Eric Foner has recently explained how, throughout their history, Americans have defined their liberty and freedom largely in racial terms, self-servingly contrasting Anglo-Saxon independence and capacity for self-government with the innate inferiority of other races and peoples. Emerson was no different. As late as the publication of *English Traits* in 1856, he relied on the prevalent "scientific" racism of the day to explain American success and prophesize about its future, inevitable greatness. Any discussion of Emerson and abolition that ignores or minimizes his racial assumptions and their impact upon his views and activities is necessarily flawed. The best recent book on Emerson and antislavery by Len Gougeon is a case in point. A fine work of scholarship, *Virtue's Hero* devotes only a few pages to Emerson's racist worldview and the fact that for half of his life he believed Africans "did not exceed the sagacity of an elephant." See West, *American Evasion of Philosophy*, 28; and Eric Foner, *The Story of American Freedom* (New York, 1998).

14. "Dedication," *Works* 11:106.

15. Emerson writes: "our good friend S. J. May may instruct us in many things." See *JMN* 5:73.

16. *JMN* 2:42–43.

17. In his *Proslavery*, Larry Tise has shown how proslavery writings were hardly the sole provenance of southerners. See *Proslavery: A History of the Defense of Slavery in America, 1701–1840* (Athens, Ga., 1987).

18. *JMN* 2:43.

19. *JMN* 2:43.

20. *JMN* 2:44.

21. *JMN* 2:48–49.

22. *JMN* 2:48.

23. Some contemporary philosophers argue that as far back as Kant's "hierarchy of personhood," European identity has been defined in relation to and above the inhabitants of the nonwhite, non-European world. See, for example, Theodore Allen, *The Invention of the White Race* (London, 1994) and Lucius Outlaw Jr., *On Race and Philosophy* (New York, 1996). The most recent analysis of Kant and race is Mark Larrimore, "Sublime Waste: Kant on the Destiny of the 'Races,' " *Canadian Journal of Philosophy* (1999), Supplementary Vol. 25 on "Civilization and Oppression," ed. Catherine Wilson.

24. In his ruminations at the age of nineteen, Emerson takes up the basic issue that numerous scholars have noted as the central issue of antislavery thought. David Brion Davis, for example, writes: "slavery has always raised certain fundamental problems that originate in the simple fact that the slave is a man." See *The Problem of Slavery in Western Culture* (Ithaca, 1966), 31.

25. *JMN* 2:57.

26. In 1834 Emerson called slavery "the unpardonable outrage it is" precisely on the basis of his conviction that "every man has within him somewhat really divine." He also called this undefined divinity "the only equality of all men." See *JMN* 4:357.

27. *JMN* 7:393.

28. George F. Fredrickson, *The Black Image in the White Mind: The Debate on Afro-American Character and Destiny, 1817–1914* (Middletown, Conn., 1987), 159.

29. The racial basis of Emerson's thought manifests itself most clearly when his comments about the "African race" are compared to his soaring rhetoric about human equality in other contexts. In an 1834 journal entry he noted that "because every man has within him somewhat really divine therefore is slavery the unpardonable outrage it is." Emerson was very clear in pointing out in this same passage, however, that this "somewhat really divine" element was "the only equality of all men," that it did not extend to intellectual ability or capacity. Slavery was an egregious sin, but a biracial society was utterly implausible. See *JMN* 4:357.

30. Cited in Larrimore, "Sublime Waste," 14.

31. *JMN* 13:127 (1853).

32. "Power," *Works* 6:64.

33. "Power," *Works* 6:64.

34. "Power," *Works* 6:64.

35. In a journal entry dating from 1852, Emerson remarks that it is "puerile to insist on nationalities over the edge of individualities." There is considerable irony in the timing of this shift. Emerson adopted his antislavery voluntarism at precisely the moment when his philosophical bearings were moving from the autonomy of the individual toward various forms of determinism. From freedom to fate, Stephen Whicher characterized it.

36. *English Traits*, in *Works* 5:50.

37. Nicoloff, *Emerson on Race and History*, 151.

38. *English Traits*, in *Works* 5:50.

39. *English Traits*, in *Works* 5:47; see Robert Knox, *The Races of Man: A Fragment* (Philadelphia, 1850).

40. Emerson's most detailed published thoughts on race and history are his first pages of his chapter, "Race," in *English Traits*. See *Works* 5:47–74.

41. Carlyle's view of history was also informed by his prediction of an approaching "judgment day"; *JMN* 2:4.

42. *JMN* 2:39.

43. *JMN* 9:299–300.

44. *JMN* 4:92 (1833); the citation is from Saint Pierre's condemnation of slavery, *Studies of Nature*, published in 1796.

45. Emerson to Ezra Ripley, 1/17/27, *Letters* 7:155. For an extended discussion of the relationship of economic attitudes and abolitionism, see David Brion Davis, *The Problem of Slavery in the Age of Revolution, 1770–1823* (1975; rep., New York, 1999); as well as Thomas Bender, ed., *The Antislavery Debate: Capitalism and Abolitionism as a Problem in Historical Interpretation* (Berkeley, Calif., 1992).

46. *JMN* 12:154 (1837).

47. *JMN* 2:42.

48. *JMN* 3:10.

49. *JMN* 2:57.

50. Conway, *Emerson at Home and Abroad*, 242.

51. Conway, *Emerson*, 242. Martineau would get even in her scathing review of Boston in her militantly abolitionist *Society in America* (London, 1837).

52. Maria Weston Chapman, ed., *Harriet Martineau's Autobiography* (Boston, 1877), 1:375; and in *Letters* 2:24n. The two brothers had met Martineau at the home of Henry Ware on August 25.

53. Lidian's antislavery sentiments were buttressed by the Concord visit of Angelina and Sarah Grimké in the fall of 1837, to which she attributed a lasting impact. See Alma Lutz, *Crusade for Freedom: Women of the Anti-Slavery Movement* (Boston, 1968), 103–6.

54. Ellen Tucker Emerson, *The Life of Lidian Jackson Emerson*, ed. Delores Bird Carpenter (Boston, 1980), 84.

55. *JMN* 5:382 (1837).

56. *JMN* 5:382 (1837).

57. Cited in Phyllis Cole, *Mary Moody Emerson and the Origins of Transcendentalism* (New York, 1998), 233–34.

58. Gilman Ostrander notes that many men joined the movement as a result of "militantly abolitionist wives and sweethearts" in *Republic of Letters: The American Intellectual Community, 1776–1865* (Madison, Wis., 1999), 229.

59. *JMN* 12:152.

60. See Conway, *Emerson*, 243.

61. "Heroism," *Early Lectures* 2:338; see also *JMN* 5:437; for popular reaction to the lecture, see Conway, 243, for the comments of George Bradford, an Emerson friend in attendance at one of the "Heroism" lectures.

62. "To me," Emerson wrote in the opening paragraph of "Fate," one of his greatest essays, "the question of the times resolved itself into a practical question of the conduct of life. How shall I live?" See "Fate," *Works* 6:9.

63. *JMN* 12:152 (1837).

64. All citations in this paragraph from *JMN* 12:151–52 (1837).

65. All citations from *JMN* 12:152 (1837).

66. *JMN* 12:154 (1837).

67. His view would change with the proslavery turn in national politics after 1845.

68. All quotes from *JMN* 12:151–58 (1837).

69. In words evocative of Amasa Delano, the self-satisfied republican captain in Melville's *Benito Cereno*, Emerson called blacks an "amiable joyous race who for ages have not been permitted to unfold their natural powers." See Herman Melville, *Benito Cereno*, first published in *Putnam's* in 1855.

70. All quotes from *JMN* 12:152 (1837).

71. All quotes from *JMN* 12:154.

72. On American destiny and race, see Reginald Horsman, *Race and Manifest Destiny: The Origins of American Racial Anglo-Saxonism* (Cambridge, 1981); and Anita H. Patterson, *From Emerson to King: Democracy, Race, and the Politics of Protest* (New York, 1997).

73. *JMN* 5:505.

74. *JMN* 5:505.

75. As have Ann Douglas and Anne Rose more recently. See Rose, *Transcendentalism as a Social Movement, 1830–1850* (New Haven, 1981); and Douglas, *The Feminization of American Culture* (New York, 1977), ch. 1.

76. *JMN* 7:31 (1838).

77. See Charles Capper, *The Private Years*, vol. 1 of *Margaret Fuller: An American Romantic Life* (New York, 1992), esp., 224–25.

78. See Richard F. Teichgraeber, *Sublime Thoughts/Penny Wisdom: Situating Emerson and Thoreau in the American Market* (Baltimore, 1995), 93–95.

79. "New England Reformers," *Collected Works* 3:154.

80. *JMN* 9:134 (1844).

81. Quoted in Frank Preston Stearns, *Cambridge Sketches* (Philadelphia, 1905), 203.

82. "War," delivered on April 12, 1838, as "The Peace Principle," in *Works* 11:198.

83. *JMN* 8:116.

84. *JMN* 9:102.

85. *JMN* 9:103.

86. There is some dispute about this; see James Eliot Cabot, *A Memoir of Ralph Waldo Emerson* (Cambridge, 1887), 2 vols., 574.

87. Reprinted in [Ward] *Letters from Ralph Waldo Emerson to a Friend, 1838–1853*, ed. Charles Eliot Norton (Boston, 1900), 60. See also the note in *Letters* 3:279.

88. *JMN* 4:281.

89. *JMN* 9:266–67.

90. See *JMN* 9:382, 400, 410–11.

91. Emerson to John Greenleaf Whittier, 9/13/44, *Letters* 3:261.

92. See *JMN* 5:479n concerning the publication of the letter.

93. Letter is Appendix D in Cabot, *Memoir*, 699.

94. *JMN* 5:475.

95. *JMN* 5:479.

96. *JMN* 5:477.

97. *JMN* 5:15.

98. *JMN* 7:129.

99. *JMN* 7:139.

100. *JMN* 9:126–27.

101. *JMN* 7:405.

102. See Irving Bartlett, ed., "The Philosopher and the Activist: New Letters from Emerson to Wendell Phillips," *New England Quarterly* 62:2 (1989), 280–81.

103. Loren Baritz goes way overboard in his hopelessly flat characterization in *City on a Hill: A History of Ideas and Myths in America* (New York, 1964), 252. He writes that "faced with slavery, Emerson stood solidly on a cloud and insisted that the only possibilities were intellectual ones. It was unimportant if a man's body was enslaved as long as his mind was free. No slaveowner could have desired a more satisfactory defense of slavery, a defense that insisted that the institution was too insignificant even to notice."

104. *JMN* 9:62 (1844).

105. *JMN* 8:10 (1841).

106. Cited in Cabot, *Memoir*, 2:428.

107. Cabot, *Memoir*, 2:432.

108. On emancipation statistics for the British West Indies, see Stiv Jakobsson, *Am I Not a Man and a Brother? British Missions and the Abolition of the Slave Trade and Slavery in West Africa and the West Indies 1786–1838* (Uppsala, Sweden, 1972), 621–24.

109. Will Gravely, "The Dialectic of Double-Consciousness in Black American Freedom Celebrations, 1803–1863," *Journal of Negro History* (winter 1982), 302–17.

110. "An Address . . . on . . . the Emancipation of the Negroes in the British West Indies (1844)," *Emerson's Antislavery Writings*, 7.

111. *Emerson's Antislavery Writings*, 7.

112. *Emerson's Antislavery Writings*, 8.

113. *Emerson's Antislavery Writings*, 8.

114. *Emerson's Antislavery Writings*, 9–10.

115. See Joseph Slater, "Two Sources for Emerson's First Address on West Indian Emancipation," *Emerson Society Quarterly* 44 (1966), 97–100.

116. *Emerson's Antislavery Writings*, 29.

117. *Emerson's Antislavery Writings*, 30.

118. *Emerson's Antislavery Writings*, 30.

119. *Emerson's Antislavery Writings*, 19.

120. *Emerson's Antislavery Writings*, 31.

121. *Emerson's Antislavery Writings*, 31.

122. For the epistolary exchange between Emerson and Phillips, see Bartlett, "The Philosopher and the Activist," 280–96.

123. *Emerson's Antislavery Writings*, 31. Some scholars view the 1844 address less as a turning point than as a singular expression of Emerson at his least racist. Cornel West makes this argument in *American Evasion of Philosophy* but undermines his case with a faulty chronology (30–31).

124. *Emerson's Antislavery Writings*, 20.

125. *Emerson's Antislavery Writings*, 23.

126. *Emerson's Antislavery Writings*, 19.

127. *Emerson's Antislavery Writings*, 25.

128. *JMN* 9:134 (1844).

129. *JMN* 9:126 (1844).

130. *JMN* 9:126 (1844).

131. It is unclear whether Emerson read these remarks at the meeting; see Cabot, *Memoir*, 752.

132. "Thoreau," *Works* 10:427.

133. On Thoreau's activism, see Nick Ford, "Henry David Thoreau, Abolitionist," *New England Quarterly* 19 (1946), 359–71.

134. *JMN* 9:445.

135. *JMN* 11:255.

136. Emerson to Carlyle, 12/31/44, *CEC* 373.

137. "Address to the Citizens of Concord—on the Fugitive Slavery Law," delivered May 3, 1851, in *Emerson's Antislavery Writings*, 53.

138. Wilbur H. Seibert, "The Under-Ground Railroad in Massachusetts," *Proceedings of the American Antiquarian Society* 45 (1935), 25–100; Seibert called Concord "an Underground haven"(57).

139. Al von Frank seems to have this right when he claims that the recapture of fugitive slaves contributed far more to the "pocket revolution" in Boston than did the 1854 Kansas-Nebraska Act. See Albert von Frank, *The Trials of Anthony Burns: Freedom and Slavery in Emerson's Boston* (Cambridge, 1998), xi–xiii.

140. See Joanne Pope Melish, *Disowning Slavery: Gradual Emancipation and "Race" in New England, 1780–1860* (Ithaca, 1998).

141. *JMN* 11:354–55 (1851); I have changed "thus" to "this" in the third sentence.

142. *JMN* 11:360 (1851).

143. See von Frank, *The Trials of Anthony Burns*.

144. *JMN* 13:48–49 (1852).

145. *JMN* 11:361 (1851).

146. Cited in Cabot, *Memoir,* 2:425.

147. *JMN* 11:349 (1851).

148. Cabot, *Memoir*, 2:587.

149. Moody, "Emerson as an Abolitionist," 16.

150. It was not published until 1995.

151. Cabot, *Memoir*, 2:593.

152. "Assault on Charles Sumner," *Emerson's Antislavery Writings*, 107.

153. See von Frank, *Trials of Anthony Burns*.

154. See Franklin Benjamin Sanborn, *Recollections of Seventy Years*, 2 vols. (Boston, 1909).

155. *JMN* 14:125 (1857).

156. *JMN* 14:334 contains a draft of the letter (1859).

157. "Speech at a Meeting to aid John Brown's Family (1959)," *Emerson's Antislavery Writings*, 119.

158. This activism included making speeches on behalf of John Gorham Palfrey's 1851 Free-Soil bid for a congressional seat.

159. F. O. Matthiessen, *American Renaissance: Art and Expression in the Age of Emerson and Whitman* (New York, 1941), 3–75.

160. "Success," *Works* 7:267.

161. Emerson to James Eliot Cabot, 8/4/61, *Letters* 5:253.

162. *JMN* 15:182.

163. *JMN* 11:362.

164. Emerson to James Eliot Cabot, 8/4/61, *Letters* 5:253.

165. Years earlier, in 1845, Emerson had declined to speak at the New Bedford lyceum because of its decision to exclude free blacks from its lectures. In a letter to the lyceum, Emerson noted that since "the Lyceum exists for popular education," its exclusion of "the humblest and most ignorant" was precisely the wrong course of action. See "Letter to William Rotch, 17 November 1845," *Emerson's Antislavery Writings*, 39–40.

166. Frederick Douglass, *Douglass' Monthly* 5 (August 1863), 852.

167. *JMN* 9:126 (1844). I am indebted to Eduardo Cadava's penetrating reading of this poem. See his *Emerson and the Climates of History* (Stanford, Calif., 1997), 188–201.

168. "Voluntaries," *Works* 9:179.

169. "Voluntaries," *Works* 9:179.

170. Emerson to Oliver Wendell Holmes, March 1856, *Letters* 5:18.

171. *JMN* 15:187 (1862).

172. *JMN* 15:494 (1863).

173. "The President's Proclamation (1862)," *Emerson's Antislavery Writings*, 130.

174. *Emerson's Antislavery Writings*, 132.

175. *Emerson's Antislavery Writings*, 131.

176. *Emerson's Antislavery Writings*, 130.

177. *Emerson's Antislavery Writings*, 135, 131.

178. A good review of the literature on Emerson's political views is Cyrus Patell, "Emersonian Strategies: Negative Liberty, Self-Reliance, and Democratic Individuality," *Nineteenth Century Literature* (March 1994), 440–79. See also Russell B. Good-

man, "Moral Perfectionism and Democracy: Emerson, Nietzsche, Cavell," *ESQ* 43 (1997), 159–78.

179. George Kateb's brilliant reading of Emerson's anti-statism fails to take Emerson's Reconstruction views into account, thus overemphasizing Emerson's antipathy, I think, to state power. See George Kateb, *Inner Ocean: Individualism and Democratic Culture* (Ithaca, 1992).

180. "Resources," *Works* 8:138.

181. Kateb, *Inner Ocean*, 241.

182. "Address to the Citizens of Concord (1851)," *Emerson's Antislavery Writings*, 70.

7

ASSESSING EMERSON AS DEMOCRATIC INTELLECTUAL

> The end of all political struggle, is, to establish morality as the basis for all legislation. 'Tis not free institutions, 'tis not a republic, 'tis not a democracy, that is the end,—no, but only the means.[1]

E merson's public career did not end with the Civil War and his participation in the fight to abolish slavery. Blessed with longevity, the Concord sage continued to lecture through his sixties and even as he approached his seventieth year. He commanded handsome fees, averaging almost seventy-five dollars per appearance, and spoke out on such issues as "Social Aims," "Character," and the "Fortune of the Republic."[2] Although he traveled extensively, even delivering a lecture in California where he met John Muir and toured Yosemite Valley, his now well-deserved reputation as a public intellectual conspired with his slowly ebbing energies to turn him into more of a reassuring, avuncular American elder statesman than the fiercely independent intellectual gadfly he had been in previous decades. Emerson could not escape his celebrity, which tied him to fights waged and won before the Civil War. Antagonists within the Unitarian establishment and Harvard Yard as well as the defenders of slavery had been vanquished, just as Margaret Fuller, Theodore Parker, and Henry Thoreau had succumbed to early deaths. Even as he continued to fulfill his self-assigned role as public intellectual, calling for reforms in education and immigration policy and cajoling Americans to fulfill their national destiny, Emerson found himself increasingly hindered by his unshakable association with past triumphs. His irenic style and flagging mental powers also contributed to his transformation in the public mind from Transcendentalist radical to Concord sage.[3] No longer engaged in that challenging vocational search, which had led him from schoolteacher to ordained minister to public lecturer, Emerson had by the last decade or so of his life comfortably reconciled himself to semiretirement. St. Louis Hegelian Denton Snider ironically noted that by the end of his life the Concord sage had realized his own objective or synthetic freedom in becoming an institution himself. Emerson's popularity seemed to signal that the impact of the man and his message was on the wane.[4]

The slow and inevitable decline of the man, who rather comfortably settled into the role of gray eminence, was punctuated by a type of dementia that all but silenced him for the last years of his life. This mental degeneration cast something of a pall over his earlier activism. More importantly, without the creative energy derived from the singular search for a vocation that marked the critical years of his professional life, Emerson's message seemed to lose its caustic, challenging edge. As the foregoing chapters have sought to highlight, it was this ardent quest to become a democratic intellectual that formed the basic framework of his ideas. For more than a half-century, Emerson's vocational odyssey provided that special spark for a unique and still-resonant articulation of the potential of the individual as well as the role of the intellectual to cajole Americans to make the most of themselves. The urgency and relevance of his message had hinged on the professional struggles of the man.

Spanish American philosopher George Santayana once wrote that Emerson "is never a philosopher, but always Emerson philosophizing."[5] Santayana's apt observation can equally be applied to politics. Emerson was never a politician and for the most part disavowed direct participation in political and reform movements, especially in his later years. Nonetheless, he was always politicking and reforming. So much of Emerson's intellectual project addressed the relationship of private and public and the role of the intellectual in a democratic society. "To me," Emerson wrote in the opening paragraph of "Fate," one of his greatest essays, "the question of the times resolved itself into a practical question of the conduct of life. How shall I live?"[6] In all of his published writings, public lectures, and occasional addresses, Emerson insisted on the ultimate unity of public and private, as well as the interconnection of ideas and action, of ethics and politics. Perhaps no other American intellectual in the nineteenth century so consciously and effectively endeavored to have an impact upon both contemporary thought and public behavior as Emerson.[7] This was the meaning of the last line in his essay "Experience," in which he committed himself to "the transformation of genius into practical power."[8] Emerson's genius was always political, even as he viewed politics as just one means to exalted ethical ends. Although he never ran for office nor authored political treatises or campaign speeches, Emerson nevertheless proved to be one of the most trenchant and astute students of the American public and its political machinations. The slow decline of his later years should not obscure this fact.

By Emerson's own calculation, to be useful all thinking had to be practical. Intellectual endeavors had to have some point of utility, or they were just so much posturing and waste of time. "Do not accuse me of sloth," he had written acerbically in his journal in 1840. "I have been writing with some pains Essays on various matters as a sort of apology to my country for my apparent idleness."[9] Because of his aloofness from direct participation in or technical theorizing about American electoral politics, even in his lifetime Emerson's words and deeds often appeared somehow incongruous. Many a reformer and politician lamented the sage of Concord's stance above the melee of Jacksonian parties and electioneering, always apparently maintaining a certain hermetic distance from the excitements of the day.[10] Similarly, some scholars, building on Henry Nash Smith's unfortunate distinction between action and contemplation in Emerson's "American Scholar" address, have interpreted his aloofness as a sign of "alienation."[11] For them, Emerson, as a white middle-class male insensitive to the great injustices of antebellum American society, could afford to play the detached observer, cleverly camouflaging inaction by largely insignificant rhetorical displays.[12] Eschewing direct action, Emerson nevertheless believed to his very core that he had forsaken a life of contemplation and noble exile when he quit the ministry in 1832. He went on to travel more miles and address more Americans than virtually any of his contemporaries. Santayana, for example, could not have been more wrong when he wrote in 1900 that Emerson "fled to the woods or to his 'pleachèd garden,' to be the creator of his own worlds in solitude and freedom."[13] Few intellectuals seemed more engaged in the life of the nation than did Emerson.

Emerson devoted himself to reforming American society but had his doubts about most reformers. What he wrote about Montaigne being "equally at odds with the evils of society, and with the projects that are offered to relieve them" applied as much to himself as to the great French doubter.[14] "The wise skeptic is a bad citizen; no conservative, he sees the selfishness of property and the drowsiness of institutions. But neither is he fit to work with any democratic party that ever was constituted; for parties wish every one committed, and he penetrates the popular patriotism."[15] Whether he kept his distance from politicians, campaigns, and the like out of fear and insensitivity or out of an acute sense of discipline and honesty is a question to which Emerson repeatedly returned. "I must act with truth, though I should never come to act, as you call it, with effect," he wrote in his "Lecture on the Times" in 1841. "I must consent to inaction."[16] Insistent always that ingenuous inaction trumped dishonest and precipitous movement, Emerson dedicated himself to the pursuit of a life of political participation that neither succumbed to conformity nor entailed the loss of individual integrity. He was convinced that his articulation of a philosophy of self-reliant individuality in the face of Jacksonian boosterism on the one hand and various types of socialism on the other was his rendition of radical politics.

Emerson was acutely aware that for the typical American the danger of overblown activism always outweighed that of thoughtful inaction. An unavoidable flaw of a democratic polity in which "all persons take part" is that of doing more than conviction dictates, which is always so much falsity. The United States (then as now) was comprised of activists who tended to be short on individual thinking and long on a desire to join movements to perfect the world. Tocqueville eloquently noted this danger in the second volume of *Democracy in America*, while Emerson also wrote of the awesome pressure multitudes exerted on individual conscience. "[W]hen a quarter of the human race assume to tell me what I must do," he wrote, "I may be too much disturbed by the circumstances to see so clearly the absurdity of their command."[17] Ever eager, energetic, and impatient, Americans preferred decisive action to reasoned contemplation, fearing that the latter, more often than not, resulted in ambivalence and indecision. In a journal entry in 1847 on the "Irresistibility of the American," Emerson noted both the obtuseness and the elemental energy of his overeager fellow citizen who joined the fight with

> no conscience; his motto like nature's is, "our country right or wrong." He builds shingle palaces and shingle cities; yes, but in any altered mood perhaps this afternoon he will build stone ones, with equal celerity. Tall, restless Kentucky strength; great race, but tho' an admirable fruit, you shall not find one good sound well-developed apple on the tree. Nature herself was in a hurry with these hasters & never finished one.[18]

Americans in Emerson's day—and in our own—were nothing if not prepared to undertake almost anything on a moment's notice: to settle a new territory, to engage in mass demonstrations, to enact new laws, or to stage elaborate elections. Ceaseless activity was the coin of the realm just as seeking "the best chance" was elementally bound up with the nature of American society. Emerson proved to be one of the nation's great political resources for the exact reason that his critics often bemoaned. Like Hamlet, he believed that "nothing is good or bad but thinking makes it so."[19] He steadfastly lived by the conviction that right thinking was both a form of action in itself and a critical precursor to any purposeful engagement. Residing in a nation teeming with a preternatural energy, Emerson largely defined his vocation as one of reflection that ran counter to the spirit of the times. In his essay "Spiritual Laws," he candidly defended his ponderous mode of operation:

We call the poet inactive, because he is not a president, a merchant, or a porter. We adore an institution, and do not see that it is founded on a thought which we have. But real action is in silent moments. The epochs of our life are not in the visible facts of our choice of a calling, our marriage, our acquisition of an office, and the like, but in a silent thought by the way-side as we walk; in a thought which revises our entire manner of life and says,—"Thus hast thou done, but it were better thus."[20]

Emerson understandably believed that Jacksonians blithely sallying forth into engagements without deliberation constituted a distinct national danger, and usually resulted in premature initiatives and wasted effort, as well as unnecessary wanton destruction. Such was the case with the dreadful Cherokee removal, the annexation of Texas, the Mexican War, and other aggressive calamities.[21] In contrast, Emerson, "the student of the world," sought to do his patriotic part by offering his country what it so palpably lacked.[22] Emerson's activism was his thinking, which he strove to make relevant. Perhaps the most un-American statement in his entire career was his bold assertion that "To think is to act."[23]

Often harshly disdainful of his erstwhile intellectual colleagues in Boston and Cambridge, whom he believed isolated and irrelevant, Emerson distinguished between an effete, superannuated scholarship and his own practical intellectual activity devoted to utility.

What right, cries the good world, has the man of genius to retreat from work, and indulge himself? The popular literacy creed seems to be, "I am a sublime genius; I ought not therefore to labor." But genius is the power to labor better and more availably. Deserve thy genius: exalt it, . . . learn to act, and carry salvation to the combatants and demagogues in the dusty arena below.[24]

In his political life, Emerson carved out an intellectual middle ground of the sort to which he had made reference in his college essay on "The Character of Socrates." With what he styled a Socratic prudence, Emerson insisted that all thinking must lead to action and that all action must be based on honest, sober thought. Simultaneously dismissive of thinkers who demanded certainty before acting and politicians and other leaders who acted without reflection, Emerson doggedly pursued the relationship of consistency and integrity. He maligned the futile quest for certainty and absolutes characteristic of so many indecisive intellectuals in New England's churches and colleges. This spurious demand proved to be nothing more than a ruse by which idle speculators avoided their civic duty. "A foolish consistency," about which Emerson famously wrote "is the hobgoblin of little minds," could be distinguished from honesty insofar as the former was internal and merely speculative—and therefore all but fruitless—while the latter was practical and related to the world of action.[25] On consistency, Emerson assumed the Kierkegaardian posture that proofs were not only impossible but worse than useless because they negated self-reliance. A logical consistency was merely intellectual, while Socratic probity was personal and political. The circumspect individual acted both honestly and with an unavoidable insecurity that derived from lack of certainty. Emerson emulated what he styled "the prudence of Socrates," about which he wrote so eloquently as an undergraduate. Prudence his Athenian hero "possessed abundantly in the philosophical signification of the term,—but none of that timorous caution which might interfere with the impulses of patriotism, duty, or courage."[26] Ever the thinker, Emerson never manifested a timorous caution, but created himself as an activist savant in a nation of doers. Emerson devoted his public life to creating the intellectual means to advance the nation. By the time he reached adulthood, Emerson resolved to live and act upon his participatory ethic.

Emerson's problem of vocation related distinctly to his commitment to activism. From the first entries in his journals during his college days, Emerson clearly yearned for the kind of fame so typical of ambitious adolescents. Unlike that of his classmates, Emerson's hunger for renown was tempered by a distinct alienation from his elite surroundings. Particularly after his trip to Europe subsequent to the death of his first wife, he yearned for a more visceral bond with a broader segment of the American people. His fateful decisions to quit the ministry, to challenge the solemn tenets of the Unitarian hierarchy, to crisscross the nation as a public lecturer, and to take up the cause of freedom in the abolitionist movement attested to his struggle to fit out the vocation of the intellectual in an open society. Emerson sought to define his role as an intellectual in a democratic society. Such a calling could not be answered in a pulpit or a classroom. It necessitated a more broadly based appeal than any Unitarian minister or Harvard professor could ever hope to attain even if he so desired. The democratic intellectual respected the great mass of Americans, confident that they were capable, creative, and competent to control their destiny. Such an intellectual served the people with whatever gifts he possessed.

Like Plato, Emerson lived in a period of political transition. Whereas Plato largely assumed a reactionary posture, sympathizing with the stability of the despotic regime of Sparta, Emerson by temperament and intellect sided with the new.[27] The United States in the middle third of the nineteenth century faced domestic problems and challenging foreign dealings but had neither suffered through a catastrophic war nor faced grave external menace. The nation witnessed the capitulation of the last vestiges of an explicitly deferential society during an era largely devoid of foreign threats. The opening of American society, a trend that engendered profound misgivings in Emerson's former Brahmin colleagues, unfolded during such propitious circumstances that only the most conservative elements in society feared an impending crisis. Emerson embraced the nation's economic and political developments as part of the inevitable, progressive march of history.[28] "Personal rights [are] universally the same," he explained in a lecture delivered only weeks after the disappointing 1836 presidential election, "and demand always a democratic government."[29] With Alexis de Tocqueville, Emerson grasped that he was alive at an exciting moment, at a time of great social change. "If there was any period one would desire to be born in," Emerson exuberantly explained to an audience of staunch conservatives at the 1837 Harvard commencement, "is it not the age of Revolution?"[30] With the spectacle before him of a barely literate American president, of "pet banks," Indian removal, log cabin and hard cider campaigns, and "Tippecanoe and Tyler Too," Emerson steadfastly explored and extolled the transformative potential inhering in a free and participatory form of government. Even if Emerson meant by American democracy nothing more than, as Tocqueville wrote, "a government where people more or less participate in their government," he expressed the sentiment in a way that his contemporaries both on the right and the left considered radical.[31] Among the "superstitions of our age" that he enumerated in a journal entry in August of 1847 and that he hoped to dispel was "the fear of radicalism or democracy."[32] At a moment when the United States was still a fledgling constitutional republic with an uncertain future, Emerson believed himself uniquely situated to articulate the transcendent possibilities of a regime that seemed to be based on a fundamental equality.

Emerson's "eager apprehension of the possibilities of democracy," as F. O. Matthiessen put it, had its paradoxical side.[33] Son of a prominent minister, ninth in a line of Puritan clerics, the product of Boston Latin School and Harvard College, it seems almost inexplicable that Emerson did not join the ranks of the Longfellows, Holmes, Quincys, Eliots, Ticknors, and the rest of the Brahmins. Perry Miller claimed his radicalism was the result of genius. For Miller, genius entailed breaking rules, so that was inevitably what Emerson the genius did.[34] Emerson's early years were characterized less by genius than by a social and intellectual isolation that contributed mightily to his antipathy toward Brahmin conservatism. Emerson himself remarked on the genealogy of radicalism in several passages in his journals. He insightfully noted, or admitted, that "conservatism, ever more timorous and narrow, disgusts the children [of conventional parents] and drives them for a mouthful of fresh air into radicalism."[35] Far more critical to the growth of his anti-Brahmin sentiments than genius or abstract mental capacity were the experiences of his youth. If wealth strengthens patrimony, then it is little wonder that Emerson threw off his elitist inheritance. Not Emerson's genius but his alienation from Brahmin Boston and unquenchable thirst for making himself relevant played the crucial role in the pursuit of his public life. His disenchantment at Harvard and in the Unitarian church, his fateful decision to forsake his formal education by quitting the ministry, his exploration of Europe in search of America, and his creation of the vocation of public lecturer all testify to his popular aspirations. As John Dewey perceptively observed, Emerson dedicated himself to fabricating a democratic conception of education, art, and culture as the delight and duty not of a single class or constituency but of all Americans.

Highly ambitious, Emerson understandably grew disenchanted with the insular attitudes of a Brahmin elite that was wedded to a hierarchical social order. Sensitive to the great changes afoot in the nation, and altogether indifferent to the lure of money and status, Emerson craved a more elemental connection to his countrymen. Unlike his parents, professors, and pastors, Emerson came to believe that community, cohesion, culture, and creativity could survive in a democracy with the guidance of intellectuals like himself who inspired the development of that self-reliance instilled by participatory government. If his congregation at Boston's Second Church was any example, these ideals were far more likely to flourish in the rest of Jacksonian America than in Boston. In the face of rapid and unpredictable change, the critical expedient for teachers and lecturers like himself was to conjure up the courage needed to transform their antiquated professions into a new expansive vocation. Temperamentally, Emerson was unwilling to consign himself to what he deemed to be irrelevance.

That Emerson believed the only course open to him was to embrace the open political culture of the United States by no means implies that he was a Democrat, nor even an unqualified believer in human equality. He did believe that all people shared the basic ability to look after their own interests while simultaneously being aware of the shortcomings of most ordinary people. Indeed, Emerson's writings offer an incisive commentary on the problems of conformity, materialism, and alienation equaled only by Tocqueville. Emerson never held that the advent of a democratic polity would necessarily result in human excellence, an equitable social order, or a perfect society. That he sustained the ultimate justice, necessity, and inevitability of an open, participatory regime did not make him oblivious to other incipient dangers. His writings and lectures addressed no issues more fervently and repeatedly than those of materialism and conformity, the two intractable evils of his age. A sworn enemy of the materialistic and unoriginal urges of democratic society in all its guises, Emerson was sufficiently thoughtful and reflective to never become a simple apologist for the existing social order.[36] His peculiar youth, awesome ambition, critical mind, intellectual honesty, and awareness of the pivotal moment in which he lived all combined to make him more than merely the prophet of the unfolding social order. Rather, Emerson emerged as a sort of optimistic meddler who, as Oliver Wendell Holmes described, embodied a rebellion "so calm and serene that its radicalism had the accents of the gospel of peace."[37] As much as Emerson identified his expectant vision with the destiny of one nation—an intellectual move that inevitably transformed his ideas into ideology—he nevertheless resolutely challenged the American people to fulfill their collective "mission." Consciously assuming the treacherous political terrain of domestic censor, Emerson to this day stands out as simultaneously canonical and one of the nation's staunchest social critics.[38] Holmes dubbed him "an iconoclast without a hammer."[39]

In the course of his career Emerson extensively examined political issues in both his public and private writings. As with other topics, he never offered a definitive, systematic treatment of politics, even in his essay of that name, preferring instead to relegate most of his observations to the relative privacy of his journals and correspondence. Nevertheless, the sheer volume of the political commentary and occasional asides in his unpublished works amply testify to his abiding fascination with the study of American political institutions. Emerson delivered many lectures and addresses relating to public issues, from "Man the Reformer" and "New England Reformers" in the early 1840s and his numerous essays concerning national issues as well as the abolition of slavery in the 1850s to the "Fortune of the Republic" in 1868. His most extended examination of the issue was the lecture "Politics," which he read to eager audiences at least a half-dozen times before its publication in *Essays: Second Series* in 1844.[40] In the printed version, Emerson explicated far more than the prevailing state of Jacksonian politics in the nation. "Politics" represented his most systematic statement of his estimation of the elemental nature and peculiar place of politics in society. It is here that the author explained why politics—and the state—could never be an end in themselves, but only a necessary means to realizing an incomparably broader design.

In many ways, the author of "Politics" was at his most ironic. Clearly, this essay remains overshadowed in *Essays: Second Series* by "Experience" and "The Poet," whose themes so strongly subordinate politics and the state to more pressing, personal matters. Poets intrigued Emerson far more than politicians or presidents. Indeed, the primary theme of "Politics" is that as worthy a subject for examination as political theory and practice were, they commanded entirely too much attention from the American public. Here was Emerson composing and delivering a work entitled "Politics" in no small measure to admonish his audience that parties and campaigning and elections should not be taken overly seriously. He was intent on chiding his readers for their misplaced enthusiasm in such a way as to betray his grudging admiration for the very vitality of the political process in all its Jacksonian excess. "Politics" disparaged neither politicians nor the American electoral process, as the opening paragraph offered that "politics rest on necessary foundations, and cannot be treated with levity."[41] Undertaking a frank analysis of the topic with demystification as his primary objective, Emerson explained that politics merely reflected larger forces at work in society. The best that could be said about the state was that at the present stage of American cultural development it was expedient.

Emerson published "Politics" not long after his fortieth birthday, having delivered some form of the lecture on numerous previous occasions. He refined his views of politics in several ways over the ensuing decades, particularly in light of the fight for abolition and the coming of the Civil War. Nevertheless, Emerson remained wedded to the basic themes expressed in the essay. The state constituted solely a means, never an end. "The main duties of government," he wrote, included "the duty to instruct the ignorant, to supply the poor with work and with good guidance."[42] Dismissive of the American tendency to fetishize politics, Emerson unwaveringly urged his fellow citizens to redirect their energies more properly toward self-improvement and culture. The political apparatus of the state could only offer marginal help with what in the end proved to be a personal quest. "Politics is an after-work, a poor patching," Emerson declared in his lecture on culture. "We are always a little late. The evil is done, the law is passed, and we begin the up-hill agitation for repeal of that of which we ought to have prevented the enacting. We shall one day learn to supersede politics by education."[43] In the meantime, politics ought not to be taken too seriously because, after all, citizens should not serve the state. The state existed for the individual.

The single greatest benefit of participatory politics rested with its advancing of citizens' sense of individual self-worth. Fascinated by the relationship of politics and *bildung*, Alexander von Humboldt's term for self-education, Emerson manifested throughout his life a keen interest in the operation of American political institutions and their implications for the growth of the individual. References, observations, critiques, and praise of republican institutions proliferated in his journals in virtually every year of his life, with the greatest commentary coming during the tumultuous decades of the heyday of the second party system. As disparaging as the author of "Politics" was concerning his fellow citizens' misdirected exuberance for campaigns, candidates, and political causes, he remained intrigued and impressed by the effervescent or adolescent energy that Jacksonian democracy engendered in the nation.[44] It seems that he preferred the Democrats to the Whigs precisely for their possession of that elemental raw energy he observed in his "rural Jacobin" neighbors.[45]

Emerson believed that no form of government was good or bad in itself. By no means was a republican regime necessarily superior to monarchy, aristocracy, or other political arrangements. In several places Emerson chastised Americans for their unthinking jingoistic endorsement of republicanism as the one and only best system of government, fervently dismissive of such universal claims.[46] "In this country we are very vain of our political institutions," Emerson the historicist explained, "which are singular in this,"

> that they sprung, within the memory of living men, from the character and condition of the people, which they still express with sufficient fidelity,— and we ostentatiously prefer them to any other in history. They are not better, but only fitter for us. We may be wise in asserting the advantage in modern times of the democratic form, but to other states of society, in which religion consecrated the monarchical, that and not this was expedient. Democracy is better for us, because the religious sentiment of the present time accords better with it. Born democrats, we are nowise qualified to judge of monarchy, which, to our fathers living in the monarchical idea, was also relatively right. But our institutions, though in coincidence with the spirit of the age, have not any exemption from the practical defects which have discredited other forms.[47]

Emerson structured his analysis and endorsement of the American regime not around its universal or transcendent qualities, but around what he believed to be its practical consequences for his compatriots. Constitutionally sympathetic to the prior claims of an elemental equality, which stemmed from his Christian-Platonist view of individuals' capacity to look after themselves, Emerson pursued rationales for advancing the cause of republicanism that were more substantive than mere personal predisposition against artificial distinctions.

Although he did not systematically explore or explain the efficacy of republicanism in any one place or to a final conclusion—he never did that with any proposition—over many years he did focus on two basic, interrelated tendencies of the American form of participatory government. First, for all its defects, it constituted the most just system, since it was based on the supposition of the basic equality of all citizens. "There is one mind common to all individual men," Emerson eloquently claimed. "Every man is an inlet to the same and to all of the same. He that is once admitted to the right of reason is made a freeman of the whole estate."[48] Emerson believed that "the one basic" equality of all people in a world of difference was their ability to use reason to pursue self-interest, a conviction that not only validated his unconditional disdain for the orthodox Congregationalist advocacy of innate human depravity but, even more importantly, served as the basis for his emerging sense of the justness of participatory regimes. "There is imparted to every man," he wrote in 1834, "the Divine Light of reason sufficient not only to plant corn & grind wheat by but also to illuminate all his life his social, political, [and] religious actions."[49] For Emerson, as for John Dewey, the moral legitimacy of the American polity hinged on the proposition that individuals (both prior to and above the state) act as the best agents for themselves. Like the passage from the *Meno* in which Socrates demonstrated how even an uneducated slave boy could readily undertake geometric proofs, Emerson based his political ideas upon the apparent fact that in the United States so much of the nation's elemental power derived from the average man or woman's instinctive and rational pursuit of self-interest. Not that Emerson ever proposed that all persons were identical; in fact, his vision of individuality suggested precisely the opposite, that "we boil at different degrees of the thermometer."[50] The legitimacy of democracy rested upon only a very few, identifiable universal traits about which Emerson was highly specific. "Reason is potentially perfect in every man," Emerson once explained to his brother and, as a result of its ubiquity, "demands a democracy."[51]

Second, in the United States at least, popular rule proved to be the best means to promote self-reliance. For Emerson, participatory government instilled the value of self-worth; it was instrumental in creating "the wise man" and fostering what might best be called democratic individuality.[52] Intent on much more than merely legitimating a form of government, Emerson extolled the American political system for its ability to promote self-culture. Political participation was indispensable to the development of the self-reliant individual who would make government of any kind obsolete. "'Tis not free institutions," Emerson wrote in "The Fortune of the Republic," one of his last great lectures, delivered many times between 1868 and 1878, only four years before his death, "'tis not a democracy that is the end,—no, but only the means."[53] Self-government encouraged the growth of self-reliant individuals, who respected their own humanity to such an extent that they would have no use for the state, the school, the seminary, or extracted surplus value. "In this fact, that we are a nation of individuals," Emerson continued, "that we have a highly intellectual organization, that we can see and feel moral distinctions, and that on such an organization sooner or later the moral laws must tell, to such ears must speak,—in this is our hope."[54]

Emerson's consanguinity rested upon a virtually axiomatic anti-institutional bias. The radical individuality for which he fought leapt out of that line of "Self-Reliance" in which the author stated that "Society everywhere is in a conspiracy against the manhood of every one of its members."[55] The revolution through which he was living, and for which he believed he was fighting, was nothing less than the struggle to convince everyone of his own unique, intrinsic worth. Emerson, the prophet of the ego, sided with this revolution and sought allies wherever he could. In the democratic regime, Emerson believed he found a crucial means toward that end.

The self-reliant individuality that Emerson valorized contrasted sharply with the contemporary definition of individualism.[56] From the moment he first used the word in a journal entry in 1842, Emerson clearly set out to distinguish his view of individualism from its current vogue. For his contemporaries, individualism was "the vice of the age," which if left unchecked would result in a disastrous conflagration of all against all.[57] Emerson's co-optation of the term proved at once both more and less utopian than that of his European socialist contemporaries.[58] Emerson based his vision of the self-reliant individual on a thoroughly idealist conception of an "Oversoul" to which all humans had access or in which they all participated. Nevertheless, his idealism only informed his politics, which was skeptical and pragmatic, at the most basic level. He retreated before the utopianism of the socialists who sought to translate their communal ideals into reality, convinced that socialism could subdue the dangerous centrifugal forces unleashed by individualism only by destroying human dignity altogether. "For the matter of Socialism," he wrote after touring Europe in 1848, "there are no oracles. The oracle is dumb. When we would pronounce anything truly of man, we retreat instantly on the individual."[59] For Emerson, any system that did not make the self-reliant individual its ultimate objective unconsciously or consciously conspired "against the manhood of everyone of its members."[60] Opposing the self-reliant individual to the socialists' negative individualism proved to be more than an intellectual task. It also entailed Emerson's ultimate decision to reject an invitation to join the Brook Farm experiment of his friends Sophia and George Ripley. In the end, Emerson concluded that remaining aloof from such collective experiments was the only course he could pursue honestly.

The self-reliant individual was neither the egoist of Joseph de Maistre, nor isolated and utterly unattached as later critics would have it, nor the materialistic possessive bourgeois man of twentieth-century social critics like C. B. Macpherson.[61] Self-reliant individuality relied upon a theory of human rights and capacities that engendered respect of others as unique, dignified human beings. For Emerson, there could be no self-reliant individual outside of the community, because self-reliance rested upon the foundation that all humans deserved respect and dignity. With Tocqueville, Emerson considered the American polity to be far more than merely a new form of government; it was one crucial part of a revolutionary change in society and culture. Tocqueville reasoned that democratic institutions would produce isolated and alienated beings, but hoped for some sort of amelioration from religious and other sources. Emerson, on the other hand, extolled the nation's participatory politics precisely because of its potential to advance individuality, while still cognizant of its latent dangers. The "new importance given to the single person" Emerson celebrated as "a sign of the times."[62] In *Nature* he wrote "everything that tends to insulate the individual,—to surround him with barriers of natural respect, so that each man shall feel the world is his, and man shall treat with man as a sovereign state with a sovereign state,—tends to true union as well as greatness."[63]

Emerson believed that the American system of government promoted self-reliance in that the routine aspects of personal participation as well as the regular working of the political system materially altered the human psyche in a way that at once encouraged respect for individual rights and engendered a salubrious use of those rights in people's lives. The process of voting itself transformed masses into individual citizens with responsibilities and rights. American electoral politics clearly brought out an elemental energy in the citizens. "The same energy in the Greek *Demos* drew the remark that the evils of popular government appear greater than they are," Emerson declared in his lecture "Power" which he repeated many times; "there is compensation for them in the spirit and energy it awakens. The rough-and-ready style which belongs to a people of sailors, foresters, farmers, and mechanics, has its advantages."[64] From merely paying attention to civic issues to organizing and participating in party machinations, citizens routinely acted in such a way as to raise their sense of self. This monumental benefit of such participation far outweighed the "hardship" thrust upon the self-styled elite of having to participate in a process that had its obvious shortcomings. Emerson preferred to focus on the uplifting elements of political involvement instead of its manifest messiness: "I like that every chair should be a throne, and hold a king."[65] The Concord sage understood that "the true test of civilization is, not the census, nor the size of cities, nor the crops,—no, but the kind of man the country turns out. I see the vast advantages of this country," Emerson observed, in the unfolding of participatory constitutional government.[66]

The new way of life encouraged by, among other things, the routine participation in electing leaders constituted the true end of politics. Emerson consistently claimed that the consummation of what he called the "American idea" of government was not better laws or better congressmen, but self-reliant individuals. From his first reading of "Politics" in 1837 to his lectures on "The Natural History of Intellect" in 1871, Emerson regularly repeated the theme that the state only exists to make the citizen wise, which it accomplishes not solely by funding education and building schools but by constituents' participation in politics and reform movements of all kinds that tended to "educate the conscience and intellect of the people."[67] As early as his first European trip in 1832–33, Emerson came to understand that such participation liberated not only the political person but the social one as well. His seminal experience abroad, repeated in 1848, ineluctably contributed to Emerson's identification of self-reliant individuality with the United States. "The American idea, Emancipation, appears," Emerson wrote in 1861, "in our bad politics; it has, of course, its sinister side, which is most felt by the drilled and scholastic, but if followed it leads to heavenly places."[68] This participatory freedom emancipated the individual, elevating citizens from the masses and convincing them of their self-worth. In the same 1861 lecture Emerson most eloquently expressed his sense of the uplifting egalitarianism confirmed in the daily operation of "our bad politics":

> There is a little formula, couched in pure Saxon, which you may hear in the corners of streets and in the yard of the dame's school, from very little republicans: "I'm as good as you be," which contains the essence of the Massachusetts Bill of Rights and of the American Declaration of Independence. . . . What is very conspicuous is the saucy independence which shines in all their eyes. They could say to themselves, Well, at least this yoke of man, of bishops, of courtiers, of dukes, is off my neck. We are a little too close to wolf and famine than that anybody should give himself airs here in the swamp.[69]

Americans made manifest what Emerson called the "theology and instinct of freedom" in every election, party meeting, and expressed political opinion.[70] Emerson's protégé and successor, Walt Whitman, exceeded his mentor in this line of thought in *Democratic Vistas*. Whitman went so far as to insist that direct participation was not even necessary for the citizen. Only the opportunity and the self-awareness of the opportunity to have one's say were needed.[71] The mere fact of enfranchisement moved the citizen toward self-reliant individuality.

For Emerson and Whitman both, the enfranchised citizen was only a subspecies of the cultured individual. "One man, one vote" translated to one person among equals. This was the invisible and constantly expressed directive of constitutional democracy, whether in the franchise, the fleeting and tenuous power of elected officials, or the ability to remove the lofty from office simply by regular election. The potential power invested in the citizen as a citizen had a profound impact upon social relations, because self-consciousness of one's own constitutional endowments of necessity inspired respect for others. Each and every citizen possessed the same rights. Self-respect suggested regard for others. Far from becoming isolated, the self-reliant individual projected her or his elemental ascendancy onto others. Self-reliance, Emerson believed ferociously, fostered a respect for universal human dignity. "The fact that a new thought and hope have dawned in your breast," he recited in "Man the Reformer" in 1841, "should apprise you that in the same hour a new light broke in upon a thousand private hearts."[72]

Time and again on the lecture circuit Emerson noted with a profound and abiding admiration just how reasonable, industrious, and clever Americans could be. "There is also something excellent in every audience, capacity of virtue; it is expectant & greatly expectant," he noted in a journal entry in 1846 after many weeks of lecturing. "They know so much more than the orators. And are so just."[73] The course of American history, especially as it manifested itself among the "Hoosier, Sucker, Wolverine, [and] Badger" in the new states on the far side of the Appalachians, where he lectured annually, validated Emerson's hopes for the nation.[74] One needed to look no farther than the American West, Emerson believed, to grasp the exigency of conceiving of humans as rational problem solvers eminently capable of self-government. In his popular lecture "Civilization," which he published in *Society and Solitude*, Emerson explained how his travels had contributed so vitally to his egalitarian political beliefs.

> But when I look over this constellation of cities which animate and illustrate the land, and see how little the government has to do with their daily life, how self-helped and self-directed all families are,—knots of men in purely natural societies, societies of trade, of kindred blood, of habitual hospitality, house and house, man acting on man by weight of opinion, of longer or better-directed industry; the refining influence of women, the invitation which experience and permanent causes open to youth and labor:—when I see how much each virtuous and gifted person, whom all men consider, lives affectionately with scores of excellent people who are not known far from home, and perhaps with great reason reckons these people his superiors in virtue and in the symmetry and force of their qualities,—I see what

cubic values America has, and in these a better certificate of civilization than great cities or enormous wealth.[75]

In what might be called a virtuous circle, Emerson reasoned that the "American idea" of emancipation unshackled the creative energies of the common citizen, while in turn the orderly and energetic settlement of the Midwest and upper Mississippi Valley in his own lifetime validated the nation's emancipatory political system. "We wish to put the ideal rules into practice, to offer liberty instead of chains," Emerson opined optimistically in one of his lectures, "and see whether liberty will not disclose its proper checks; believing that a free press will prove safer than the censorship; to ordain free trade, and believe that it will not bankrupt us; universal suffrage, believing that it will not carry us to mobs, or back to kings again. I believe that the checks are as sure as the springs."[76] Emerson portrayed himself in his lectures and essays as nothing more than the recorder of a people in the process of proving the efficacy of democratic institutions.

Analogous to and coterminous with Emerson's faith in the individual's reasonable pursuit of self-interest was his profound conviction that there existed a universal moral foundation of human nature, a common reason that undergirded universal access to the divine, to God, to a shared morality. This conviction proved central to the basic justness of an open society and a participatory political regime. "For there is somewhat spheral and infinite in every man, . . . which, if you can come very near him, sports with all your limitations. For rightly every man is a channel through which heaven floweth," Emerson liked to believe.[77] Having quit the ministry and abandoned organized religion altogether, Emerson hardly cast aside religion or his faith in the divine. He preached his new divinity, his abiding faith in the "Over-soul" as the crucial building block of a nation of free and self-reliant individuals:

> The Supreme Critic on the errors of the past and the present, and the only prophet of that which must be, is that great nature in which we rest as the earth lies in the soft arms of the atmosphere; that Unity, that Over-soul, within which every man's particular being is contained and made one with all other; that common heart, of which all sincere conversation is the worship, to which all right action is submission; that overpowering reality which confutes our tricks and talents, and constrains every one to pass for what he is, and to speak from his character and not from his tongue, and which evermore tends and aims to pass into our thought and hand, and become wisdom, and virtue, and power, and beauty. We live in succession, in division, in parts, in particles. Meantime within man is the soul of the

whole; the wise silence; the universal beauty, to which every part and parti-
cle is equally related; the eternal ONE.[78]

Eclectically combining elements of his reading of Plato, Neo-Platonists, Christians, and Romantics, Emerson articulated a simultaneously religious and philosophical argument against any system based on inequality, be it of wealth, education, bloodlines, or whatever. The fact that there existed a single "universal mind [of which] each individual man is one more incarnation" proved sufficient and irrefutable grounds for a type of equality manifested in American political institutions.[79] By means of the "Over-soul" Emerson in his secular sermons championed the divine aspect in all people.[80]

"The State is a poor good beast who means the best," Emerson once noted; "it means friendly."[81] For fifty years he sang the praises of the American system of government for its social and psychological effects on the individual, from his first published work to his last lecture roundly declaring that "the world is nothing; the man is all."[82] Precisely because it undermined blind institutional faith, discouraged an excessive respect for laws, and helped to internalize a sense of equality and personal capacity did democracy promise to be an incomparably better regime than aristocracy or any other system based upon inequality. Emerson championed that "eager, solicitous, hungry, rabid, busy-body America attempting many things," exactly because those were the traits, despite their estimable pitfalls, that fostered the growth of democratic individuality.[83] For all its problems, democracy more than any other regime was for Emerson the government of the self-reliant individual. As the state-sponsored disasters of the twentieth century have made abundantly clear, the one reliable source for valuing human dignity and respecting others is the self-reliant individual.

Never really a radical and as much a champion as a critic of American society, Emerson resolutely insisted that intellectuals like himself had to fulfill their responsibility to the nation by reminding their fellow citizens of the importance, potential, and awesome obligation of every individual. Emerson would surely have agreed with Louis Sullivan when he declared that "in a democracy there can be but one test of citizenship, namely: Are you using such gifts, such powers as you possess . . . for or against the people? For or against Democracy?"[84] Today, as Americans seem to get swallowed up in a world that is simultaneously "masterless" and overwhelming, Emerson's championing of individuality often appears both hopelessly ineffectual and the source of an elemental American selfishness. At once individuals seem power-less against multinational corporations and mass media conglomerates and entirely wrapped up in their own narrow pursuits. It is easy to equate the hackneyed lines of "Self-Reliance" with one famous multinational's jingle to "Just do it," which implies that Emerson wants us to find ourselves at the shopping mall. The intellectual, then, becomes the effete outsider, fighting a losing battle against the mass of quietly desperate individuals who unwittingly serve the interests of the giant corporations.

The preceding chapters have argued that as ill-equipped as Emerson might have been to confront the challenges of a postindustrial order, it would be a sad mistake to reduce Emerson to being the pied piper of a clichéd message of crass individualism. His vision of the fiercely independent, constantly reflective self-reliant individual hardly resembles the self-centered, alienated, and materialistic individualism of our own time. Part of the blame for our woeful lack of self-reliance Emerson would surely explain as the fault of narrow-minded, careerist intellectuals, who have failed to bridge the gap between themselves and the popular culture of the nation. Emerson's legacy of the democratic intellectual laboring to do her or his part to foster self-reliance remains an optimistic and demanding vision for all educated Americans.

NOTES

1. "Fortune of the Republic," in *Emerson's Antislavery Writings,* ed. Len Gougeon and Joel Myerson (New Haven, 1995), 153.

2. He received one hundred dollars for a talk at New Albany, Indiana. See William Charvat, "A Chronological List of Emerson's American Lecture Engagements, Part IV," *Bulletin of the New York Public Library,* 657–63.

3. For a sympathetic and insightful treatment of Emerson after the Civil War, see Richard F. Teichgraeber III, " 'Our National Glory': Emerson in American Culture, 1865–1882," in *Transient and Permanent: The Transcendentalist Movement and Its Contexts,* ed. Charles Capper and Conrad Edick Wright (Boston, 1999), 499–526.

4. See Herbert W. Schneider, *A History of American Philosophy* (1946; rep., New York, 1963), 245.

5. George Santayana, "The Optimism of Ralph Waldo Emerson," in *George Santayana's America: Essays on Literature and Culture,* ed. James Ballowe (Urbana, Ill., 1967), 83.

6. "Fate," *Works* 6:9.

7. "Emerson may not have been what is conventionally called a political philosopher," writes Judith Shklar, "but political considerations played a more subtle part in his thinking than mere expressions of opinion on public affairs suggest." See "Emerson and the Inhibitions of Democracy," *Political Theory* 18.4 (1990), 601–14.

8. "Experience," *Collected Works* 3:49.

9. *JMN* 7:404. Gay Wilson Allen and Cornel West offer very different readings of this passage. See Allen, *Waldo Emerson: A Biography* (New York, 1981), 363; and

West, *The American Evasion of Philosophy: A Genealogy of Pragmatism* (Madison, Wis., 1989), 22.

10. The sole exception to Emerson's avoidance of direct political campaigning was his efforts on behalf of John Gorham Palfrey's Free-Soil campaign for Congress in 1851.

11. Henry Nash Smith, "Emerson's Problem of Vocation: A Note on the 'American Scholar,' " *New England Quarterly* 12 (1939), 52–67; and Carolyn Porter, *Seeing and Being: The Plight of the Participant Observer in Emerson, James, Adams, and Faulkner* (Middletown, Conn., 1981).

12. An extreme critic of Emerson as detached from politics is David Marr. In his *American Worlds Since Emerson* (Amherst, 1988), Marr argues that Emerson's antinomian ethos of supreme individualism "sanctions the reckless attack of the very idea of public life" (4).

13. George Santayana, *Interpretations of Poetry and Religion* (1900; rep., New York, 1922), 220.

14. "Montaigne," *Collected Works* 4:97.

15. "Montaigne," *Collected Works* 4:97.

16. "Lecture on the Times," *Collected Works* 1:177.

17. "Politics," *Collected Works* 3:125.

18. *JMN* 10:95–96.

19. See Emerson's comparison to Hamlet in an 1855 letter to his brother in *Letters* 4:484.

20. "Spiritual Laws," *Collected Works* 2:93.

21. Emerson greatly admired Americans for their awesome energy and youthful exuberance. These were signs of unstoppable promise and a creative vitality unmatched in human history. Emerson no more wanted to inhibit this "march of progress" than he believed it remotely possible to do so. All the more, then, this nation of adolescents demanded someone like him, a democratic intellectual who was not about to rage against the inevitable.

22. "Literary Ethics," *Collected Works* 1:100.

23. "Spiritual Laws," *Collected Works* 2:94.

24. "The Transcendentalist," *Collected Works* 1:211.

25. "Self-Reliance," *Collected Works* 2:33.

26. "The Character of Socrates," *Two Unpublished Essays* (Boston, 1895), 23.

27. See Alvin Gouldner, *Enter Plato: Classical Greece and the Origins of Social Theory* (New York, 1965).

28. Emerson wrote: "According to De Tocqueville, the column of our population on the western frontier from Lake Superior to the Gulf of Mexico (1200 miles as the bird flies) advances every year a mean distance of seventeen miles. He adds 'This gradual & continuous progress of the European race towards the Rocky Mountains has the solemnity of a providential event; it is a like a deluge of men rising unabatedly & daily driven onward by the hand of God.' " See *JMN* 7:433.

29. "Politics," *Early Lectures* 2:72.

30. "The American Scholar," *Collected Works* 1:67.

31. Alexis de Tocqueville, *The European Revolution and Correspondence with Gobineau,* ed. and trans. John Lukacs (New York, 1959), 102.

32. *JMN* 10:143–44.

33. F. O. Matthiessen, *American Renaissance: Art and Expression in the Age of Emerson and Whitman* (New York, 1941).

34. Miller wrote that Emerson "was a genius. This was his burden, his fate, and the measure of his disseverance from the ethos of his clan" (29). See Perry Miller, "Emersonian Genius and the American Democracy," *New England Quarterly* 26 (1953), 27–44.

35. "Power," *Works* 6:65.

36. See John Andrew Bernstein's acute criticism of identifying Enlightened optimism with conservatism in *Progress and the Quest for Meaning: A Philosophical and Historical Inquiry* (Cranbury, N.J., 1993), 78–101.

37. Holmes is cited in Carlos Baker, *Emerson among the Eccentrics: A Group Portrait* (New York, 1996), 472.

38. See Sacvan Bercovitch, "Emerson, Individualism, and Liberal Dissent," in *The Rites of Assent: Transformations in the Symbolic Construction of America* (New York, 1993), 307–52.

39. See Baker, *Eccentrics*, 472.

40. Charvat identifies the number of times Emerson was known to have delivered the lecture in "A Chronological List of Emerson's American Lecture Engagements," *Bulletin of the New York Public Library* 65 (1961), 500–507. See also Albert J. von Frank, *An Emerson Chronology* (New York, 1994), 120–33.

41. "Politics," *Collected Works* 3:117.

42. "The Young American," *Collected Works* 1:235.

43. "Culture," *Works* 6:135–36.

44. This facile exuberance George Caleb Bingham brilliantly captured in his paintings. On Bingham, see Nancy Rash, *The Painting and Politics of George Caleb Bingham* (New Haven, 1991).

45. *JMN* 7:99.

46. "Patriotism is balderdash," Emerson wrote in his journal. "Our side, our state, our town is boyish enough. But it is true that every foot of soil has its proper quality, that the grape on either side of the same fence has its own flavor, and so every acre on the globe, every group of people, every point of climate has its own moral meaning whereof it is the symbol. For such a patriotism let us stand." *JMN* 10:161.

47. "Politics," *Collected Works* 3:121–22.

48. "History," *Collected Works* 2:3.

49. *JMN* 4:356.

50. *JMN* 8:57.

51. Emerson to Edward Bliss Emerson, 5/31/34, *Letters* 1:413.

52. See George Kateb, *The Inner Ocean: Individualism and Democratic Culture* (Ithaca, 1992) and *Emerson and Self-Reliance* (Thousand Oaks, Calif., 1995).

53. "The Fortune of the Republic," *Works* 11:422.

54. "The Fortune of the Republic," *Works* 11:412.

55. "Self-Reliance," *Collected Works* 2:29.

56. See Cyrus R. K. Patell, "Emersonian Strategies: Negative Liberty, Self-Reliance, and Democratic Individuality," *Nineteenth Century Literature* 48.4 (1994), 440–79.

57. *JMN* 8:249.

58. For a discussion of the origins and articulation of individualism, see Gregory Claes, " 'Individualism,' 'Socialism,' and 'Social Science': Further Notes on a Process of Conceptual Formation 1800–1850," *Journal of the History of Ideas* 47 (1986), 81–93; and Koenraad Swart, "Individualism in the Mid-Nineteenth Century (1826–1860)," *Journal of the History of Ideas* 32 (1962), 77–90.

59. *JMN* 10:310.

60. "Self-Reliance," *Collected Works* 2:29.

61. C. B. Macpherson, *The Political Theory of Possessive Individualism: Hobbes to Locke* (1962; rep., New York, 1969).

62. *Nature, Collected Works* 1:68.

63. *Nature, Collected Works* 1:68.

64. "Power," *Works* 6:63.

65. "Manners," *Collected Works* 3:80.

66. "Civilization," *Works* 7:34.

67. "Lecture on the Times," *Collected Works* 1:172.

68. "Boston," *Works* 12:101.

69. "Boston," *Works* 12:102.

70. "Boston," *Works* 12:103.

71. See Walt Whitman, *Leaves of Grass and Democratic Vistas* (London, 1930), 301–4.

72. "Man the Reformer," *Collected Works* 1:146.

73. *JMN* 9:430.

74. "Power," *Works* 6:64.

75. "Civilization," *Works* 7:35.

76. "Progress of Culture," *Works* 8:219.

77. "Nominalist and Realist," *Collected Works* 3:142.

78. "The Over-Soul," *Collected Works* 2:160.

79. "History," *Collected Works* 2:4.

80. Emerson also converted "romantic natural theology [into] an expression of the national dream," as Sacvan Bercovitch so aptly styled it in *The Puritan Origins of the American Self* (New Haven, 1975), 162.

81. *JMN* 9:446.

82. *Nature, Collected Works* 1:69.

83. *JMN* 10:79.

84. Louis Henri Sullivan, *Kindergarten Chats and Other Writings* (New York, 1947), 151.

SELECTED BIBLIOGRAPHY

BY RALPH WALDO EMERSON

Manuscript Sources

The great majority of Emerson manuscripts (journals, letters, sermons, poems) are on deposit in the Emerson Family Papers at the Houghton Library at Harvard University. Other holdings include those in the Andover-Harvard Theological Library at the Harvard Divinity School. Several collections, including the Emerson Family Papers, the Farnham Family Papers, and the Wortis Collection, are at the Massachusetts Historical Society.

Emerson's Publications

Beginning with his 1836 publication of *Nature,* Emerson published many volumes of writings, including essays, poetry, and occasional lectures. These writings have been published in several editions. These collected works are in the process of being edited and reissued by Harvard University Press as *The Collected Works of Ralph Waldo Emerson.* Five volumes have been published so far.

The Collected Works of Ralph Waldo Emerson. Vols. 1–5. Ed. Robert E. Spiller, Alfred E. Ferguson et al. Cambridge, 1971–.
The Complete Works of Ralph Waldo Emerson. 12 vols. Riverside Edition. Ed. Edward Waldo Emerson. London, 1898–1900.

Collections of Emerson's Unpublished Work

The Complete Sermons of Ralph Waldo Emerson. 4 vols. Ed. Albert J. von Frank et al. Columbia, Mo., 1989–92.
The Correspondence of Emerson and Carlyle. Ed. Joseph Slater. New York, 1964.
The Early Lectures of Ralph Waldo Emerson. 3 vols. Ed. Stephen E. Whicher, Robert E. Spiller, and Wallace E. Williams. Cambridge, 1961–72.

Journals of Ralph Waldo Emerson. 10 vols. Ed. Edward Waldo Emerson. Cambridge, 1909–14.

The Journals and Miscellaneous Notebooks of Ralph Waldo Emerson. 16 vols. Ed. William H. Gilman et al. Cambridge, 1960–82.

The Letters of Ralph Waldo Emerson. Vols. 1–6. Ed. Ralph L. Rusk. Vols. 7–10. Ed. Eleanor M. Tilton. New York, 1939 and 1990–95.

The Poetry Notebooks of Ralph Waldo Emerson. Ed. Ralph Orth et al. Columbia, Mo., 1986.

The Topical Notebooks of Ralph Waldo Emerson. 3 vols. Ed. Susan Sutton Smith. Columbia, Mo., 1990–94.

Two Unpublished Essays: The Character of Socrates and The Present State of Ethical Science. Boston, 1895.

Edited Volumes of Emerson's Work and Topical Sources Material

Concordance to the Poems of Ralph Waldo Emerson. Ed. George S. Hubbell. New York, 1932.

Emerson's Antislavery Writings. Ed. Len Gougeon and Joel Myerson. New Haven, 1995.

Emerson in His Journals. Edited and selected by Joel Porte. Cambridge, 1982.

Emerson's Literary Criticism. Ed. Eric W. Carlson. 1979. Rep., Lincoln, Nebr., 1995.

Emerson's Transcendental Vocabulary: A Concordance. Ed. Mary Alice Ihrig. New York, 1982.

Letters from Ralph Waldo Emerson to a Friend, 1838–1853. Ed. Charles Eliot Norton. Boston, 1899.

Ralph Waldo Emerson. Ed. Richard Poirier. New York, 1990.

Ralph Waldo Emerson: A Descriptive Bibliography. Ed. Joel Myerson. Pittsburgh, 1982.

Ralph Waldo Emerson: An Annotated Secondary Bibliography. Ed. Robert E. Burkholder and Joel Myerson. Pittsburgh, 1985.

The Selected Letters of Ralph Waldo Emerson. Ed. Joel Myerson. New York, 1997.

Young Emerson Speaks: Unpublished Discourses on Many Subjects. Ed. Arthur Cushman McGiffert Jr. Boston, 1938.

WORKS ON EMERSON

Biographies

Allen, Gay Wilson. *Waldo Emerson: A Biography.* New York, 1981.

Baker, Carlos. *Emerson among the Eccentrics: A Group Portrait.* New York, 1996.

Cabot, James Elliot. *A Memoir of Ralph Waldo Emerson.* Boston, 1887.

Ireland, Alexander. *Ralph Waldo Emerson.* London, 1882.

McAleer, John. *Ralph Waldo Emerson: Days of Encounter.* Boston, 1984.

Richardson, Robert. *Emerson: The Mind on Fire.* Berkeley, 1995

Rusk, Ralph L. *The Life of Ralph Waldo Emerson.* New York, 1949.

Sanborn, Franklin B. *Ralph Waldo Emerson.* Boston, 1901.

Whicher, Stephen E. *Freedom and Fate: An Inner Life of Ralph Waldo Emerson.* Philadelphia, 1953.

Collections of Essays on Emersons

Bloom, Harold, ed. *Ralph Waldo Emerson.* New York, 1985.

Bode, Carl, ed. *Ralph Waldo Emerson: A Profile.* New York, 1968.

Buell, Lawrence, ed. *Ralph Waldo Emerson: A Collection of Critical Essays.* Englewood Cliffs, N.J., 1993.

Burkholder, Robert E., and Joel Myerson, eds. *Critical Essays on Ralph Waldo Emerson.* Boston, 1983.

Konvitz, Milton R., ed. *The Recognition of Ralph Waldo Emerson: Selected Criticism Since 1837.* Ann Arbor, 1972.

Myerson, Joel. *Emerson Centenary Essays.* Carbondale, Ill., 1982.

Porte, Joel, and Saundra Morris, eds. *The Cambridge Companion to Ralph Waldo Emerson.* New York, 1999.

Works on the Emerson Family

Emerson, Ellen Tucker. *The Life of Lidian Jackson Emerson.* Ed. Delores Bird Carpenter. Boston, 1980.

Cole, Phyllis. *Mary Moody Emerson and the Origins of Transcendentalism: A Family History.* New York, 1998.

Haskins, David Greene. *Ralph Waldo Emerson: His Maternal Ancestors.* Boston, 1887.

Kalinevitch, Karen. "Ralph Waldo Emerson's Older Brother: The Letters and Journal of William Emerson." Unpublished Ph.D. dissertation, University of Tennessee, 1982.

Pommer, Henry F. *Emerson's First Marriage.* Carbondale, Ill., 1967.

Simmons, Nancy Craig, ed. *The Selected Letters of Mary Moody Emerson.* Athens, Ga., 1993.

Thematic Studies of Emerson

Barish, Evelyn. *Emerson: The Roots of Prophecy.* Princeton, 1989.

Bishop, Jonathan. *Emerson on the Soul.* Cambridge, 1964.

Cadava, Eduardo. *Emerson and the Climates of History.* Stanford, 1997.

Cavell, Stanley. *Conditions Handsome and Unhandsome: The Constitution of Emersonian Perfectionism.* LaSalle, Ill., 1990.

————. *This New Yet Unapproachable America.* Albuquerque, 1989.

Cayton, Mary Kupiec. *Emerson's Emergence: Self and Society in the Transformation of New England, 1800–1840.* Chapel Hill, N.C., 1989.

Conway, Moncure. *Emerson at Home and Abroad.* New York, 1883.

Ellison, Julie. *Emerson's Romantic Style.* Princeton, 1984.

Emerson, Edward. *Emerson in Concord.* Cambridge, 1888.

Gelpi, Donald. *The Religious Quest of Ralph Waldo Emerson.* Lanham, Md., 1991.

Gonnaud, Maurice. *An Uneasy Solitude: Individual and Society in the Work of Ralph Waldo Emerson.* Princeton, 1987.

Gougeon, Len. *Virtue's Hero: Emerson, Antislavery, and Reform.* Athens, Ga., 1990.

Harris, Kenneth Marc. *Carlyle and Emerson: Their Long Debate.* Cambridge, 1978.

Hodder, Alan D. *Emerson's Rhetoric of Revelation.* University Park, Pa., 1989.

Holmes, Oliver Wendell. *Ralph Waldo Emerson and John Lothrop Motley.* Boston, 1884.

Kateb, George. *Emerson and Self–Reliance.* Thousand Oaks, Calif., 1995.

Lange, Lou Ann. *The Riddle of Liberty: Emerson on Alienation, Freedom, and Liberty.* Atlanta, 1986.

Lopez, Michael. *Emerson and Power: Creative Antagonism in the Nineteenth Century.* DeKalb, Ill., 1996.

Loving, Jerome. *Emerson, Whitman, and the American Muse.* Chapel Hill, N.C., 1982.

Marr, David. *American Worlds Since Emerson.* Amherst, Mass., 1988.

Mattheissen, F. O. *American Renaissance: Art and Expression in the Age of Emerson and Whitman.* New York, 1841.

Michael, John. *Emerson and Skepticism: The Cipher of the World.* Baltimore, 1988.

Mott, Wesley T., and Robert E. Burkholder, eds. *Emersonian Circles: Essays in Honor of Joel Myerson.* Rochester, 1997.

Newfield, Christopher. *The Emerson Effect: Individualism and Submission in America.* Chicago, 1996.

Nicoloff, Phillip. *Emerson on Race and History: An Examination of English Traits.* New York, 1961.

Packer, B. L. *Emerson's Fall: A New Interpretation of the Major Essays.* New York, 1982.

Paul, Sherwin. *Emerson's Angle of Vision: Man and Nature in the American Renaissance.* Cambridge, 1952.

Poirier, Richard. *Poetry and Pragmatism.* Cambridge, 1992.

————. *The Renewal of Literature: Emersonian Reflections.* New York, 1987.

Porte, Joel. *Representative Man: Ralph Waldo Emerson in His Time.* 1979. Rep., New York, 1988.

Porter, David. *Emerson and Literary Change.* Cambridge, 1978.

Roberson, Susan L. *Emerson in His Sermons: A Man-Made Self.* Columbia, Mo., 1995.

Robinson, David. *Apostle of Culture: Emerson as Preacher and Lecturer.* Philadelphia, 1982.

——. *Emerson and the Conduct of Life.* New York, 1993.

Rowe, John Carlos. *At Emerson's Tomb: The Politics of Classic American Literature.* New York, 1997.

Sealts, Merton M. *Emerson on the Scholar.* Columbia, Mo., 1992.

Stoehr, Taylor. *Nay-Saying in Concord: Emerson, Alcott, and Thoreau.* Hamden, Conn., 1979.

Teichgraeber, Richard F. III. *Sublime Thoughts/Penny Wisdom: Situating Emerson and Thoreau in the American Market.* Baltimore, 1995.

Van Leer, David. *Emerson's Epistemology: The Argument of the Essays.* New York, 1986.

Wilson, Eric. *Emerson's Sublime Science.* New York, 1999.

Topical Source Materials

Cameron, Kenneth W. *Ralph Waldo Emerson's Reading.* 1941. Rep., Hartford, Conn., 1962.

Harding, Walter. *Emerson's Library.* Charlottesville, Va., 1967.

von Frank, Albert J. *An Emerson Chronology.* New York, 1994.

OTHER SOURCES CITED IN THE TEXT

Published Primary Sources

Alcott, A. Bronson. *The Journals of Bronson Alcott.* Ed. Odell Shepard. Boston, 1938.

Beecher, Lyman. *The Autobiography of Lyman Beecher.* 2 vols. Ed. Barbara Cross. Cambridge, 1961.

Bentley, William. *Diary of William Bentley.* 4 vols. Salem, Mass., 1905–1914.

Buckminster, Joseph Stevens. *Works.* 2 vols. Boston 1854.

Emerson, William. *A Sermon on the Decease of Peter Thacher, D.D.* Boston, 1803.

Martineau, Harriet. *Harriet Martineau's Autobiography.* Ed. Maria Weston Chapman. Boston, 1877

——. *Society in America.* London, 1837.

Murat, Achille. *The United States of North America.* London, 1833.

Quincy, Josiah IV. *Figures of the Past, from the Leaves of Old Journals.* 1883. Rep., Boston, 1926.

Books

Adams, Henry. *The Education of Henry Adams.* Boston, 1918. Rep. 1989.

——. *History of the United States during the Administration of Jefferson and Madison.* 1921. Rep., Chicago, 1967.

Allen, Theodore. *The Invention of the White Race.* 2 vols. London, 1993.

Amory, Cleveland. *The Proper Bostonians.* New York, 1947.

Ballowe, James, ed. *George Santayana's America.* Urbana, Ill., 1967.

Baritz, Loren. *City on a Hill: A History of Ideas and Myths in America.* New York, 1964.

Bender, Thomas, ed. *The Antislavery Debate: Capitalism and Abolitionism as a Problem in Historical Interpretation.* Berkeley, 1992.

Bercovitch, Sacvan. *The Puritan Origins of the American Self.* New Haven, 1975.

———. *The Rites of Assent: Transformations in the Symbolic Construction of America.* New York, 1993.

Bernstein, John Andrew. *Progress and the Quest for Meaning: A Philosophical and Historical Inquiry.* Cranbury, N.J., 1993.

Bloom, Harold. *The Anxiety of Influence: A Theory of Poetry.* New York, 1973.

———. *The Ringers in the Tower.* Chicago, 1971.

Bode, Carl. *American Lyceum: Town Meeting of the Mind.* New York, 1956.

Brown, Jerry Wayne. *The Rise of Biblical Criticism in America, 1800–1870: The New England Scholars.* Middletown, Conn., 1969.

Buell, Lawrence. *Literary Transcendentalism: Style and Vision in the American Renaissance.* Ithaca, 1973.

Capper, Charles. *Margaret Fuller: An American Romantic Life, the Private Years.* New York, 1992.

Capper, Charles, and Conrad Edick Wright, eds. *Transient and Permanent: The Transcendentalist Movement and Its Contexts.* Boston, 1999.

Charvat, William. *The Origins of American Critical Thought.* Philadelphia, 1936.

Colbert, Charles. *A Measure of Perfection: Phrenology and the Fine Arts in America.* Chapel Hill, N.C., 1997.

Conkin, Paul. *Puritans and Pragmatists: Eight Eminent American Thinkers.* Bloomington, Ind., 1968. Rep., 1976.

Crocker, Matthew. *The Magic of the Many: Josiah Quincy and the Rise of Mass Politics in Boston, 1800–1840.* Amherst, Mass., 1999.

Curley, Edwin, ed. *A Spinoza Reader.* Princeton, 1994.

Davis, David Brion. *The Problem of Slavery in the Age of Revolution, 1770–1823.* 1975. Rep., New York, 1999.

———. *The Problem of Slavery in Western Culture.* Ithaca, 1966.

Donald, David. *Lincoln Reconsidered: Essays on the Civil War Era.* New York, 1956.

Elkins, Stanley M. *Slavery: A Problem in American Institutional and Intellectual Life.* Chicago, 1959.

Foner, Eric. *The Story of American Freedom.* New York, 1998.

Fredrickson, George. *The Black Image in the White Mind: The Debate on Afro-American Character and Destiny, 1817–1914.* Middletown, Conn., 1987.

———. *The Inner Civil War: Northern Intellectuals and the Crisis of the Union.* New York, 1965.

Frothingham, P. R. *Edward Everett: Orator and Statesman.* Boston, 1925.

Gouldner, Alvin. *The Dialectic of Ideology and Technology: The Origins, Grammar, and Future of Ideology.* New York, 1979.

———. *Enter Plato: Classical Greece and the Origins of Social Theory.* New York, 1965.

Gramsci, Antonio. *The Modern Prince and Other Writings.* New York, 1957.

Gura, Philip. *The Wisdom of Words: Language, Theology, and Literature in the New England Renaissance.* Middletown, Conn., 1981.

Hofstadter, Richard. *Anti-Intellectualism in American Life.* New York, 1964.

Horsman, Reginald. *Race and Manifest Destiny: The Origins of American Racial Anglo-Saxonism.* Cambridge, 1981.

Howe, Daniel Walker. *The Unitarian Conscience: Harvard Moral Philosophy, 1805–1861.* Cambridge, 1970.

Jakobsson, Stiv. *Am I Not a Man and a Brother? British Missions and the Abolition of the Slave Trade and Slavery in West Africa and the West Indies 1786–1838.* Uppsala, Sweden, 1972.

James, Henry. *Partial Portraits.* 1888. Rep., Westport, Conn., 1970.

Kateb, George. *The Inner Ocean: Individualism and Democratic Culture.* Ithaca, 1992.

Knox, Robert. *The Races of Man: A Fragment.* Philadelphia, 1850.

Lang, Amy Schrager. *Prophetic Women: Anne Hutchinson and the Problem of Dissent in the Literature of New England.* Berkeley, Calif., 1987.

Lowell, James Russell. *My Study Windows.* Boston, 1884.

Lutz, Alma. *Crusade for Freedom: Women of the Antislavery Movement.* Boston, 1968.

Macpherson, C. B. *The Political Theory of Possessive Individualism: Hobbes to Locke.* 1962. Rep., New York, 1969.

Melish, Joanne Pope. *Disowning Slavery: Gradual Emancipation and "Race" in New England, 1780–1860.* Ithaca, 1998.

Melville, Herman. "Benito Cereno," *Putnam's.* 1855.

Miller, Perry, ed. *The Transcendentalists: An Anthology.* Cambridge, 1950.

Ostrander, Gilman. *Republic of Letters: The American Intellectual Community, 1776–1865.* Madison, Wis., 1999.

Outlaw, Lucius, Jr. *On Race and Philosophy.* New York, 1996.

Patterson, Anita H. *From Emerson to King: Democracy, Race and the Politics of Protest.* New York, 1997.

Perry, Lewis. *Boats Against the Current: American Culture Between Revolution and Modernity, 1820–1860.* New York, 1993.

Porter, Carolyn. *Seeing and Being: The Plight of the Participant-Observers in Emerson, James, Adams, and Faulkner.* Middletown, Conn., 1981.

Railton, Stephen. *Literary Performance in the American Renaissance.* Princeton, 1991.

Rash, Nancy. *The Paintings and Politics of George Caleb Bingham.* New Haven, 1981.

Rose, Anne C. *Transcendentalism as a Social Movement, 1830–1850.* New Haven, 1981.

Sanborn, Franklin B. *Recollections of Seventy Years.* 2 vols. Boston, 1909.

Santayana, George. *Interpretations of Poetry and Religion.* 1900. Rep., Gloucester, Mass., 1969.

———. *The Last Puritan: A Memoir in the Form of Novel.* 1935. Rep. Boston, 1991.

Sewel, William. *The History of the Rise, Increase, and Progress of the Christian People Called Quakers.* 3rd ed. 2 vols. Philadelphia, 1823.

Smith, Harmon. *My Friend, My Friend: The Story of Thoreau's Relationship with Emerson.* Amherst, Mass., 1999.

Sprague, William. *Annals of the American Pulpit.* Vol. 8. New York, 1865.

Stearns, Frank Preston. *Cambridge Sketches.* Philadelphia, 1905.

Story, Ronald. *Harvard and the Boston Upper Class: The Forging of an Aristocracy, 1800–1870.* Middletown, Conn., 1980.

Thayer, James B. *Reverend Samuel Ripley of Waltham.* Cambridge, 1897.

———. *A Western Trip with Mr. Emerson.* Boston, 1884.

Thornton, Tamara Plakins. *Cultivating Gentlemen: The Meaning of Country Life among the Boston Elite, 1785–1860.* New Haven, 1989.

Tise, Larry. *Proslavery: A History of the Defense of Slavery in America, 1701–1840.* Athens, Ga., 1987.

von Frank, Albert J. *The Trials of Anthony Burns: Freedom and Slavery in Emerson's Boston.* Cambridge, 1998.

Ware, William. *American Unitarian Biography.* Boston, 1850.

West, Cornel. *The American Evasion of Philosophy: A Genealogy of Pragmatism.* Madison, Wis., 1989.

Whitman, Walt. *Leaves of Grass and Democratic Vistas.* London, 1930.

Wright, Conrad Edick, ed. *American Unitarianism, 1805–1865.* Boston, 1989.

Yoder, R. A. *Emerson and the Orphic Poet in America.* Berkeley, 1978.

Zwarg, Christina. *Feminist Conversations: Fuller, Emerson, and the Play of Reading.* Ithaca, 1995.

Articles

Ahlstrom, Sidney, "Theology in America: A Historical Survey." In *The Shaping of American Religion,* ed. J. W. Smith and A. L. Jamison. Princeton, 1961.

Bartlett, Irving, ed. "The Philosopher and the Activist: New Letters from Emerson to Wendell Phillips," *New England Quarterly* 62:2 (1989): 280–81.

Bowditch, Nathaniel. "Did Mr. Emerson Sympathize with the Abolitionists?" *Index* (November 1885).

Cameron, Kenneth W. "Emerson, Thoreau, Parson Frost, and 'The Problem,' " *ESQ* 6 (1957): 16.

Cayton, Mary Kupiec. "The Making of an American Prophet: Emerson, His Audiences, and the Rise of the Culture Industry in Nineteenth-Century America," *American Historical Review* 92 (1987): 597–620.

Charvat, William. "A Chronological List of Emerson's American Lecture Engagements," *New York Public Library Bulletin* 64 (1960): 492–507.

Claes, Gregory. " 'Individualism,' 'Socialism,' and 'Social Science': Further Notes on a Process of Conceptual Formation 1800–1850," *Journal of the History of Ideas* 47 (1986): 81–93.

Cushing, John D. "Notes on Disestablishment in Massachusetts," *William And Mary Quarterly*, 3rd. ser. 26 (1969): 169–90.

Douglass, Frederick. *Douglass' Monthly* 5 (August 1963): 852.

Downs, Lenthiel H. "Emerson and Dr. Channing: Two Men of Boston," *New England Quarterly* 20 (1947): 524–26.

Field, Peter S. "The Birth of Secular High Culture in America: The *Monthly Anthology and Boston Review* and Its Critics," *Journal of the Early Republic* 17 (1997): 575–609.

————. "The Strange Career of Emerson and Race," *American Nineteenth Century History* 2:1 (2001): 1–32.

Flanagan, John. "Emerson and Communism," *New England Quarterly* 10 (1937): 243–61.

Ford, Nick. "Henry David Thoreau, Abolitionist," *New England Quarterly* 19 (1946): 359–71.

Glicksberg, Charles I. "Bryant on Emerson the Lecturer," *New England Quarterly* 12 (1939), 530–34.

Goodman, Russell B. "Moral Perfectionism and Democracy: Emerson, Nietzsche, Cavell," *ESQ* 43 (1997): 159–78.

Gortis, Lisa. "Consecrating a Rebellion: Emerson's Divinity School Address, David Friedrich Strauss, and the Historical Jesus," *The Journal of Unitarian Universalist History* 24 (1997): 1–16.

Gravely, Will. "The Dialectic of Double-Consciousness in Black American Freedom Celebrations, 1803–1863," *Journal of Negro History* (winter 1982): 302–17.

Habich, Robert D. "Emerson's Reluctant Foe: Andrews Norton and the Transcendental Controversy," *New England Quarterly* 65 (1992): 208–37.

Hill, William Bancroft. "Emerson's College Days," *The Literary World,* 5/22/1880.

Jensen, Tim. " 'Their own thought in motley . . .': Emerson's Divinity School Address and Henry Ware, Jr.'s *Hints on Extemporaneous Preaching*," *The Journal of Unitarian Universalist History* 24 (1997): 17–28.

Larrimore, Mark. "Sublime Waste: Kant on the Destiny of the 'Races,' " *Canadian Journal of Philosophy*, Supplementary Vol. 25 (1999): 81–98.

Lippy, Charles H. "The 1780 Massachusetts Constitution: Religious Establishment or Civil Religion?" *Journal of Church and State* 20 (1987): 533–49.

Lowell, James Russell. "Emerson The Lecturer." In *The Recognition of Ralph Waldo Emerson*, 43–47.

McClay, Wilfred M. "Mr. Emerson's Tombstone." In *Community and Tradition: Conservative Perspectives on the American Experience*, ed. George W. Carey and Bruce Frohnen. Lanham, Md.: 1998.

Miller, Perry. "Emersonian Genius and the American Democracy," *New England Quarterly* 26 (1953): 27–44.

Miller, Perry. "Jonathan Edwards to Emerson," *New England Quarterly* 13 (1940): 589–617.

Moody, Marjory M. "The Evolution of Emerson as an Abolitionist," *American Literature* 17 (1945–46): 1–21.

Patell, Cyrus. "Emersonian Strategies: Negative Liberty, Self–Reliance, and Democratic Individuality," *Nineteenth Century Literature* (March 1994): 440–79.

Robinson, David. "Poetry, Personality, and the Divinity School Address," *Harvard Theological Review* 82:2 (1989): 185–99.

Rose, Anne. "Social Sources of Denominationalism Reconsidered," *American Quarterly* 38 (1986): 251.

Santayana, George. "The Optimism of Ralph Waldo Emerson." In *George Santayana's America,* ed. James Ballowe. Urbana, Ill., 1967.

Scott, Donald M. "The Public Lecture and the Creation of a Public in Mid-Nineteenth-Century America," *Journal of American History* 66 (1980): 791–809.

Seibert, Wilbur H. "The Under-Ground Railroad in Massachusetts," *Proceedings of the American Antiquarian Society* 45 (1935): 25–100.

Shklar, Judith. "Emerson and the Inhibitions of Democracy," *Political Theory* 18.4 (1990): 601–14.

Silver, Rollo G. "Emerson: Abolitionist," *New England Quarterly* 6 (March 1993): 151–57.

Slater, Joseph. "Two Sources for Emerson's First Address on West Indian Emancipation," *Emerson Society Quarterly* 44 (1966): 97–100.

Smith, Henry Nash. "Emerson's Problem of Vocation: A Note on the 'American Scholar,' " *New England Quarterly* 12 (1939): 52–67.

Swart, Koenraad. "Individualism in the Mid-Nineteenth Century (1826–1860)," *Journal of the History of Ideas* 32 (1962): 77–90.

Teichgraeber, Richard F. III. " 'Our National Glory': Emerson in American Culture, 1865–1882." In *Transient and Permanent: The Transcendentalist Movement and Its Context,* ed. Charles Capper and Conrad Edick Wright. Boston, 1999: 499–526.

Thorp, Willard. "Emerson on Tour," *Quarterly Journal of Speech* 16 (1930): 19–34.

Tolles, Frederick B. "Emerson and Quakerism," *American Literature* 10 (1938): 142–66.

Turpie, Mary. "A Quaker Source for Emerson's Sermon on the Lord's Supper," *New England Quarterly* 17 (1944): 95–101.

Woodall, Guy R. "The Journals of Convers Francis (2)." In *SAR,* ed. Joel Myerson. New York, 1981.

Wright, Conrad. "Emerson, Barzillai Frost, and the Divinity School Address," *Harvard Theological Review* 49 (1956): 19–43.

Other Published Sources

Christian Disciple
Cincinnati Gazette

Harvard College *Records of the College Faculty*
Kenosha (Wisconsin) *Democrat*
Providence *Manufacturers' and Farmers' Journal*
Monthly Anthology and Boston Review
Milwaukee *Sentinel*

INDEX

ABOUT THE AUTHOR

PETER S. FIELD teaches history at the University of Canterbury in Christ-church, New Zealand. He is the author of *The Crisis of the Standing Order: Clerical Intellectuals and Cultural Authority in Massachusetts, 1780–1833* and coauthor of *The Promise and Paradox of American Freedom*. He has pre-viously taught at Columbia University and Vanderbilt University, and in 1998–99 he was a fellow at the Center for the Study of Religion at Princeton University.